Sarojini Naidu.
Selected Poetry and Prose

Sarojini Naidu:
Selected Poetry and Prose

Edited with an introduction and commentary by
MAKARAND PARANJAPE

Rupa & Co

Copyright © Makarand Paranjape 2010

Published 2010 by
Rupa • Co
7/16, Ansari Road, Daryaganj,
New Delhi 110 002

Sales Centres:
Allahabad Bengaluru Chandigarh Chennai
Hyderabad Jaipur Kathmandu
Kolkata Mumbai

All rights reserved.
No part of this publication may be reproduced, stored
in a retrieval system, or transmitted, in any form or
by any means, electronic, mechanical, photocopying, recording
or otherwise, without the prior permission of the publishers.

The author asserts the moral right to be identified
as the author of this work.

Typeset in Aldine721 by
Mindways Design
1410 Chiranjiv Tower
43 Nehru Place
New Delhi 110 019

ISBN 978-81-2911-580-5

Printed at Repro Knowledgecast Limited, Thane

To my students

CONTENTS

Preface — xiv
Chronology — xvi

INTRODUCTION — 1
POETRY
Juvenilia — 73
Mehir Muneer

From *The Golden Threshold* — 108
Folk Songs
  Palanquin-Bearers — 108
  Wandering Singers — 108
  Indian Weavers — 109
  Corn-Grinders — 109
  Village-Song — 110
  Indian Love song — 111
  Suttee — 112

Songs for Music
  Autumn Song — 113
  Alabaster — 113
  Ecstasy — 113

Poems

Ode to H.H. The Nizam of Hyderabad	114
Leili	115
In the Forest	116
Past and Future	117
To the God of Pain	117
Indian Dancers	118
My Dead Dream	119
Damayanti to Nala in the Hour of Exile	120
The Queen's Rival	121
The Poet to Death	123
The Indian Gipsy	124
The Pardah Nashin	124
Nightfall in the City of Hyderabad	125
Street Cries	126
To India	127
The Royal Tombs of Golconda	127
To a Buddha Seated on a Lotus	128

From *The Bird of Time*
Songs of Life, Death & The Spring

The Bird of Time	130
Dirge	131
An Indian Love Song (*Written to an Indian, tune*)	132
Love and Death	133
At Twilight	134
A Rajput Love Song	135
A Song in Spring	136
Vasant Panchami	137
In a Time of Flowers	138
In Praise of Gulmohur Blossoms	139
Nasturtiums	140
Golden Cassia	140
Champak Blossoms	141
Ecstasy	142

Indian folk songs
    Village Songs   142
    Songs of My City   143
    Song of Radha, The Milkmaid   145
    Spinning Song   146

Songs of Life
    The Hussain Sagar   147
    The Faery Isle of Janjira   148
    The Soul's Prayer   148
    The Old Woman   150
    An Anthem of Love   151
    The Call to Evening Prayer   151
    Guerdon   152

From *The Broken Wing: Songs of Life, Death & the Spring*
Songs of Life and Death
    The Broken Wing   154
    The Gift of India   155
    The Temple   156
    The Imam Bara   157
    A Song from Shiraz   158
    Memorial Verses   159
    Wandering Beggars   160
    The Lotus   161
    The Prayer of Islam   162
    Bells   163
    The Pearl   164
    Kali the Mother   165
    Awake!   166

The Flowering Year
    The Magic of Spring   167
    June Sunset   167

The Time of Roses	168

The Peacock Lute
Caprice	169
Destiny	169

The Temple
I. The Gate of Delight	170
II. The Path of Tears	175
III. The Sanctuary	180

From *The Feather of The Dawn*
The Bird Sanctuary	186
The Amulet	187
Blind	188
Entreaty	188
Renunciation	189
Immutable	190

Poems of Krishna
Ghanashyam	191

Songs of Radha
At Dawn	191
at Dusk	182
The Quest	193

PROSE
Mah Rukh Begum	197
Nilambuja: The Fantasy of a Poet's Mood	202
Women's Education and the Unity of India	206
Gokhale the Man	211
The Soul of India	223
Ideals of Islam	230

Indian Women and the Franchise	237
Speech at Trichur	247
Speech at Durban Town Hall	256
Presidential Address 40th Indian National Congress	267
Presidential Address Asian Relations Conference	278
My Father, Do Not Rest, Homage to Mahatma Gandhi on His Death	285
Convocation Remarks	290
Select Bibliography and Works Cited	301
Abbreviations used in the Commentary	306
Commentary	307

PREFACE

The first edition of *Sarojini Naidu: Selected Poetry and Prose* was published in 1993. This was a hardback, with rare photographs, samples of the author's handwriting, and much unpublished or inaccessible material. Sarojini's* primary works had long been out of print; in fact, they were practically impossible to come by except in some pirated or unauthorized editions. The effort to produce a coherent and authoritative volume, as I indicate in the Introduction, involved considerable labour over several years. However, I was fortunate not only to be able to access manuscripts, letters, and other valuable personal papers of the author, but also examine the first and subsequent editions of Sarojini's works in order to arrive at my own selection. It was therefore gratifying that that first, limited, hardcover edition quickly sold out. The publisher then issued a paperback version for which I carried out quite a few corrections and changes. After remaining in circulation for a few years, that edition too went out of print. Once again, Sarojini's work became difficult to obtain. In the meanwhile, the publishing house changed its ownership, management and editorial staff. My attempts to bring out a new edition, thus, did not bear fruit.

Appearing nearly seventeen years afterwards, this second edition remains largely unaltered in its contents. I have found no reason to add or subtract from my original selection not just because I still believe it constitutes her best work, but also because no new material has come to light. Even my approach remains fundamentally the same. Although, some post-colonial and feminist scholars have shown interest in Sarojini's work, this has not translated into new readings. Indeed, no substantial new research has been done during these years except for the first volume of Sarojini's selected letters which I edited and published in 1996. I have, however, extended my own line of thinking in the Introduction, making it more detailed and, I hope, thought-provoking. I have incorporated some of the material which appeared in Commentary in the first edition, also adding some new ideas and interpretations. Some errors that had remained in the first edition have also been corrected.

I am very pleased that Rupa & Co. have shown keenness in bringing out this second edition. I am grateful to both the management and the editorial staff for their encouragement and support. I would also like to thank those who read and commented on the Introduction. Most of the work on this second edition was done when I was a Shivdasani Fellow at the Oxford Centre for Hindu Studies. I am obliged to them for the opportunity to return to a life that I enjoy most—that of a graduate student at a first-rate university.

Makarand R. Paranjape
1 December 2009

---

*Meena Alexander, a former member of the Department of English, University of Hyderabad, offers her own account of her connection with Sarojini Naidu in *The Shock Of Arrival: Reflections On Postcolonial Experience*. See her chapter, 'In Search of Sarojini Naidu,' especially the section on pages 172-181.

CHRONOLOGY

1879 13 February	Sarojini Chattopadhyaya is born in Hyderabad, Deccan, the eldest of eight children of Aghorenath Chattopadhyaya and Varada Sundari.
1890	Begins her poetic career at the age of eleven, when instead of an algebra sum, she writes a poem.
Up to 1890	Educated at home by governesses. Then sent to Madras to prepare for the Madras Matriculation Examination.
1891	Passes the Madras Matriculation Examination in the First Division, a feat that makes her famous.
1892	Writes *Mehir Muneer* at the age of thirteen.
1893	*Mehir Muneer* a poem in three cantos by 'A Brahmin Girl' printed by Srinivasa, Varadachari and Co., Madras.
1894	Falls in love with Dr M. Govindarajulu Naidu.
1895	Receives a scholarship of £300 per annum plus a passage to England from the Nizam of Hyderabad. Leaves for England. Becomes the ward

	of Miss Manning and attends lectures at King's College, University of London. Meets Edmund Gosse and starts sending him letters and poems. Also writes to Govindarajulu Naidu, enclosing poems.
1896	Joins Girton College, Cambridge University. Meets Arthur Symons and members of the Rhymer's Club. Writes several poems, some of which will be later published in *The Golden Threshold*.
September	Visits Burgdorf in Germany.
October	*Songs* by S. Chattopadhyaya published privately in Hyderabad; contains poems written from 1892-1896.
1898	Falls ill. Visits Switzerland and Italy. Returns to India.
September October	Marries Dr Naidu in Madras in a Brahmo ceremony with Veerasalingam Pantulu officiating as the minister.
1901-1904	Birth of her children: Jayasurya (1901), Padmaja (1902), Randheera (1903), and Leilamani (1904).
1901	Starts travelling and speaking in public.
1905	*The Golden Threshold* published by Heinemann, London. Partition of Bengal. Plunges into public life, championing the cause of Hindu-Muslim unity.
1906	Speaks at the annual session of the Indian National Congress in Calcutta. By now she knows the major public figures of her day including Sir Pherozeshah Mehta, G.K. Gokhale, and M.A. Jinnah. Addresses the Indian Social Conference

	in Calcutta on 'The Education of Indian Women.'
1908	Awarded the Kaiser-e-Hind gold medal by the Government of India.
1912	*The Bird of Time* published by Heinemann, London.
March	Addresses the Muslim League in Lucknow.
May	Leaves for England because of her ill-health.
1912-1914	Often meets Gokhale in London.
1914 8 August	Meets Mahatma Gandhi. World War I breaks out. Assists Gandhi in the war effort.
October	Returns to India. Fellow of the Royal Society for Literature.
1915 February	Both Aghorenath and Gokhale die; publishes a tribute to the latter in *The Bombay Chronicle*. Virtually leaves Hyderabad, setting herself up at the Taj Mahal hotel, Bombay.
1916	Varada Sundari dies. Meets Jawaharlal Nehru at the Lucknow session of the Congress. Publishes 'The Soul of India.'
1917	*The Broken Wing* published by Heinemann, London. Campaigns for the abolition of Indentured Labour.
December	Leads a delegation of women to Lord Chelmsfold and E.S. Montagu asking for educational, social, and political rights for women.

1918-19	Works for women's franchise through various forums.
1919	Campaigns against the Rowlatt Act as Gandhi's follower.
July	Leaves for England as member of the India Home Rule League. Returns her Kaiser-e-Hind medal in protest against the Jallianwala Bagh massacre.
1920	Speaks extensively on Punjab and the Khilafat movement in England.
1921	Returns to India after travelling through Sweden, Switzerland, and France. Campaigns for Gandhi's non-cooperation movement all over India.
1922	Gandhi's famous trial and conviction; writes on it in *The Bombay Chronicle*. During Gandhi's imprisonment, tours the country spreading the gospel of Khadi. Visits Malabar after the Moplah rebellion. Visits Sri Lanka on a holiday; lectures throughout the island.
1923	Sides with the 'No-Changers' (Gandhian faction) in the rift in the Congress.
1924	Visits Kenya and South Africa, lecturing extensively.
1925	Succeeds Gandhi as President of the Indian National Congress; the first native woman to occupy the high office and the second woman ever after Annie Besant.
1927	Helps in the founding of the All India Women's Conference.
July-August	Composes most of the poems that go into the posthumously published *The Feather of the Down*

1928	The AIWC delegate to the Pan-Pacific Women's Conference at Honolulu; sails for America in May.
1929	Returns to India after a successful tour of the USA and Canada.
	Leaves in November to preside over the East African Congress.
1930	President of the AIWC.
12 March	Gandhi's Dandi March commences.
May	After the arrest of Gandhi and Abbas Tyabji, leads the salt satyagraha at the Dharasana Salt Works.
16 May	Arrested and sent to jail.
1931 January	Released from jail.
September	Accompanies Gandhi in August to the Second Round Table Conference in London. The Conference fails. Naidu travels to the continent.
1932 January	Returns to London; sets sail for Cape Town. Joins the Indian Delegation to South Africa.
	On her return to India, becomes 'acting President' of the Congress because all the other leaders are in prison.
22 April	Arrested; interned at the Arthur Road jail, Bombay, with Kasturba Gandhi and Mira Behn; transferred to Yeravada where Gandhi was imprisoned.
8 August	Communal Award announced on 8 August.
20 September	Gandhi commences his fast unto death against the communal award; nurses Gandhi and oversees his appointments.

1933 April	Released from jail.
8 May	Gandhi commences a 21-day fast and is released from jail; attends on him through the fast and the recuperation afterwards. Plays an important role in the founding of the Lady Irwin College, New Delhi, by the AIWC.
1934 August	Addresses the Women's India Association in Madras.
1935 4 March	Presides over the All India Music Conference, Delhi. As President of the Bombay Provincial Congress Committee, unveils a plaque celebrating the Golden Jubilee of the Indian National Congress.
1936	Is removed from and brought back into the Congress Working Committee by Nehru.
1937	Visits Gandhi at Sevagram, near Wardha.
1938	In Calcutta for months; visits Allahabad.
1939 April	Chairs the special session of the Congress which saw election of Rajendra Prasad as President after the resignation of Subhas Chandra Bose.
1940 October	Joins the individual *satyagraha* movement against the enforced participation of India in World War II; arrested along with Gandhi and other leaders.
December	Released.
1942 9 August	Arrested along with Gandhi and the rest of the CWC after Gandhi's 'Quit India' speech of 8 August; interned in the Aga Khan Palace, Pune.

15 August	Mahadev Desai dies of heart attack; helps keep up Gandhi's spirits.
1943 10 Feb-3 March	Gandhi's twenty-one-day fast.
21 March	Discharged from prison upon contracting malaria; retires to Hyderabad.
1943-1944	Assists in the relief efforts in Hyderabad for the victims of the Bengal famine.
1945 May	Randheera, her youngest son, dies.
1944-1947	Often visits Bengal.
1947 23 March	Presides over the Asian Relations Conference, New Delhi, and delivers the Presidential address.
15 August	India becomes free.
July-November	Officiates as the Governor of United Provinces in place of Dr B.C. Roy.
November	Continues as Governor because of Roy's resigning the post.
1948 30 January	Gandhi assassinated; offers a moving tribute on his death; accompanies the ashes to Allahabad with other national leaders.
1949 28 January	Presides over the convocation on the occasion of Silver Jubilee of Lucknow University.
2 March	Dies at 3-30 a.m.

INTRODUCTION

I
Reclaiming a Kinship

I began working on Sarojini Naidu purely by accident. No doubt I had read and, unlike many others of my generation, actually enjoyed her poetry. I had even ventured to write something on it. But all this was to be expected of someone specialising in Indian English literature for his Ph.D. It was only after I joined the University of Hyderabad in February 1986 as a Fellow in English that I formed a serious interest in Sarojini's life and work.*

Again, how this happened was almost a matter of chance. In those days, the Schools of Humanities and Social Sciences operated from the city, before the large campus at Gachi Bowli, on the outskirts of Hyderabad, where the University has been located for several years now, was developed. In those days, we were housed at 'The Golden Threshold,' which had been Sarojini's home. *The Golden Threshold*, of course, was also the title of Sarojini's first collection of poems, published in 1905. This once beautiful house, now much altered and spoiled by the needs of its new occupants, still retained traces of its old grace and charm. Located on Nampally Station Road, near Abids,

---

*Meena Alexander, a former member of the Department of English, University of Hyderabad, offers her own account of her connection with Sarojini Naidu in *The Shock Of Arrival: Reflections On Postcolonial Experience*. See her chapter, 'In Search of Sarojini Naidu,' especially the section on pages 172-181.

Hyderabad's busiest downtown business district, it was at the very heart of the city, in a tree-lined and fairly large compound. There was a fountain in the middle, now defunct. In addition to the main house, there were annexes for classrooms.

The house itself had had a chequered history. It was donated to the nation by Padmaja Naidu, the last surviving heir of the Naidu family. Indira Gandhi, one of the executors of Padmaja's will and India's Prime Minister, gave it to the newly started Central University of Hyderabad. Prior to that it had been leased out to the Neo Mysore Café, which had now shifted next door. Even earlier, it had been let out to a training college in 1938 after the family moved to Zaheer Manzil in Red Hills. Later, probably in 1942, the family moved again to Sukh Niwas in Ramkote. Behind the main house in the compound of the 'Golden Threshold,' was a large extension built by Govindarajulu for his son, Dr Jaisoorya Naidu, who was also a doctor. Unfortunately, the father and the son could not get along. 'Jaisoorya Clinic,' as it was called, was hardly used by the person it was named after, though he did practice from these premises after the death of his parents. It now housed the library and some faculty offices upstairs.

Jaisoorya, Sarojini's the eldest son, and his German wife, died without heirs. The youngest son, Ranadheera, led a rather sad life; an alcoholic and drifter, he died young, during his mother's own lifetime. The two sisters fared better. The younger, Leilamani, a civil servant, was known to be rather overbearing and acerbic; she lived for several years in Government accommodation on Janpath (formerly Kingsway), New Delhi, and died a spinster. I heard stories of her imperious ways from some who had taken her classes at Nizam College, where she taught English briefly before moving to Delhi. The eldest, Padmaja Naidu, came closest to inheriting her mother's mantle. A confidante of Jawaharal Nehru, India's first Prime Minister, she served as the Governor of West Bengal, before retiring to a bungalow on the Prime Minister's estate at Teen Murti house, New Delhi. It was here that she passed away. She too did not marry nor leave any heirs behind.

Strangely enough, as a younger teacher of English in India, I felt that people like me were now the heirs of Sarojini Naidu, if not literally, then at least literarily. I felt this way because the offices of the English Department were in one of the bedrooms of the main house. Though much partitioned and divided into little cubicles, this suite of rooms with an attached bathroom, had obviously been well designed and must have once been rather elegant. It was the many hours that I spend here that provided me the somewhat irreverent answer to repeated questions about my rather unfashionable and otherwise inexplicable involvement with Sarojini Naidu: 'I started my career in bedroom, you know.'

More seriously, the house did have an effect on me. The non-functioning fountain, unkempt garden, stinking lavatories, crowds of students, and continuous clamour of the traffic outside—none of these could fully efface its special charm. Especially in the evenings or on holidays, the mansion seemed to return to itself, resonating with memories of all the brilliant and important people who visited it. 'The Golden Threshold,' though not quite as much as Anand Bhavan, was definitely one of the famous houses of our national struggle for independence. Sarojini herself in a letter to Nehru boasted about 'the most truly cosmopolitan society in India which . . . haunts The Golden Threshold even unto four generations. . . .' Why, even the mango tree in the backyard planted by Mahatma Gandhi attested to the significance of the house. It was a different matter that the tree bore little fruit.

My office, which I first shared with the late and distinguished Professor Meenakshi Mukherjee, then with Professor Narayana Chandran, was in the 'Jaisoorya Clinic.' I loved this space, partly because you had to pass through the library to access it. What better place to have a faculty office than the university library? Surrounded by easily accessible books, in a quiet and secluded corner of a busy city campus, I soaked in this old neighbourhood, with the small sounds of the back alley where my window opened and the more insistent calls to prayer from the nearby mosques. When the sun was not too harsh, I began to explore this part of Hyderabad, wandering about its streets and lanes.

Soon I discovered 'The Sarojini Naidu Memorial Trust,' in an old bungalow behind the General Post Office. I walked in very tentatively to ask what it housed. To my surprise I found it had copies of important archival material and the manuscripts of the poet. This house was also resonant with history. The slabs of its granite floor had been trodden over by many distinguished guests and visitors. It was here that Sarojini and her siblings had been born. I thought that if I ever wrote a biography of Sarojini, I would, in one of its early scenes, depict her in the back garden of this house, on a swing slung from a tall mango tree, dreaming of a glorious future for herself, each time the swing rose high in the languid mid-afternoon air. This house originally belonged to the great Aghorenath Chattopadhyay, D.Sc. (Edinburgh), founder of modern education in Hyderabad state, philosopher, savant, and alchemist. He and his wife Varada Sundari Devi had, in their own way, done so much for the national cause. Each of their eight children distinguished himself or herself in some manner or the other. Incidentally, this house was on the Jawaharlal Nehru Road, which began just after the Mahatma Gandhi Road ended at the General Post Office. Gandhi, Sarojini, and Nehru—born exactly ten years apart, in 1869, 1879, and 1889 respectively, certainly were part of the same story of modern India.

The city of Hyderabad itself had many memorials to Sarojini besides these two houses. There was the Sarojini Devi Eye hospital near Mehdipatnam and the Sarojini Devi Road in Secunderabad, besides the Sarojini Devi Vanita Mahavidylaya, a leading college for women. With all these associations and resources, it was sad if not surprising that none was interested in Sarojini Naidu. The decision to do something about this neglect gradually stole upon me. Suddenly, so many connections with her life and work began to emerge, almost wherever I looked.

The incongruity of my situation struck me. We were surrounded by history but did little about it. Here I was, a specialist in Indian English literature, actually sitting day after day in the house of an important poet and national leader, next door to a Trust set up in her memory, yet making little use at all of my opportunities. I remembered how well the houses of poets and writers, not to speak of other historical monuments, were maintained in England. In contrast, how callous and careless we were! What was the point of talking about 'decolonisation' or 'post-colonialism' in our classrooms when we were neglecting to study the very writer in whose house we worked? I was not, then, especially interested in Sarojini Naidu, but I thought I *had to* look at her life and work seriously. It was my way of engaging with my immediate environment, of trying to be directly relevant to my location as an English teacher in India.

The Sarojini Naidu Memorial Trust contained copies of Sarojini's letters, besides a fairly good collection of the primary and secondary materials on her poetry. The letters had not yet been published. There were also several unpublished poems, including juvenilia. Though there were at least two good biographies, both were outdated and inadequate. So much new material had now become available which was these biographers had not taken note of. I quickly realised that a lot could and need be done on Sarojini Naidu.

The problem was, however, of the means. The Trust had very little funds. They barely managed to function from day to day. The University had no separate budget to sponsor projects, even in the memory of someone who's multi-crore rupee property had been bequeathed to them. I therefore began to spend some time on my own in the Trust, acquainting myself with its contents. Photocopies were expensive and had to be specially authorised from a shop nearby. There were no personal computers in India in those days. Often letters and other material had to be hand written, then given to a job typist to be turned into a fair copy. I realised that I would have to plough a lonely furrow. I began by teaching a special optional course on Sarojini, perhaps the only one in any university to do so. Later I got a Homi Bhabha Fellowship for Literature to work on Sarojini Naidu. It supported my two year stay in Delhi, where most of the original papers were located, either at the Nehru Memorial Library or at the National Archives. Before the Fellowship ended in 1993, I had published this first edition of this collection of Sarojini's poetry and prose, with the hitherto unknown or unpublished pieces. I also began to collect and organise her letters for a separate volume, I published with Kali for Women three years later, in 1996.

Looking back at my early days as a university Lecturer in English, I can only be grateful for that unexpected contact with Sarojini's life, which later was to open up a much wider range of interests in India's national struggle for independence. I am happy that I pursued that lead, for though many are called it is given only to the fortunate few to answer.

II
The Life

Sarojini Naidu (1879-1949) was perhaps the most prominent woman among the leaders of the mass movement who fought for the independence of India. As a nationalist leader, poet, activist for women's rights, orator, and celebrity, she was certainly one of the most memorable and colourful Indian women of the 20th century. She was not only the first native woman to become the President of the Indian National Congress, but also became the first woman Governor of any state in independent India when she assumed charge of the largest and most important United Province (now Uttar Pradesh). As one of the principal aides and followers of Mahatma Gandhi she was often in the limelight and was among the best-known Indian woman of her time. She also had an international presence as India's unofficial cultural ambassador and spokesperson of the freedom movement. In her life converge some of the dominant cultural, social, and political currents of pre-independence India. Thus, both in her own right and as a representative of her times, Sarojini deserves to be remembered and studied.

She was born on 13 February 1879 in Hyderabad. Her parents were Dr Aghorenath Chattopadhyaya and Varada Sundari. She was the eldest of eight children. Aghorenath, besides being a D.Sc. from Edinburgh and the founder of modern education in the Hyderabad State, was an extraordinary person. A social reformer, alchemist, spiritualist, and savant, he was a pioneer in all kinds of radical movements including Swadeshi, women's education, and the indigenisation of modern science long before they became popular elsewhere. Twice deported from the Nizam's dominions for his unorthodox views, Aghorenath nevertheless commanded great respect for his uprightness, nobility, and kindliness. Varada Sundari, who had been educated in a Brahmo home for women while her husband was abroad, was also a remarkable woman. Not just a skilled homemaker, she was abreast with the happenings of the world, besides being a talented singer and storyteller. The eight children they produced were vibrant individualists. Virendranath became a revolutionary. An internationally well-known figure in world communism who knew Lenin and Stalin, he lived abroad in exile because he was a wanted man in British India. Mrinalini, or Gunnu Auntie, was a renowned educationist who, after studying in Cambridge, was for many years the Principal of a leading girls' college in Lahore. Harindranath, the youngest son, was a poet, dramatist, actor, and Member of Parliament. Suhasini, the youngest daughter, married a trade union leader and was active in the movement. All told, it was an interesting, talented, and diverse family that occupied a home that was one of the centres of every kind of intellectual adventurism and freethinking in Hyderabad.

Sarojini grew up in such an atmosphere. Her unconventionality, utter lack of prejudice, curiosity and openness can perhaps be traced to upbringing she received as a child. Soon, however, her innate precocity asserted itself. Indeed, she was somewhat of a prodigy, passing the Madras Matriculation Examination at twelve, composing a 1300-line poem when she had barely entered her teens, and falling in love with a man from a different caste when she was fourteen. Her father, sensing trouble, arranged to send her abroad on a scholarship given by the Nizam of Hyderabad. Though she spent three years in England, first in London and then at Girton College, Cambridge, she proved to be a poor scholar. Instead, she spent most of her time reading and writing poetry. Through Edmund Gosse, she met some of the most important poets of the 1890s. Before she returned to India, she travelled on the Continent.

On returning she contracted a marriage when she was barely nineteen with the man she loved, Dr Govandarajulu Naidu. The ceremony was performed by Pandit Veerasalingam Pantulu under the provisions of the Special Marriages Act which enabled people from different castes, communities, or religions to marry. It was one of the first such unions in Hyderabad state. Her husband was a medical doctor, employed by the Nizam's Medical Services. Sarojini settled down to an upper-middle class life of domestic duties and social drudgeries. From 1901 to 1904 she gave birth to four children in quick succession—Jaisoorya, Padmaja, Leilamani, and Ranadheera. Her duties as a wife, mother, and hostess occupied most of her time. However, her restless spirit rebelled against such a quotidian existence. She began to publish her poems and her first collection, *The Golden Threshold*, appeared in 1905. This was followed by *The Bird of Time* (1911) and, later, by *The Broken Wing* (1917). In the meanwhile, she had begun to receive invitations to address the several social organisations, especially those devoted to the welfare of youth and of women, which had proliferated all over India since the renaissance of the nineteenth century. Both she and her audiences quickly discovered her innate gift for oratory; soon she became a popular speaker, very much in demand all over the country.

It was through her friendship with Gopal Krishna Gokhale, whom she met frequently in London from 1912 to 1914, that she entered the mainstream of national political life. Gokhale extracted a pledge from her to dedicate herself and her gifts to the nation. This, arguably, was the turning point of her life. Soon afterwards, she met Gandhi, Nehru, Jinnah, and all the important leaders of her time. After Gokhale's death, she became a devoted associate of Gandhi. Largely through his influence, she succeed him as the President of the Indian National Congress in 1925. Prior to her, the only woman to have occupied this high post was Annie Besant. Soon afterwards in 1927, she become one of the founder-members of the All India Women's Conference, later becoming its President. Sarojini participated whole-heartedly in the freedom struggle under Gandhi's leadership. She also travelled extensively both in India and abroad, not just as a spokesperson of the Congress but as an outstanding extempore orator and an internationally recognised poet. She was jailed four times by the British, participated in the Civil Disobedience, Non-cooperation, Salt Satyagraha, Quit India and other movements, was a member of the Congress Working Committee, nursed Gandhi during some of his fasts, and in general, bore witness to some of the most important events of the first half of the twentieth century. After India achieved independence, she became, as already mentioned, the first Governor of India's most populous state, the United Provinces (now Uttar Pradesh).

She led a rich, varied, hectic, and satisfying life, dying in 1949 at the age of seventy. Longevity was not the least of her achievements because she was plagued by ill-health nearly all her life and suffered a variety of ailments including heart disease, rheumatism, lumbago, malaria, nervous disorders, broken limbs, spinal injury, fevers, headaches, and so on. Sarojini was aware of her own unusual zest for life which would triumph over all illnesses. In a letter of 5th October 1911 to her publisher William Heinemann, she says:

> You'll be sorry to hear that I am rather seriously ill. . . . Govind, my husband, is very anxious and very cross with me. But I cannot unless I am really dangerously ill, lie abed and 'cease activities.' He says I shall truly die young, but I don't believe it: I have far too much vital energy of the soul and can stand, without making a sign, any amount of pain—and besides, good God—how can I die—I who love life and all humanity?

(Paranjape, *Sarojini Naidu: Selected Letters* 70)Addressing Gopal Krishna Gokhale on the 30th of November 1914, she says: 'My health is shattered completely but I have some wonderful vitality in me that makes me even younger than my own children in their years! (Paranjape, *Sarojini Naidu: Selected Letters* 100). But, sick or healthy, Sarojini made the most of what she got from life. She was a personality full of energy and laughter, someone who in spite of tremendous suffering retained a comic view of life. As she wrote to Ranadheera soon after her sixty-fourth birthday, 'one is not so concerned with a long life as with a 'merry one'—merry as the sum of worthwhile, rich, full, interesting, and who can say that mine has not been and is not in that sense 'merry' as well as long?' (ibid 308). The letter, incidentally, was written from the Yervada jail. In another letter written to Padmaja over ten years earlier, also from the Yervada jail, she had declared: 'In the course of a long and most variegated life I have learned one superlative truth . . . that the true measure of life and oneself lies not in the circumstances and events that fill its map but in one's approach and attitude and acceptance of those things' (ibid 278). She certainly lived by these words till the end of her days.

III
Works

Sarojini Naidu's works have long been hard to get or out of print. *Sarojini Naidu Select Poems*, edited by H. G. Dalwey Turnbull, was published by Oxford University Press, Calcutta, in 1930. But, besides being outdated, it has never been reprinted. Today it is almost impossible to find a copy of this book. During her lifetime, Sarojini supervised the publication of *The Sceptred Flute*, which includes all the poems from her three major collections, *The Golden Threshold* (1905), *The Bird of Time* (1912), and *The Broken Wing* (1917). This served in lieu of an edition of her collected poems. It was first published by Dodd, Mead and Co., New York, in 1937. An Indian edition was issued by Kitabistan, Allahabad, in 1943, and reprinted several times up to 1979. However, today a copy even of the reprint is difficult to obtain; not just the Indian edition, but the publishing house itself is defunct. Moreover, there are several of her poems which *The Sceptred Flute* does not contain, including two juvenile compositions and *The Feather of the Dawn*, a volume of poems edited by her daughter Padmaja Naidu and published in 1961, twelve years after the poet's death. Thus, there has been neither a complete edition of her poems, nor a truly representative selection.

But such has been the continuing demand for her poetry, especially after it began to be prescribed in some universities, that there have been several unauthorised 'quickie' editions of her poems; of these I have looked at one by A. N. and Satish Gupta, and another by the indefatigable Raghukul Tilak (see Works Cited), a well known writer of bazaar notes. Such *kunjis* or 'keys' constitute a genre of their own; they are cheap, examination-oriented, and though badly edited and produced, are popular substitutes for texts among a majority of students of English literature in India. These 'guides' have performed a function similar to anthologies in keeping the poet alive in the minds of a new generation of students. Today, however, even these *kunjis* are not easily available.

Sarojini's prose is even less in circulation; it is practically inaccessible. The fullest collection can be found in *Speeches and Writings of Sarojini Naidu*, published by the great nationalist publisher, G. A. Natesan in Madras; its third edition came out in 1925. But even this was woefully incomplete because Sarojini remained in the public realm for another twenty-four years, until she died in 1949, during which period she must have given hundreds of speeches. This edition, moreover, has been out of print for decades. Hence, her prose is practically unknown, so much so that the fact that she wrote some memorable pieces is almost forgotten today.

In this Introduction, while not making any special claims for the value or significance of her writings, I do wish to offer a new way of reading them. To begin with, we must remember that Sarojini was an important figure in India's recent history and that her work therefore deserves to be available to present and future readers. As a politician, nationalist leader, poet, activist for women's rights, orator, and celebrity, she was certainly one of the most memorable and colourful Indian women of the last century. Thus, both in her own right and as a representative of her times, Sarojini deserves to be remembered and studied.

Yet, her career exhibits an intriguing paradox. She was one of those great people whose greatness is most difficult to identify and substantiate. Historians of the freedom movement invariably assign to her a minor role in the formation of the Indian nation. Important as a lieutenant and acolyte of Gandhi, by herself and on her own terms, she becomes relatively less so. Certainly, she made no epoch-making original contribution to either the ideology or practice of the struggle against colonialism. Even within the Congress, such an evaluation of her was not uncommon. This was evident even in the manner in which she became the Governor of United Provinces, India's largest state, which later came to be known as Uttar Pradesh. It was Bidhan Chandra Roy who was first offered the Governorship by Jawaharlal Nehru in July 1947. Roy was in the USA at that time. Sarojini agreed to officiate in his place. When Roy returned to India in November, he decided to accept the more challenging office of the Chief Minister of West Bengal and consequently resigned his Governorship. It was only after his resignation that she was 'confirmed' as the Governor of U.P.; otherwise, she was to have handed over charge by the end of October 1947. Through her entire public life, she never ran for any elected office; most likely, she had no grassroots support or base in any part of the country. It is easy, therefore, to see her contribution as merely that of a celebrity publicist and public relations officer of the Congress in general and Gandhi in particular.

Similarly, in the women's movement, Sarojini's contribution is more that of a supporter and populariser than an original thinker or activist. When one examines the documents of the All-India Women's Conference or the Indian suffragette movement, for instance, one notices that Margaret Cousins and not Sarojini was the prime mover to begin with. Sarojini was a non-controversial and famous *Indian* figurehead who could lend the cause legitimacy and acceptance.* Similarly, in the realms of ideas and activism, Sarojini was no radical like Pandita Ramabai nor a great organiser like Annie Besant in the field of religion and politics.

Nowhere is this paradox more obvious than in her poetry. Sarojini's poetry occupies a very limited realm of lyricism and is deliberately ephemeral thematically. Her indisputable metrical felicity and technical mastery have not prevented some of her poems from sounding like childish jingles. Indeed, with the

---

*For an account of the formation of the AIWC, see *Women's Struggle: A History of the All India Women's Conference 1927-2002* by Aparna Basu and Bharati Ray (New Delhi: Manohar, 2003).

modernist turn in Indian English poetry in the 1950s, a whole generation of poets grew up despising her poetry. Among them are P. Lal, Nissim Ezekiel, R. Parthasarathy, Adil Jussawalla, A. K. Mehrotra, and Keki Daruwalla. Some of them have also been influential anthologists, editors, and patrons of Indian English poetry. To them Sarojini was a particularly soft target: not only did she represent a dead aesthetic, but her romanticism was of a particularly meretricious kind. Whereas Rabindranath Tagore or Sri Aurobindo were harder to demolish or dismiss, Sarojini was a pushover because she had no pretensions to the depth or intellectual range of the other two figures. But despite her sinking reputation among a whole generation of poets and poet-makers, she has remained one of the most popular, widely-anthologised and studied of Indian English poets. Indeed, there are more books, papers, and articles on her poetry than on any Indian English poet except .Sri Aurobindo.

I would attempt to solve the riddle of the greatness of Sarojini by suggesting that she was a minor figure in a major mode. In other words, though whatever she did was not necessarily profound or significant in itself, it was nevertheless performed on a scale which was extraordinary and central to the formation of the Indian nation. She could sustain this seeming contradiction not only because of the special circumstances in which she lived and which made her qualities rare and sought-after, but because she was truly outstanding in one sphere. Her unusual energy contributed to an extraordinary public presence, which was both dynamic and catalytic. In other words, her unique greatness lay in aspects of her life and personality which are no longer accessible to us through her written words. The text of Sarojini's greatness was live, not written like that of great male leaders like Gandhi or Nehru.

One instance of this lost greatness needs special mention. Sarojini was one of the most eloquent and moving orators of her time, though most of what she spoke had emotional appeal and sentiment rather than 'solid' thought or argumentation. She was not really a great thinker, but an able one; it was, instead, the force of her personality that created the impact that she was remembered for. She was, perhaps, the most effective purveyor of the sublime, transforming public speaking into poetry. Moreover, Sarojini was an unorthodox and irrepressibly candid person, one who could poke fun at Gandhi himself, not to speak of his more solemn, humourless and puritanical coterie. Her letters to her children, especially to Padmaja, reveal her as a chatty correspondent, revelling in caricature and witty gossip. Finally, her greatness is most evident in her unconventional life. Throughout her eventful and busy years, she overcame extraordinary odds and pushed the realms of activity for Indian women farther than perhaps anyone had done before her. She achieved all this without being especially privileged by birth or upbringing.

Thus, while it is easy not to take seriously the adoring and cloying praise of her contemporaries and admirers, it is equally necessary not to swing to the other extreme in dismissing her out of hand. A critical examination of her life and works reveals not only that crucial aspects of her achievement may not be easily accessible to us, but that we need to look afresh at whatever of her life and work is available to us. A career such as Sarojini's not only calls into question how great she really was, but also forces us to re-examine our received notions of 'greatness', which are mostly patriarchal and intellectually elitist.

Sarojini's poetic career began when she was just eleven. Arthur Symons quotes her in his Introduction to *The Golden Threshold:*

> One day, when I was eleven, I was sighing over a sum in algebra: it *wouldn't* come right; but instead a whole poem came to me suddenly. I wrote it down.
>
> From that day my 'poetic career' began. At thirteen I wrote a long poem *a la* 'Lady of the Lake'—1300 lines in

six days. At thirteen I wrote a drama of 2000 lines . . . I wrote a novel, I wrote fat volumes of journals. I took myself very seriously in those days. (9)

Of these early works, only the first, the long poem '*a la* Lady of the Lake,' survives today. It was published when Sarojini was fourteen. Perhaps, it was the presentation of this book to the Nizam which resulted in her being awarded a scholarship by him for higher studies in England.

I found a printed copy of this poem in the Padmaja Naidu papers, Nehru Memorial Library. The title page reads: '*Mehir Muneer. A Poem in Three Cantos by a Brahmin Girl*. Madras: Printed by Srinivasa, Varadachari and Co., 1893.' There are corrections made throughout the book in a handwriting that resembles Sarojini's, including the title page, where 'A Brahmin Girl' has been scored out and 'A Hindu Lady' written in its place. A revised edition, though, was never brought out. It is interesting to see how Sarojini did not wish to be identified as the author of the poem and used, first, the more traditional disguise of 'Brahmin girl,' then struck it out and wrote over it, 'A Hindu Lady,' for a possible second, revised edition, which never came out. Despite the camouflage, she wished to highlight both her gender and her religion or community because these would make the poem all the more remarkable for its time.

This is Sarojini's earliest published poetic work and among the first she wrote. While Padmini Sengupta makes no mention of it, Tara Ali Baig, in *Sarojini Naidu* Tara Ali Baig, mistakenly calls it a play:

> She also wrote a little Persian play called 'Meher [sic] Muneer' which her father got printed in a local journal. A few copies of this play written in English were sent to friends. Among them was the Nizam of Hyderabad who was so charmed that he made a typically princely gesture . . . in 1895 His Exalted Highness endowed her with a scholarship granting her passage to England and

£300 a year.

It is clear that neither Sengupta nor Baig got to see the printed copy of *Mehir Muneer*. In its present form, the work is clearly a poem and not a play. However, the fact that Sarojini herself referred to it, mentioning its precise number of lines, that the text showed up in the Padmaja Naidu Papers, that it has corrections in Sarojini's handwriting, and that Baig says it earned her endowment, proves that Sarojini was indeed its author. My theory is that it was written originally in English as a poem, and that perhaps a Persian version was also prepared and presented to the Nizam. Though Sarojini had learned Persian and translated from it, I wonder if she knew it well enough to write an original literary work of considerable length in it at the age of thirteen.

Artistically, the poem is interesting, but flawed. The verses and rhymes are mostly childish, though there are bursts of inspired writing through the work. The poem, moreover, lacks unity and coherence. The first canto, about the birth of Mehir Muneer, seems to drag on for too long, and has little to do with the main plot concerning the romance between Mehir and Badar, which takes place in Cantos II and III. The most interesting aspects of the poem are its depiction of adult love in pre-adult terms. Here we have all the passion and innocence of such love without its guilt-inducing sexuality. This is also a children's world in that there are no disciplining and repressive authority figures in it to obstruct Mehir and Badar's first night together. Sarojini's creation of unreal and magical worlds is also noteworthy; not only is the poem set in an exotic locale, but the exoticism is further heightened in the enchanted forest world in Canto II. About it possible source, while Sarojini herself says she was writing a la

Walter Scott, Izzat Yaar Khan observes that 'its story was adapted from one of Sir Edwin Arnold's stories' (6).*

Her next collection, *'Songs* by S. Chattopadhyaya,' was printed privately by her father Aghorenath Chattopadhyaya in Hyderabad in 1896 and contains poems which she wrote from 1892-1896. The collection was, thus, published when she was in England. We know that she sent letters and poems to her would-be husband, Govindarajulu, from England. Some of these poems found their way into *Songs*, along with a number of older pieces. This collection is the weakest of all her books. In fact, I have not found a single poem in it which is worth quoting or studying except as juvenilia. Its publication was not supervised by her, though the printed copies of both *Mehir Muneer* and *Songs* show correction marks in her handwriting. Perhaps, she intended to republish both later, but then dropped the idea. The poems in these two juvenile collections are hardly ever discussed by critics. I believe that I made *Mehir Muneer* available for the first time to the general audience by reprinting it here.

It was with *The Golden Threshold* in 1905 that Sarojini's career as a poet really took off. Arthur Symons was responsible for the publication of this book. The poems in it belong almost wholly to two periods: 1896 and 1904. Sarojini had sent Symons some new poems in 1904 and he had already seen her earlier work in 1896. Symons says, 'As they seemed to me to have an individual beauty of their own, I thought they ought to be published' (9). Sarojini then wrote to Edmund Gosse asking for his advice and permission in publishing the collection. Sarojini's dedication of the book to 'Edmund Gosse who first showed me the way .to the Golden Threshold' indicates how deeply she was influenced

---

*Anisur Rahman in a more detailed study says that her poem draws heavily on an Urdu *mathnavi*, *Sehr-ul-Bayan* (The Magic of Narration) by Meer Ghulam Hasan Dehlavi, published by Fort William College in 1805. How and whether Sarojini had access to this work, however, remains to be established.

by him. Ironically, when Gosse had seen many of these very poems in 1896, he had been disappointed as he tells us in his Introduction to *The Bird of Time*. Now, thanks to Symons they were being published anyway. There was, however, yet another difficulty which no biographer or critic to my knowledge has mentioned. William Heinemann was unwilling to risk his money on the book, though it was recommended by Gosse and Symons, and would carry an Introduction by the latter. The poet had actually to pay the publisher a tidy sum of £ 14 to cover the printing costs. As she says in her letter of to Gosse of 4 September 1905:

> Some time I heard from Arthur Symons that Mr Heinemann would publish it and that an edition of 50-100 copies would cost £14—the binding extra. I at once wrote and asked him if I should send £14 immediately or wait till he let me know the total cost . . . So I have made up my mind to write direct to Mr Heinemann and send him the £14 this week so that there need be no delay in the printing.
>
> (*Selected Letters* 47)

The book, of course, went on to be a huge success; the first edition. was sold out by the end of 1905 and a new edition was published and quickly snapped up in 1906. Several poems were also set to music.

The Golden Threshold is, arguably, Sarojini's finest collection. The title is significant, hinting at the kind of romanticism that Sarojini practiced. What is the collection a threshold to? Does it refer to a key theme in the collection, that of growing up, bidding goodbye to one's dreams, and of maturing person and woman? Or is it a threshold to her poetic career, which she hopes will be golden? Or, yet again, is the collection a sort of threshold or passage to India itself for Western readers? And as a nationalistic poet, she would want to introduce her readers not to an earthen or clayey India, but a magnificent, golden India, embellished by her imagination and carefully ornamented so as to be pleasing and delectable to her foreign readers. At any rate, the title foregrounds the problem of representation which is at the heart of Sarojini's poetic project. Khan could not find the MS of *The Golden Threshold* at the National Library, Calcutta; he concludes that it is lost. But multiple manuscripts of several poems are at the National Archives, New Delhi.

This collection contains many of Sarojini's best known and loved poems, including several of the 'folk songs.' Of these, 'Palanquin Bearers,' is certainly the best-known and most-anthologised. The poem has an intricate metrical composition. Each line has four feet, with three anapaests, followed by a shorter iambic foot at the close. The dominant foot is the anapaest, which gives the poem its springy effect.

> Lightly, O lightly, we bear her along,
> She sways like a flower in the wind of our song;
> She skims like a bird on the foam of a stream
> She floats like a laugh from the lips of a dream.
> Gaily, O gaily we glide and we sing,
> We bear her along like a pearl on a string. (108)[*]

This poem can be central to a symptomatic re-reading of Sarojini's poetry in terms of what it leaves out—the toil, sweat, and oppression of the palanquin bearers. Hence, it presents a 'pretty picture' of a dying feudal order under colonialism. The poem, moreover, is in a section called, 'Folk Songs.' Sarojini makes the 'folk' sing of their reality in terms which would please the gentry. The folk are shown in idealised and idyllic postures, in effect, celebrating and glorifying their own oppression.

The poem does represent accurately some features of the situation depicted, though. Palanquin bearers were, indeed, known to sing as they worked, their verses meant to lighten the

---

[*]The page numbers after the poems refer to this volume.

burdens that they carried. But the labour was heavy and hard. The verses were often repetitive and meaningless. Sarojini, too, tries to bring a similar formulaic repetitiveness to the poem. Once the first stanza defines a workable structure, it can be reused with slight variations. The two stanzas, hence, do not present any real development of thought but do constitute a sort of balanced whole. Though the situation is authentic, what the bearers are made to say is not. There is therefore a tension between the structure and texture of the poem, quite characteristic of her other folk songs. The folk cannot break out of the idealised mould into which they are cast.

An 'Indian Love Song' (132-133) from this collection presents a heavily mannered and conventionalised love poem with the images tailored for the contrasting masculine and feminine voices. The poem is a part of a cycle of love poems which include 'An Indian Love Song' and 'A Rajput Love Song' from the *Bird of Time*. All these poems show that Sarojini deliberately created masculine and feminine types, complete with appropriate gestures, clothes, accessories, and speech patterns. The masculine and feminine to her are, thus, abstract categories, opposite yet balanced, somewhat like Purusha and Prakriti; she was, like many of her generation, an essentialist in many matters relating to gender.

Another important poem that shows Sarojini's feudal orientation is 'Suttee' (112). The last line, 'Shall the flesh survive when the soul is gone?' seems to be a justification for the infamous rite, indicating that the deceased husband was like her soul, while all that remains of the widow is her flesh. Yet, the question mark makes the sense ambiguous. Obviously, Sarojini appears to romanticise sati in this poem, implying that like several other retrogressive practices from her immediate past, she found it aesthetically appealing though as a champion of women's rights, she opposed it politically. This tension between her poetry and her politics is evident throughout her work. This poem is one of other sati poems where the separation from or the death of the beloved leads to a strong death wish.

An 'Ode to H. H. The Nizam of Hyderabad' is of interest as an example of courtly poetry in praise of a king or patron, of which there is a long tradition not just in English, but in Persian and Urdu poetry. But what is most fascinating is the picture of Hyderabad that Sarojini presents. It is a city frozen in time, a medieval city, exotic and romantic, the very city of her poetic inspiration. It has a static and hierarchical social structure presided over by a humane, paternalistic, benevolent, and tolerant prince-poet. There are no conflicts, either of class or religion, in this city, nor any starvation, oppression, and suffering.

The Prince addressed is Mir Mahboob Ali Khan (1866-1911), the 6th Nizam of Hyderabad. He ruled, technically, from 29 February 1869, but more directly from his eighteenth year in 1884 until his death on 29 August 1911. His reign was characterised by peace, prosperity, and almost idyllic romance. The Hyderabad of Mahboob Ali Khan was the city the poet grew up in. For her, it remained the ideal city of her imagination like Yeats' Byzantium.*
In her papers, I found a most extraordinary letter describing the funeral of this Prince and the spontaneous outpouring of devotion and mourning that it aroused:

> In all history I know of nothing more poignantly lovely than the devotion he aroused and still arouses in the hearts of his people . . . rich and poor, cultured and ignorant, Hindu, Mohammedan, Parsi, Sikh, Jain, Christian—I wish you could have come to my city of the Arabian Nights in the lifetime of my own Haroun-al-Rashid! For Hyderabad will never be quite the same again.
>
> (*Selected Letters* 64).

That Sarojini's was an aesthetic of excess is also clear in a poem such as 'Indian Dancers' (118-119). There are two copies of MS in

---

*See 'Hyderabad in the Poetry of Sarojini' in *Kohinoor in the Crown* by K. V. Suryanarayana Murthy.

the National Archives, one with a title, 'Eastern Dancers.' Every sense is pushed to a point beyond satiety in this poem through an overabundance of lush and overripe imagery:
Eyes ravished with rapture, celestially panting,

> what passionate bosoms aflaming with fire
> Drink deep of the hush of hyacinth heavens
>   that glimmer around them in fountains of light;
> O wild and entrancing the strain of keen music
>   that cleaveth the stars like a wail of desire,
> And beautiful dancers with houri-like face
>   bewitch the voluptuous watches of the night.

The orient is painted as the theatre of an extravagant and dazzling sensuality, bordering on decadence in Sarojini's favourite metre, anapaest. The overall effect is to create a hazy and entranced mood, as might be induced by a narcotic or opiate. The images suggest the lack of sharpness, clarity, and visibility. Sarojini's idea of sensuality is a hedonistic glut. This aesthetic, which was supported by feudal luxury, was already declining during Sarojini's time. Perhaps, this was her requiem to its demise. Interestingly, it later continued in Bollywood cinema, especially in stories of the Muslim courtesan, albeit with a degree of irony or moral censure.

'Damayanti to Nala in the Hour of Exile' (120) is a fine example of what Sarojini could, but did not, do. The fragment is in, grand end-stopped, rhyming couplets in iambic pentameter. The principal *rasa* or art emotion is *vira* or heroism. Damayanti, one of the exemplary classical heroines, had to undergo many hardships along with her husband, Nala, who lost his kingdom in a game of dice. The poem shows Damayanti trying to rouse the spirits of her depressed husband. It is another matter that latter in the story she is by Nala in the forest. The story is found in the Mahabharata. The diction of the poem is Victorian as is its tone of high moral purpose. The message is that the love of a woman is no less than a kingdom for a deposed king. Such a notion of woman's love for a man being the highest value is found in several of Sarojini's poems, culminating in 'The Temple' in *The Broken Wing*.

'The Pardah Nashin' (124-125), a famous poem like 'Suttee,' shows Sarojini's ambivalence to traditional institutions that restricted the rights of women, in this case, the Muslim practice of *purdah* or seclusion and veiling. The poem begins with a romanticisation of the life of the sequestered woman; an effect of luxurious idleness, consoling and sensuous is created. But as the poem progresses, the purdah becomes as repressive as it is protective. It cannot prevent the entry of old age and sorrow into the woman's quarter. The note of pathos at the end cleady suggests that Sarojini felt more pity than approval for the *purdah nashin* or the sheltered woman. 'Nightfall in the City of Hyderabad' (125-126) is another of the Hyderabad poems, celebrating the city's grandeur and romance. The construction of Hyderabad as an enchanted, medieval fortress-city is shaped by the rich imagery in rhyming couplets. The images emphasise the pristine, secluded, secure, leisured, sensuous and opulent life of the city. 'Street Cries' (126), also a Hyderabad poem, has the typical cyclical structure of many of Sarojini's poems. The morning, when 'bread' is sold, is a time of work and activity; the afternoon when the 'fruit' sellers roam, of leisure and relaxation, and night, represented by 'flower' sellers, of love and sex. Each facet has its place and together constitutes the totality of life.

Sarojini's nationalism is reflected in poems such as 'To India' (127). The poem, not particularly effective or memorable, is a typical of the prevailing discourse. India is personified as the Mother who is both ancient and young. The burden of the poem is to awaken the slumbering nation to freedom and to a sense of her special mission as the inheritor of a great past and progenitor of a promising future, after having traversed the 'fettered darkness' of the colonial interregnum.

'The Royal Tombs of Golconda' (127-128), another Hyderabad poem, argues that Time cannot consign to oblivion the Kings and Queens buried in the tombs, an idea which goes counter to the usual argument in Romantic poetry as in Shelley's 'Ozymandias.' Curiously, Sarojini makes a different case for the men and for the women. The kings, she says, will not be forgotten as long as their fortress still stands on the hills and the queens will not die because their flower-like bodies will reawaken with every spring. For Sarojini, the latter are closer to nature and, therefore, freer from the decay of time. Oneness with nature is a key theme in her work and recurs frequently in her many spring poems. Spring, both physically and metaphorically, is Sarojini's answer to the mutability of the human condition.

The last poem of *The Golden Threshold*, 'To a Buddha Seated on a Lotus' (128-129), ensures that the collection ends on a spiritual note, a pattern followed in her other books too. Though not impressive in itself, the poem is remembered in the West because it was one of the three included in *The Oxford Book of Mystic Verse* edited by D. H. S. Nicholson and A.H.E. Lee. To me, it falls short of a significant insight into the mystical experience because the speaker merely wonders how ordinary people may reach the elusive goal of nirvana.

The *Golden Threshold* was reviewed favourably both in the Indian and, especially, in the British press. There were reviews in *The Times* (London), *The Manchester Guardian*, *The Review of Reviews*, *The Morning Post*, *Athanaeum*, *Daily Chronicle*, *Spectator*, and *T.P.'s Weekly*. *The Golden Threshold* made Sarojini a celebrity in both India and England. Never before had a book of poems by an Indian caused such a stir abroad. We might remember that it predated the English *Gitanjali* of Tagore by quite a few years. So enchanting did her English readers find her verses, that several poems were set to music by Liza Lehman. *The Golden Threshold* remains Sarojini's best and most popular book. She never quite exceeded what she achieved in it.

Sarojini's second collection of poems, *The Bird of Time*, was published by William Heinemann in 1912, with an introduction by Edmund Gosse; it was also published simultaneously in New York by John Lane. This book, too, was reviewed widely in India and in England. Sarojini was an established poet by now. Her readers in England expected both beauty and oriental glamour from her and she did not disappoint them. The title is from Omar Khayyam and the title poem (130) encapsulates Sarojini's poetic philosophy. When asked 'What are the songs you sing?' (stanza one) and 'where did you learn/ The changing measures you sing?' the singing bird replies that she sings of both the joys and sorrows of life and that she learned her songs from both nature and culture. There is a deliberate cultivation here of the minor mode; Sarojini is happy to write seemingly insignificant and ephemeral lyrics like a bird chirps its songs. The artifice is comparable to Blake's deliberate simplicity in his 'Songs of Innocence,' though not as profound in intent.

'Dirge' (131) is another sati poem. The first three stanzas seem to endorse the stripping of the widow of all her jewellery and colourful garments, forcing her to go through a sort of 'living death' now that her husband is dead. But the turn comes in the fourth stanza in a manner so devastatingly ironic that in denying the need to enforce such a ritual on the widow, Sarojini seems to reify the widow's dependence on her dead husband even more.

> Nay, let her be! . . . what comfort can we give
> For joy so frail, for hope so fugitive?
> The yearning pain of unfulfilled delight,
> The moonless vigils of the lonely night,
> For the abysmal anguish of her tears,
> And the flowering springs that mock her empty years?

The widow's life, she says, is so pathetic and sorrowful that it does not matter if she is allowed to retain her jewels and finery.

The poet does not consider setting the widow free of custom and observance, of imagining for her a new life and love. Certainly, Sarojini, the champion of women's rights, can be seen politically at her worst here. Poems such as these suggest that she never quite broke with tradition in her way of thinking, at least as far as her poetry went.

'An Indian Love Song' (132-133), has the same title as an earlier poem in *The Golden Threshold*. This poem, however, has a richer narrative content, depicting an inter-caste, inter-religious romance. The diction is reminiscent of Shakespeare's *Romeo and Juliet*. The final message is that love, the great natural force, is greater than all man-made differences. A fit plot for many a popular Hindi movie, right up to present times. Another love poem, 'Love and Death' (133-134) is, to my mind, one of Sarojini's finest poems. Its form is that of a Petrarchan sonnet, with the rhyme scheme – abbaabba ccdeed. The octave depicts the ideal of love; like Savitri, the poet dreams that her love has freed her beloved from death. But the sestet reveals the hard and cruel reality in which the poet realises that her love has not been able to mitigate even one throe of pain, let alone bring the beloved back from death. The poem is modern in spirit in that it refutes the ideal represented by Savitri. The poem makes an interesting comparison with Toru Dutt's 'Savitri,' and Sri Aurobindo's *Savitri*—it would seem that the Savitri figure is important to the Indian English imaginary.

'A Rajput Love Song' (135-136) is the finest example of the highly stylised use of convention in Sarojini's love poetry. The poem presents a *tableau vivant* of the lovers, complete with setting, costume, accessories, and appropriate imagery. A sophisticated typology of gender is constructed in the poem, with contrasting iconography for the male and female. Equal, opposite, and together complete, seems to be underlying gender ideology of the poem. According to Tod's *Annals and Antiquities of Rajasthan*, Amar Singh was the second son of Raja Jay Singh of Jodhpur.

He was banished by his father and joined Shah Jehan's service. Parvati, whom he married, was the Princess of Bundi. After Amar Singh was murdered at an early age, she committed sati (see Khan 142).

'A Song in Spring' (136-137), one of many similar poems, shows how spring is the most appropriate of seasons for love according to classical Indian aesthetics. These poems on spring appear to draw heavily on Kalidasa and on the Indian tradition of love poetry. An appropriate landscape for love is offered in them, reminding us of specifications of place, time, objects, seasons, and themes laid down in texts like the Tolkappiyam.* 'Vasant Panchami' (137-138), a poem about a spring festival, deliberately introduces a note of grief and mourning into what is otherwise a season of joy and celebration. This is typical of Sarojini who believed that life is a balance of opposites. As it happens, it turns out to be another sati poem. Lilavati, the protagonist, is a widow. The sentiments she expresses are supposedly typical and appropriate to Indian widows. The poem, once again reveals the 'revivalist' aesthetics of Sarojini, looking back and idealising traditions from the past, which many would consider not worth retaining. The insertion of the traditional interjection of grief in Hindi-Urdu, *Hai* (first line, third stanza), suggests at the kind of authenticity and 'Indianness' that Sarojini was striving to create.

'In a Time of Flowers' (138-139) is also similar in that the speaker addresses her dead lover wondering how he can continue in his grave when the spring has broken out in such riotous joy. The poem expresses the earth-bound passionate romanticism of Sarojini, reminiscent of Catherine's love for the moors in *Wuthering Heights*. 'In Praise of Gulmohur Blossoms' and the other flower poems that follow (139-142) are an attempt to bring to English verse local Indian flowers. They show her commitment to the

---

*See A. K. Ramanujan's *The Interior Landscape* for an account of the relationship between landscapes and poetic genres.

local and immediate in her attempt to 'nativise' English poetry. The poem is a celebration of transience and temporariness. Behind it is a profound philosophical conviction in their liberating power: if everything is fleeting, why worry about sorrow and death? They too, like all natural phenomena, must be temporary. Sarojini believes in revelling in the present because the present joy of spring is the overwhelming reality which shuts out all remembrance of sorrow.

'Village Songs,' (142-143) is another 'folk song,' about the Gopi from Mathura delayed on her way back from the river. Both the situation and the way the woman copes with it are typical. The problem of representation, though, is not as severe as in the earlier folk songs because the speaker does not clearly belong to an oppressed group; that is, the poem doesn't represent the experience of someone in a particular low-status profession (palanquin-bearer, fisher, weaver, and so on). The situation of the speaker is less extrinsic to her context than in the earlier folk songs. But the artificiality of the poem is equally evident in that it what might be a typical poem of Krishna and the gopis in an Indian language, appears stilted and archaic in English.

The manuscript of 'Songs of My City' (143-144) in the National Archives shows their original title as 'Two Folk Songs.' The second part is more interesting because we see an attempt, once again, to eroticise Hyderabad as a place of oriental mystery and magic. 'Song of Radha, the Milkmaid,' like the earlier 'Village Songs,' shows Sarojini pick up the Radha theme. She wrote some more Radha poems some which are published in *The Feather of the Dawn*, her last and posthumously published collection. Though the subject offers vast poetic potential and challenge to an Indian English poet, Sarojini fails to really exploit its resources. Her Radha is a weak and mindless creature, unable to express anything more than the most trivial and commonplace sentiments of distress, supplication, or devotion.

James H. Cousins, one of the most important colonial commentators on Indian literature and culture, says, 'My first contact with Mrs Sarojini Naidu's poetry was through hearing the 'Song of Radha, the Milkmaid' recited by an Oxford man in India. I shall never forget the *mantric* effect of the devotee's repetition of 'Govinda, Govinda,' as she carried the curds, her pots, and her gifts to the shrine at Mathura' (268-269). The praise seems to be exaggerated but illustrates the Orientalist agenda of Sarojini, Indianising and perhaps unintentionally exoticising her subject matter.*

'Hussain Sagar' (147) is another Hyderabad poem about the most famous lake in the heart of the city of Hyderabad. The lake becomes an object of love, wooed and courted by many, but like the poet, holding its allegiance to one lover. By identifying with the lake and by making it somewhat mysterious, Sarojini reasserts her poetic allegiance to her native city of Hyderabad, returning to it for inspiration and support. 'The Faery Isle of Janjira' (148) is just the sort of place which held fascination for Sarojini. Janjira, even more than Hyderabad, is an exotic and remote location, steeped in history and folklore; it is a romantic island where, much as she is attracted to it, she cannot stay because the larger cause of the freedom struggle ('the drum beat of destiny') calls her.

'The Soul's Prayer' (148-149) also appeared in *The Oxford Book of English Mystic Verse* and is, in my view, more complex and accomplished than the other anthologised poem, 'To a Buddha

---

*For an interesting comparison between what she calls the 'doubly orientalizing' reception of Sarojini's verse and the more recent applause that Arundhati Roy's single novel attracted, see Elleke Boehmer's 'East is East and South Is South: The Cases of Sarojini Naidu and Arundhati Roy.' Boehmer argues that certain constructions of 'singular oriental femaleness, and an extravagant oriental style' remain virtually unchanged from Sarojini's time to now.

Seated on a Lotus.' It contains a dialogue between the poet and her God. What the poet asks for is a total experience of the world, not freedom from it. God replies that such an experience will only chasten her until she desires the peace that passeth understanding. There is a genuine mystical touch in the last couplet which hints at the interconnectedness of life and death, both of which are facets of one Ultimate Reality.

'The Old Woman' (150) is one of Sarojini's finest poems. It evokes *karuna* or compassion. The refrain, which is the first article of faith for a Muslim, works very effectively, underscoring the woman's stoicism and fortitude born of her devotion. Sarojini gives us a possible history of the old woman, how she once was a wife and mother, who is now reduced to begging in the street. The second stanza is probably one of the most 'realistic' pieces of verse Sarojini ever wrote; there is very little ornamentation or embellishment in it. For once, Sarojini confronts her reality with a sober gaze. Though the structure is conventional, the representation of the woman breaks out of the predictable cast. Had Sarojini written more such poems, she might have been able to alter her idiom and enlarge her poetic capacities. Instead, with the onset of literary modernism, her verse dated rapidly, as I shall show.

'An Anthem of Love' and 'The Call to Evening Prayer' (151-152) are both nationalistic poems like 'To India.' Again, we see a clear apotheosis of the nation and a sense of divine destiny in the freedom movement. Sarojini worked for communal harmony for the better part of her life as did Mahatma Gandhi, her mentor. The poem, though not very effective as such, shows Sarojini's attempt at making religion unite rather than divide people.

The Broken Wing, her third collection, was published by Heinemann in 1917. In its opening and title poem, she poses the question 'Song-bird why dost *thou* bear a broken wing?' (154). It was actually the question that Gokhale, her mentor before Gandhi, asked her as indicated in the epigraph. Gokhale detected a hidden sorrow beneath her jovial exterior. The question posed in the first half of the poem is not answered in the second, but deflected. The poet replies that she will soar up even on a broken wing. The fact of incapacitation is not denied, nor is it explained. The conversation between Sarojini and Gokhale took place in the spring of 1914 (see 'Gokhale the Man' 211). If we read this poem as an allegory for Sarojini's poetic career, then it contains a prophecy of its impending loss of afflatus. A career which began at 'Golden Threshold,' so seemingly full of glorious possibilities, ends with singing birds' wing broken. Biographical explanations might refer to her physical disabilities or debilities or, as many of the poems themselves suggest, to loss of love which might have come with the growing estrangement with her husband. But, from the perspective of literary and cultural history, we may venture to answer the posed question rather differently: the wing is broken because the poetic fashion has changed. With the coming of modernism, there was a paradigm shift in the technique and subject of English poetry, a revolution which passed Sarojini by. She remained a singing bird in a gilded cage in age which, it would seem, had no place for her.

Another way of explaining her declining poetic output is that she was now devoted to the national cause. In another memorable encounter, this time on the terrace of the Servants of India Society in Pune, Gokhale exacted a promise from her, 'Stand here with me with the stars and hills for witness and in their presence consecrate your life and your talent, your song and your speech, your thought and your dream to the Motherland. O Poet, see visions from the hilltops and spread abroad the message of hope to the toilers in the valleys' (ibid 216-217). Perhaps, Sarojini gave up poetry for public service. Yet she did not abandon the former altogether; in fact, on many occasions, she tried to link it to the latter. For instance, her poem 'The Gift of India' (155) was read out to the Hyderabad Ladies' War Relief Association in December 1915 (Padmini Sengupta 95), with printed copies circulated; it was also recited at the Congress session of 1916 (Padmini Sengupta 91) before it appeared in *The Broken Wing*. In other words, she tried to integrate poetry with politics, wherever it was suitable. The subject of the poem is the martyrdom of those Indian soldiers who died overseas fighting for the British against the Central Powers in World War I, the blood soaking the meadows of Flanders and France. There was a common feeling at that time that Britain would show its gratitude to India for the latter's support. Sarojini's poem may be considered sentimental and superficial, substituting rhetoric for authentically felt experience, but it is nationalistic in that it urges Britain to remember the 'gift' of India. One of the reasons that Congress leaders finally decided not to support the British war effort during World War II was because the 'Gift of India' was ignored and that British promises for greater autonomy to India were never fulfilled.

Another recurring theme in Sarojini's poems is the depiction of what may be termed Muslim India. 'The Imam Bara' and 'A Song from Shiraz' (157-158) are a part of a group of 'Lucknow poems,' all of which are Shia in spirit. Both poems are highly charged and compressed in language and imagery, making them almost prophetic in manner. Ali was the son-in-law, and Hassan and Hussain, the nephews of the prophet Mohammad. They were assassinated in a struggle for succession after the latter's death. Their deaths are mourned each year by the Shias during muharram.[*] The first of the two 'Memorial Verses' (159-160), 'Ya Mahbub!' mourns the death of Mir Mahboob Ali Khan on whom she already published a poem, 'Ode to H.H. the Nizam of Hyderabad,' in *The Golden Threshold*. The Nizam was responsible for sending Sarojini to England. Again, the poem approvingly

---

*These poems are included in an anthology of such mourning poems in English by the Iranian scholar, Dr M. R. Fakhr-Rohani (see Works Cited).

evokes a picture of Hyderabad as a 'magic kingdom,' fabulous and glamorous like the 'old Baghdad' of Harun-al-Rashid. 'Wandering Beggars' (160) like 'The Old Woman' has a Muslim refrain, 'Y'Allah! Y'Allah!' The beggars are romanticised as a fearless and free band, instead of being poor and wretched. The sentiments that Sarojini makes them utter are more suitable to those *sannyasis* and *fakirs* who have voluntarily embraced poverty than to beggars. 'The Prayer of Islam' (162) is another of Sarojini's Islamic poems. Five pairs of the ninety-nine names of Allah are celebrated in it. These names are: *Hameed:* 'one to whom all praise is due'; *Hafeez:* 'the protector'; *Ghani:* 'the beautiful'; *Ghaffar:* 'the forgiver'; *Wahab:* 'the bestower'; *Waheed:* 'the unique'; *Quadeer:* 'the Almighty'; *Quavi:* 'the Powerful'; *Rahman:* 'the Merciful'; *Raheem:* 'the Compassionate,' (Khan 188-189).

The second of the two 'Memorial Verses' is dedicated to Gokhale, who, in a footnote, she calls 'the great saint and soldier of our national righteousness,' whose 'life was a sacrament, and his death was a sacrifice in the cause of Indian unity'; the verse ends the call to 'upbuild the temple' of the unity of the motherland whose cause Gokhale gave his life for and taught his countrymen and women to serve (160). Incidentally, Gokhale was revered as a political mentor by Gandhi too. It is interesting, if not uncanny, that a poem, 'The Lotus,' follows soon after, dedicated to Gandhi. In this poem, she likens Gandhi to the mystic lotus which remains inviolate even though it is rifled and plundered by 'wild-bee hordes with lips insatiate' (161). Sarojini seems to hint that the source of Gandhi's strength lay in a dimension not easily understood or accessible to mundane minds, though it was a secret she had intuited. The mantle of mentorship, thus, passed from Gokhale to Gandhi, who nominated her to the presidency of the Indian National Congress after his term ended.

'Kali the Mother' and 'Awake' (165-166) are, again, nationalistic poems. Like 'The Prayer of Islam,' the first poem contains a litany of some of the names of Shakti, the great, composite female Goddess of Hinduism. Both poems invoke the Goddess to harmonise all the sections of Indian society; of course, the Mother also refers to Mother India. Indeed, Sarojini often invoked the this idea yoking the secular goal of nationalism to religious symbolism in the tradition of Bankimchandra Chatterjee and Sri Aurobindo. 'Awake' shows all the children of Mother India, separately first as 'Hindus, Parsees, Mussulmans, Christians,' then as 'All Creeds,' kneeling before her in to demonstrate their united resolve to serve her. Ironically, this poem was dedicated to Mohammed Ali Jinnah, the architect of Pakistan. It was read at a session of the Indian National Congress in 1915 in Bombay (Padmini Sengupta 114). However, at the time of the poem's writing, Jinnah was an advocate of Hindu-Muslim unity.

'The Temple' (170-185) is a sequence of twenty-four poems with eight in each of the three parts, 'The Gate of Delight,' 'The Path of Tears,' and 'The Sanctuary.' It is her longest single composition since *Mehir Muneer* and her only mature attempt at something more ambitious than her habitual lyric muse. The three sections suggest an architecture for the sequence resembling that of a temple in which a pilgrim progresses from the gate to the sanctuary. Such an appropriation of religious symbols for earthly love is common in Indian love poetry. However, the tripartite structure is denied in the poems themselves which don't seem to show any progression at all. This sequence is Sarojini's most sustained attempt at defining the various facets of love. Overall, it is not a happy collection. The speaker seems to be trying desperately to revive a moribund or dead love. Her lover spurns her despite her repeated attempts to win him back. The poems proclaim an undying and lofty love for this broken relationship, but the lover remains unmoved. One could even go so far as to suggest that these poems document the rather sad demise of what was once a passionate relationship.

At any rate, the relationship portrayed is an unequal one. The speaker is very severe on herself, often castigating and flagellating herself in the hope of drawing the lover's attention. Throughout, there is an excess of emotion and exaggerated self-abasement. The speaker seeks to sacrifice herself completely, to subordinate herself totally to the lover. But, the very insistence and repetitiveness of this assertion suggest that the surrender is an ideal, not attainable in reality; perhaps, it is even a ruse or strategy to compel some sort of response. Thus, even when the poet invites her lover to scorn her, she is, perhaps, saying this in the hope of the opposite response from the lover. The saddest aspect of the sequence is the sense of ultimate helplessness of the speaker. All her efforts are self-generated and self-limited; the liberating recognition from the beloved never comes. The sequence also relies on several conventions of Indian love poetry, portraying various facets of a heroine in love. There are poems of love in union and in separation, with several variations in the patterns. In many poems, the flavour is distinctly Tagorean as Sarojini's epigraph from Tagore would suggest.

The Broken Wing did not receive the kind of praise that her earlier books had. Instead, by now, not only was the notices lukewarm, but there was also considerable criticism of her limitations as a poet. In Europe, the first wave of modernism was beginning to gather momentum. There were to be cataclysmic changes in poetic fashion. Though she had prepared another volume in 1927, Padmaja, her daughter, published it in 1961, long after Sarojini's death. Called *The Father of the Dawn*, this final volume of her poems, was published in 1961 by Asia Publishing House. Modernism was the ruling mode in Indian poetry. The book was panned by Nissim Ezekiel, among others. Sarojini, to all intents and purposes, had been consigned to oblivion.

Padmaja's note says that the poems were composed during July-August 1927. In another note she explains the significance of the title:

> The title of this book of poems is from a dance by the

DENISHAWN DANCERS based on the Hopi Indian legend that a feather blown into the air at dawn, if caught by a breeze and carried out of sight, marks the opening of an auspicious day.

In her letter to her younger daughter, Leilamani Naidu, dated 13 August 1927, Sarojini says: 'Bebe [Padmaja Naidu] is so pleased and excited about my new poems. It seems so strange for the mood to have returned suddenly after all these years! I have half a volume, ready in these few weeks and some of the poems are I think very beautiful,' (*Selected Letters* 196). But Sarojini never published the collection during her lifetime. Was she aware that the tastes and changed and the book would no longer be received well?

Overall, the collection clearly shows a decline in poetic inspiration and quality. The enthusiasm of the earlier verses has flagged and the themes seem more tired. 'Songs of Radha' (191-194), the most interesting poems in the collection, attempt to bring the rich tradition of Krishna poetry into Indian English, but fail to do so. Here we see Sarojini turning from human to divine love in a fashion that is not unusual in Indian poetry. Yet, she does not quite succeed in pulling it off. Writing Radha poems in English, it would seem, is much more difficult and complicated than Sarojini's attempts seem to consider. It becomes all the more clear that a simple appropriation of such native poetic traditions and practices into English will not succeed without in some degree remaking and re-experiencing the spirit of the originals. This Sarojini has been unable to do. Instead, the poems seem to be weighed down by much more mundane lover's complaints, embellished with the stage dressings of pining lover's paraphernalia:

> My bridal veils are flung upon the floor,
> My bridal garlands drop across the door.
> The buds that on my bed their fragrance spilt,
> Grief-scattered, wane and wilt.

(192)

Of these Radha poems, 'The Quest' (193-194) is the most 'mystical' to my mind because it seems to actualise the transcendence of duality in its last couplet. In all her poetry so far, we have never witnessed such a moment when Sarojini seems to have glimpsed what lies beyond the separation and pining of the lover for her beloved.

If we were to examine the poetic career graph of poet, it is clear that her reputation was at its highest from 1905 to 1907 and then there was a steady decline afterwards. In India she continued to have a following until her death. But in the 1950s when modernism took over Indian English poetry, her reputation as a poet dipped to its lowest. This contempt for her poetry persists in at least two entire generations of poets and critics, some of whom are now dead, but several others still active. Yet, throughout, her poetry has remained 'popular' among the common readers in India; there is scarcely anybody with an English-medium education in India who doesn't know her 'Palanquin-Bearers' or has not, at least, heard of her. As I have tried to show, the tide, however, is turning, with at least some serious interest in her work from post-colonial and feminist perspectives.

That is why I would argue that the most effective way of reviving an interest in Sarojini's poetry is by shifting the critical focus from an evaluation of individual poems to an engagement with the underlying material and cultural conditions in which her poetry was produced and interpreted. The question then is not how good or effective a poet she was or even what the major themes and techniques of her poetry were, but what the nature of her poetic project was and how it was shaped by the dominant ideological structures of her time. We can then begin to appreciate the inner tensions and conflicts in her poetry. Thus situated, Sarojini's poetry becomes a rich and complex text which reproduces the contradictions and debates of her age.

Sarojini's poetry mediates between the usually opposing but sometimes complimentary forces of the English poetic tradition and her Indian sensibility, between the politics of nationalism and the aesthetics of feudalism, between the overwhelming power of modernity and the nostalgia for a threatened and fast vanishing residual culture, between the security of a comfortable patriarchy and the liberating power of the women's movement. Thus, Sarojini's texts display both resistance to and collusion with the dominant ideology of her time, which was colonialism. There is in them both a compromise with and resistance to prevailing power structures, whether literary or political. Unlike Tagore, Sarojini was unable to liberate her poetry from these contradictions. Her work remained coloured by them; hence, the vague sense of 'betrayal' and eventual hostility of the Indian English literary establishment after the initial adoration.

It has been a commonplace assumption that Sarojini's poetry is imitative of British romantic poets. There is no doubt that her poetry bears the stamp of British lyricism, yet the exact nature of this influence has never been worked out. The result is a plethora of possible and suggested influences, often not confined to the romantic poets. Sarojini herself identifies Sir Walter Scott as the model for *Mehir Muneer*. Gosse, her literary mentor and first critic, mentions the influence of Shelley and Tennyson. Turnbull speaks of Swinburne among other possible influences. Later critics have located her sources in the poetry of the pre-Raphaelites and of the 1890s. Such claims have never been backed up by exacting scholarship but merely aired as self-evident verities. I believe that the question of the influences on Sarojini's poetry must be traced with more precision and accuracy.

As a beginning in that direction, I shall quote from a letter which Sarojini wrote to Govindarajulu on 13 January 1896:

> Shelley and Byron, Moore and Scott, Keats and Campbell and Wordsworth were a brilliant starry coterie, but even

as brilliant as their coterie, though rather differently, are the new poets. Fancy the young, passionate, beautiful poets gathered together in a radiant galaxy. William Watson with his sublime, starry genius, Davidson with his wild, riotous, dazzling superabundant brilliance, Thompson with his rich, gorgeous, spiritual ecstasy of poetry, Yeats with his exquisite dreams and music, Norman Gale, redolent of springtime in the meadows and autumn in the orchard, Arthur Symons, the marvellous boy, with his passionate nature and fiery eyes, all gathered together in the friendly house of that dearest and lovingest of friends and rarest and most gifted of [geniuses] Edmund Gosse. Take too the older men, with their beautiful gifts—Swinburne, with his marvellous spirit, his voluptuous ecstasy of word music, take that grand old Socialist William Morris hammering with golden thunders. Take that lovely singer Edwin Arnold and that graceful writer, the laureate of the English, Alfred Austin—who says we have no rare geniuses and true poets in these days? Of course the younger men are the more gifted, and William Watson is the greatest and noblest of them all—

(*Selected Letters* 2-3)

The note of girlish excitement can easily be explained if we remember that the poet was not yet seventeen when she wrote this. It is ironic that nearly all the poets Sarojini hails as geniuses, except Yeats, are forgotten today. The problem is not so much that she had minor poets for her models; she had little choice in that regard. Moreover, bad models do not necessarily make bad poetry; there are many instances of minor poets inspiring major ones. What is important is the final product not so much the source or influence. The problem in understanding the latter in Sarojini's poetry is that most of the poets she mentions in her letter are practically unavailable in India. These poets will have to be read in the original and then compared with Sarojini to get a clearer picture of how sensibility was shaped in her formative years in England. At any rate, it will not do to underestimate the extent of Sarojini's familiarity with English poets and literary fashions. An interesting example of this is an as yet unpublished poem she wrote to Yeats:

Alul

He is a Druid-Child of mystic dreams
In the dim twilight of deep Celtic woods
He maketh music in wild, wayward moods
Of faery fantasy by starry streams.
He bears a red rose twined on his lyre
His eyes are dark and prophet-like with fire,
Alul his name—of fays I did inquire.
(Sarojini Naidu Papers, Nehru Memorial Library)

Perhaps, she was able to appreciate Yeats' greatness long before critics did. She was also able to make discriminations because he was the only one on whom she wrote a poem, though she considered Watson to be the best poet of the batch. The poem dated 16 May 1896 is enclosed in a letter of Govandarajulu. Sarojini explains, 'It is about Yeats, though whether anyone else can recognise it I am not sure.' She adds, 'Alul is the name of a mystic dreamer like Mr Yeats himself in his 'Countess Cathleen . . .' (*Selected Letters* 17).

Even more interesting, perhaps, is the role she played, though unwittingly, in the creation of literary modernism. It was Sarojini who aided Ezra Pound in his acquisition of the Fenollosa Papers in 1913.* As we well know, Pound derived many of his ideas about the centrality and function of the image in poetry from these papers. Sarojini probably helped to arrange the meeting between Mrs Fenollosa and Pound during which the former handed over the papers to the latter in her presence.

Such study of the impact of the prevailing literary climate on Sarojini's poetry will yield several other insights too. Just one example is a better understanding of the structure of her poetry. Most of her poems have a repetitive, formulaic structure. The stanzas are almost identical in form and rhyme scheme, only the images and words are changed. Such a structure is found in the roundel, an English variation of the French rondel, a literary form popular in the poetry of the 1890s. Its key features, including a simple rhyme scheme and refrains, are found in many of Sarojini's poems. Similarly, we find in Sarojini's poetry the penchant for mood, music, and dreamy ethereality which is common in the 1890s' poets, who were reacting to the high seriousness and moral questioning of the Victorian poets.

After the issue of influences, another matter which has received the attention of Sarojini's critics is the problem of 'Orientalism' in how she represents India in her poetry. It is customary, in this context, to quote Gosse's advice to the poet:

The verses which Sarojini had entrusted to me were

---

*See J.J. Wilhelm, *Ezra Pound in London and Paris: 1908-1925*: 'When Pound was invited early that fall to the house of the Indian nationalist poet Sarojini Naidu, he was doubtlessly expecting to spend most of the evening discussing poetry with the charming 'Nightingale of India', but Saroniji had been prevailed upon by the already mentioned Mrs Mary McNeill Fenollosa to arrange the appointment so that she could look over the young American poet for the job as literary executor of her husband's estate.'

skilful in form, correct in grammar and blameless in sentiment, but they had the disadvantage of being totally without individuality, they were Western in feeling and in imagery, this was but the note of the mocking-bird with a vengeance.

I advised the consignment of all that she had written, in this falsely English vein, to the wastepaper basket. I implored her to consider that from a young Indian of extreme sensibility, who had mastered not merely the language but the prosody of the West, what we wished to receive was, not a *rechauffe* of Anglo-Saxon sentiment in an Anglo-Saxon setting, but some revelation of the heart of India, some sincere and penetrating analysis of native passion, of the principles of antique religion and of such mysterious intimations as stirred the soul of the East long before the West had begun to dream it had a soul. Moreover, I entreated Sarojini to write no more about skylarks, in a landscape of our Midland countries, with the village bells somewhere in the distance calling the parishioners to church, but to describe the flowers, the fruits, the trees, to set her poems firmly among the mountains, the gardens, the temples, to introduce to us the vivid populations of her own voluptuous and unfamiliar province; in other words, to be a genuine Indian poet of the Deccan, not a clever machine-made imitator of the English classics.

(Introduction to *The Bird of Time* 4-5)

Ironically, the passage which was meant to illustrate the end of her imitativeness is often quoted to prove its continuance. Apparently, to stop being imitative at someone else's behest is as big a sin as being imitative in the first place!

In any case, most critics agree that this is a seminal passage out of which we must construct the relationship of Sarojini's to the dominant cultural ideologies of her time. Gosse's advice provokes a number of questions, especially because Sarojini appears to have followed it faithfully. Gosse gives her the choice between being a 'machine-made imitator' and a 'genuine Indian poet of the Deccan.' However, she was never accorded the latter status though she did write about the 'vivid populations of her own. voluptuous and. unfamiliar province.' James Cousins, one of her earliest and best critics, accused her of illogic and excess as early as in 1918. Lotika Basu, whose book on Indian English poetry was published in 1933, went further, criticising her poetry for being inauthentic and unrealistic:

> In Mrs Naidu's treatment of Indian subjects she does not give a realistic picture of India; she merely continues the picture of India painted by Anglo-Indian and English writers, a land of bazaars, full of bright colours and perfumes, and peopled with picturesque beggars, wandering minstrels and snake-charmers.
>
> She is more intent on drawing an interesting picture of India than on representing India as it is. It is this which makes her verses rather disappointing. Talented and with not a little of the gift of the true poet, it seems to us Mrs Naidu has failed in becoming a true interpreter of India to the West. (94-95)

It is interesting how almost no post-colonial critic has moved beyond this early critique written over eighty years ago. But to return to Sarojini's poetic career, it would seem that following Gosse's advice damned her to a fate as bad as what he wished to save her from. The change of subject from English Midlands to the voluptuous Deccan was not of much help in proving the authenticity of her work as an Indian poet. Perhaps, what was more crucial was the underlying aesthetics of representation which Sarojini accepted rather than the topics she wrote on. While Gosse could question her choice of subjects, he could not question the very aesthetics to which both he and Sarojini subscribed. His advice, hence, masked his own limitations, putting Sarojini in a sort of double bind, which perhaps, caused more harm to her than good.

This unwitting, though hidden agenda, is evident in the task which Gosse set for Sarojini. His expectation of her for 'some revelation of the heart of India, some sincere penetrating analysis of native passion, of the principles of antique religion and of such mysterious intimations as stirred the soul of the East' betrayed the deep longings of the post-Industrial West for, some area of experience untouched by modernity, unspoiled, pristine, and authentic. In brief, a longing for its exotic Other. To escape the oppressive and overpowering advance of the machine age seemed to be the compelling challenge before Victorian poetry. The poetic medievalism of the pre-Raphaelites was one way of meeting the same need as was the search for fresh locales and topics in Browning and Tennyson. In this search Europe often turned to its vast colonial spaces. Here, it could find, to its own reckoning, all the savagery, primitivism, irrationality, and mysticism that it had suppressed within itself. To my mind, it is was more that the quest for what Graham Huggan calls 'the postcolonial exotic,' though it could easily degenerate into that. The quest, at its best, was for something quite genuine, as in Theosophy, the hidden wisdom or the secret knowledge, which was still believed to be present in the East. But for the natives themselves, such a search for Europe's Other was, no doubt, a *cul de sac*. In other words, Gosse's commission was, perhaps, impossible to fulfil because there was probably no such mysterious soul of India; in fact, any such notion of it was itself merely projection or construction from the keen reality of its absence.

In setting her such a task, Gosse was, unknowingly, also setting a trap for Sarojini. The assignment he set her, of giving the West, the 'real' India was, in a sense, impossible to accomplish because there was no 'real' India of the kind that he expected. So his injunction became a snare in which Sarojini was snagged, trying to furnish a picture of India which the West wished to see. The subsequent criticism of her poetry only proves how superbly Sarojini fulfilled her commission. Her India is more artificial, exotic, and picturesque than any account by an Anglo-Indian poet. But what is often unnoticed is that it is also less mysterious, alien, or dishonest than such Orientalist accounts, and with good reason too because she knew her India better and in a different way than a foreigner would. She not just met her brief, but exceeded it in unexpected ways; her *over*(t) Orientalising actually succeeded in subverting Gosse's original intention. Sarojini subtly but certainly complicated the apparently simple relationship of the colonised and the coloniser that was contained in Gosse's advice to her. Though ostensibly colluding with dominant metropolitan aesthetic and producing an answerable portrayal of India to suit Western tastes, she also resisted such a project by both nativising and politicising it. She thus reclaimed her right to represent herself as an India and also brought into poetic discourse the marginalised and oppressed 'folk' who constituted the bulk of the colonised populace of India. What is more, she tried to represent this folk so as to give them dignity, even grandeur, even if this meant masking their wretchedness and exploitation. A good example is 'The Indian Gypsy':

> In tattered robes that hoard a glittering trace
> Of bygone colours, broidered to the knee,
> Behold her, daughter of a wandering race,
> Tameless, with the bold falcon's agile grace,
> And the lithe tiger's sinuous majesty. (124)

In her very untamed poverty, this poor and nomadic woman resists being enslaved to the norms of society, culture, or colonialism. In effect, even if Sarojini's poetic programme is borrowed and its aesthetics derivative, the control over the representation is in native hands and the dignity of the represented is left intact, even as it is harnessed to the counter-imperialistic project of national liberation.

But the question still remains why such a project proved to be so appealing to the poet when many had seen through it and wished for more 'realistic' representations of India? The reasons, I believe, are both complicated and intriguing. First, we must remember Sarojini's position as an aspiring Indian poet writing in English in the 1890s. To put it simply, at that time there were no Indian English 'poets', no publishers, and no readers to speak of. The poets who wrote before her were confined mostly to Calcutta and Bombay, known only to a small circle of readers. There was no established tradition of writing poetry in English, thus no well-defined *place* for an Indian English poet in society. There had been, no doubt, individual poets like Henry Derozio or Toru Dutt before her who had achieved some renown. The latter, incidentally, was, like Sarojini, a prodigy and had been discovered by the same Edmund Gosse. So, the patronage of Gosse was something Sarojini could simply not resist trying to obtain. The significance that Sarojini attached to Gosse's encouragement can be inferred from this letter which she wrote to him on 6th October 1896:

> I do not dare to trust myself to thank you for what you said on Sunday. You cannot know what these words meant to me, how people always colour my life, how when I am in the very depth of self-disgust and despair—as I often am—they will give me new hope, a new courage —no, you cannot know! Poetry is the one thing I love so passionately, so intensely, so absolutely that it is my very life of life—and now you have told me *that I am a poet*—I am a poet! I keep repeating it to myself to try to realise it. Will you let me tell you a little about myself because I want you to know how you have been an influence on my life ever since I was eleven years old. (Tara Ali Baig, *Sarojini Naidu* 19; *Selected Letters* 27-28)

She tells him how he had been her literary idol for several years right until the time she came to England. Finally, after a long wait, she gets to meet him in person:

> Well, in January I first saw you—the magical legend had become a reality. I was not disappointed. Indeed I shall never forget that day because with one great bound I seemed to wake into a new large life, the life I had always longed for and so long in vain. From that day I seemed to be an altered being. I seemed to have put off childish things and put on garments of new and beautiful hope and ambition, and I have gone on growing and growing—I feel it,—seeing more clearly, feeling more intensely, thinking more deeply, and loving more passionately, more unselfishly, that beautiful spirit of art that has now become dearer than my life's blood to me—and all this I owe to you. . . .
>
> As you have been for so long so good an influence on my life I wanted you to go on for ever! I will send you everything I write and you must tell me what you think. I want you to be more severe and exacting than ever, the better I do, because I do not want to outlast the years but the centuries. That is very conceited of me, but is it not worthwhile to aim at the stars though one never gets beyond the mountain top? I don't think I am going to ask you to excuse me for taking up so much of your time, because I cannot go on being grateful to you in silence . . . without your knowing how much cause I have to be grateful to you for.
>
> (ibid)

No doubt, Gosse would have been embarrassed by Sarojini's effusiveness, or even her imposition of the burden of mentorship on him. To me the situation, however, doesn't concern two individuals as much as a recurrent type in a colonial encounter.

Without the patronage or sponsorship of a colonial master, no colonised subject could hope to break into the exalted ranks of the English-language literary immortals. More recently, did it not take a Graham Greene to discover an R. K. Narayan? Or, what has happened since, doesn't it take a Booker Prize or, at the least, a metropolitan publisher to put an Indian writer or critic on world stage? But to revert to Sarojini, so young, so ambitious, and so aware of how the real world worked, what better example can we find of the plight of the colonial subject, forever locked in a relationship of dependence and gratitude to the metropolis?! Grateful first for being colonised, for having an alien language imposed on her; grateful again when her efforts in that language were checked, evaluated, and certified by her masters as passing muster; grateful finally for the privilege of having her book published in the metropolis, even if she had to bear some of the costs, and for a subsequent re-import to her colonised country.

But even if the dynamics of colonialism explains the reverence which Sarojini felt for Gosse, it doesn't fully account for the attraction of the model of representation which he had recommended to her. To understand this, we must consider the contradictions and compulsions of her situation in India. As a sensitive Indian living in the semi-feudal state of Hyderabad, part of the larger British Empire in India, Sarojini, like other Indian artists and intellectuals, had to deal with the question of cultural preservation and identity. The onslaught of all-powerful modernity, sometimes aided, sometimes obstructed by the colonial administration, presented a contradictory and confusing picture. Under threat was the very selfhood of the subject. So threatened, Indians tried to revive and mark out those areas of experience which seemed to be untainted by colonialism and Western modernity.

Partha Chatterjee argued that the national tried to create its own domain sovereignty by separating the (inner) spiritual realm from the material (outer) one.* But the demarcation of the feminised inner domain was not the only way of creating the post-colonial *differend*; there were entire areas marked off from the relentless march of both modern capital and rationality. Indian religion and spirituality constituted one such bastion to which many of the key figures of the Indian renaissance, from Rammohun Roy to Gandhi, rallied. It offered shelter from both colonialism and modernity. Then there was adventure of geography. Whether it was the appeal of inaccessible jungles or mountains, remote regions like Tibet, princely states, or areas of experience such as the primitive or mystical, such spaces nurtured a sense of quasi-autonomy not just from colonialism, but also from modernity, and created their own discursive opportunities, whether in stories of adventurers, big game hunters, explorers, or stories set in princely India. Sarojini exploited many of these domains in an effort to create an authentic world of difference from colonial modernity. Not only did she write of the of the zenana and the sequestered veiled woman, but her home town of Hyderabad itself became one complete realm of sequestered difference, a whole world veiled in *purdah*, as it were, quasi-independent, sensuous, almost magically frozen in time and preserved from the ravages from encroaching modernity.

In addition, if Indian tradition in the shape of religion was attractive to intellectuals, several artists tried to see it in threatened lifestyles, customs, ways of living. Here was living proof that India, though 'backward' and under-developed, had managed to resist the machine age. What Sarojini tried to do was to offer an entry into this unspoiled India. Of course, it would have been too painful to portray it with all the horrors of its poverty,

---

*See *The Nation and Its Fragments: Colonial and Postcolonial Histories* 75.

inequality, disease, squalor, and suffering; if only these were glossed over, then a very attractive image of India would emerge, pre-modern, vivid, vibrant, colourful, and joyous. Moreover, in a period of almost exponential social and technological change, she could see vanishing before her eyes a way of life which the West had already lost and now pined for. She felt compelled to capture it in poetry and song because she probably longed for it herself. It was a poetic ethnography, a way of preserving through writing what was passing away before her eyes. All these factors contributed to her attempt at offering not just to Westerners, but also to Indians, a picture of themselves which they might be proud of, something that might salvage some of their crippled self-respect as a colonised and humiliated people.

Of course, Sarojini's ruse was no solution; everyone knew that her India was too romantic, too pretty, in fact too 'Orientalist,' to represent the teeming nation that was taking shape before their eyes. Perhaps, that is why her formula failed. It was based on a self-comforting cover up, if not delusion, not on self-criticism and courage to reform society. In contrast, Gandhi made no attempt to mitigate or underplay the extent of India's dependence and bondage, or the wretchedness and misery of its people. He rallied his countrymen and women against untouchability, Hindu-Muslim enmity, women's oppression, and so on, causes that Sarojini supported politically, but not poetically. Gandhi highlighted India's poverty and subjugation to remind the people of what they had lost, of the sovereignty they had ceded to the British. He transformed a nation of defeated people into rebels by reminding them of their own responsibility for their capitulation. While Sarojini made the life of the palanquin-bearers appear more attractive than it was by taking the poetic license of rendering the palanquin weightless, Gandhi's method was to inspire the bearers to stop carrying the palanquin, to stop cooperating with those who exploited them.

When viewed in such a light, the problem of representation

in Sarojini's poetry assumes the dimensions of a crisis. All her labouring folk—palanquin-bearers, wandering singers, Indian weavers, Coromandel fishers, snake-charmers, aged beggars, and so on, the happy or stoical toilers and heavers, become suspect. They are all made to deny the hardship and sweat of their occupations, hide their own dispossession and marginalisation, and celebrate their lowly and oppressed state. They become picturesque, exotic figures in tableaux, frozen in various attitudes of quaintness. These folk are pretty; they are simple; they are guileless; they are sincere. They are, moreover, in harmony with nature; the social order in which they live is seen as an extension of the natural order. Whether this order is just or unjust, whether they can rebel against it or not—such questions never occur to them. They are, it would almost seem, exactly as their masters, whether colonial or native, would want them: obedient, docile, and yet fascinating, interesting, quaint. A symptomatic reading thus hints at the rich context and subtext of these poems. Such a historicist-materialistic approach would explain the absences in Sarojini's text as examples of the overwhelmingly harsh reality of colonialism which the poems seek to repress and banish.

It is not just the ordinary folk in her poems who are thus (mis)represented. The India of her poems is similarly an exotic place. Hyderabad, where many of her poems are set, is an area of mystery, romance, and medieval chivalry. It is presented in an alluring medley of images of exquisite dancers, exotic bazaars, latticed balconies, veiled ladies, caparisoned elephants, rare spices, smooth silks, precious stones, decaying forts, timeless tombs, and an intriguingly deep lake which is the image of the poet herself. The city is ruled by a benevolent poet-prince and his courtiers. There is no conflict in this city; the various classes and religious communities live peacefully, in perfect harmony. This is so because there is no competition in the city, no capitalism, no threat to the survival of the poor. Even beggars are content with their lot, fully trusting divine dispensation to provide them their daily bread. This is an idealised and stable feudal society, where everyone is happy with his or her place, no one seeks to rise above his or her station, and playing one's designated role in the scheme of things is both natural and desirable. No wonder many poems show a repeated fascination with retrogressive social customs and practices including sati and purdah.

Not just the subject, but the language of her poetry reflects her aesthetic predilections. The more ornate, more latinate, more exotic, more unusual word or phrase is always favoured over the simple, functional, and ordinary. There is a heightening of sensuality in the imagery until every sense is stimulated to excess. Visually, the images tend to recede away from clear daylight and sharp focus to hazy, dream-like, dim, and blurred states of experience. It is as if the poet prefers not to see very clearly, prefers not to confront bare reality. The lighting is always soft, never bright enough to see objects and situations clearly. The poetic aim is not to confront the real world, but to render it pleasing to the senses when possible, or to escape from it altogether when required. One indication of this is the number of times, literally hundreds, that the word 'dream' recurs in her poetry. Overall, there is a definite tendency towards hedonistic self-abandon and escape from reality.

To sum up, then, Sarojini's aesthetics is feudal, though her politics is democratic nationalism. Her better poems like 'The Purdah Nashin,' 'Indian Dancers,' or 'The Old Woman,' are those which embody the feudal ideal. Whenever she attempted poems on nationalistic subjects, as in 'To India', or 'Kali the Mother', the result was laboured and uninteresting. It is hardly surprising that while as a national leader she lived mostly outside Hyderabad, she returned to her city for her poetic material and inspiration. Indeed, she always remained loyal to the Nizam ostensibly, never bringing her politics home, where her husband was an employee of the state. Such was her compromise with the feudal order of the society into which she was born and brought up. The isolation, stability, oriental splendour, and, one might add, unreality of Hyderabad appealed to her. It gave her the comfort to retreat into a dream world, to deny the onslaught of modernity and capitalism. It was a place without aggression or greed, full of old world grace and charm, with an unhurried pace of life—a place she found stifling as a housewife and mother, which she escaped from when she entered public life, which was for all practical intents and purposes sterile, limited, and narrow, but whose very decadence was appealing artistically. She always romanticised Hyderabad both in her poetry and letters, though it is clear that she knew this world was falling apart before her eyes. While she rejected it politically, it re-emerged as a place of order, stability, and sensory overabundance in her poetry.

Before leaving the topic of her aesthetics, I must stress on the ways in which Sarojini's poetry tried to authenticate an Indian sensibility. Just as careful research and scholarship are required in place of casual assertions of the influence of British poetry on her work, so must a similar scrupulousness be exercised in identifying the 'native' sources of her poetry. The only serious attempt in this direction has been made by P. V. Rajyalakshmi in *The Lyric Spring*. She shows how Sarojini used traditions from Sanskrit and Urdu-Persian poetry in evolving her poetics. Thus, not only in her deliberate choice of Indian subject matter, but also in her poetic technique, she enlarged the possibilities of her medium.

Nowhere is her use of Indian poetic traditions more evident than in her love poetry. Her heroes and heroines are not so many individuals as they are types and attitudes. An examination of a medieval treatise on love poetry, such as Kesavadasa's *Rasika Priya*, reveals a whole catalogue of such situations and attitudes:

1. *Nabodha:* the shy maiden frightened of meeting her lover alone.
2. *Abhisarika:* 'hastening towards'; a love-sick maiden,

venturing out of her father's house at night to keep a tryst with her lover.
3. *Vesaka Sajja:* 'dress equipped'; the heroine, fully apparelled, waiting in her chamber to receive her lover.
4. *Mugella:* 'charming'; young woman conscious of her charms.
5. *Smarandha:* 'love blind'; a woman blinded by her passion.
6. *Sambhoga:* 'united joy'; looking forward to or actually enjoying the embraces of her lover.
7. *Utka:* longing; a woman waiting with deep longing in a lonely place for her lover.
8. *Swadhina:* 'independent'; woman who is free to indulge her emotions and likings.
9. *Svadhina-patika:* woman who has her husband in subjection.
10. *Praushita-patika:* woman pining for her lover who is away.
11. *Kalaha-antanta:* 'quarrel-separated'; a woman yearning but too proud to make up.
12. *Manini:* woman sulking and rejecting her lover.
13. *Vipra labdha:* 'hurt-desire'; deceived or jilted woman.
14. *Khandita:* an 'immoral' woman whose lover is playing truant or is impotent.

(Adapted from Benjamin Walker's
The Hindu World, Vol 2: 433)

Obviously, several of these types can be found in Sarojini's poetry. A deeper study involving a comparison of original sources is required.

Similarly, a key aspect of classical Indian aesthetics was the emphasis on *alamkara* or the 'beautiful form' in poetry. There were elaborate lists of various devices and figures of ornamentation as of rules to apply them correctly. In the light of *alamkara shastra,* we can identify Sarojini's is primarily a poetry of ornamental and beautiful forms. Every line, every idea, every image is embellished elaborately. A thorough examination of the various devices that she employs may reveal her indebtedness to Indian poetry and poetics to an extent greater than is acknowledged.

It has often been remarked that Sarojini's poetry is superficial, that it lacks a philosophical content. The poet herself contributed to such an impression by her deliberate emphasis on the fleeting and momentary. Nowhere else in Indian English poetry do we find such celebration of mutability and transience. The image of the singing bird, whether soaring up or fluttering on its broken wing, recurs in her poetry. In her letter to Symons quoted in his Introduction to *The Golden Threshold* she says:

> You know how high my idea of Art is; and to me my poor casual poems seem to be less than beautiful—I mean with that final enduring beauty that I desire. (9-10)

In another letter she adds:

> I am not a poet really. I have the vision and the desire, but not the voice. If I could write just one poem full of beauty and the spirit of greatness, I should be exultingly silent for ever; but I sing just as the birds do, and my songs are as ephemeral. (10)

Such remarks provide a more challenging task to feminist critics than merely an identification of the image of women or the self-portrayal of feminine sexuality in her poems. No doubt, Sarojini's construction of femininity and masculinity is amazingly essentialist; furthermore, the women that she depicts are often not just conventional and subordinate, but appear to endorse the patriarchy themselves in their words, images, and attitudes. Yet, one could try to retrieve something of value from her aesthetics rather than arguing that there is something undeniably and uniquely 'feminist' about her poems. Sarojini's deliberate espousal of *carpe diem* and her cultivated anti-intellectualism aligns her to all those women whose voices and words were lost, who were outside the purview of the high-brow, bourgeois, male-dominated notion of 'great art.' In her letter to Symons, it is this notion that she undermines. In a sense, her own mother herself was such a woman who composed Bengali lyrics when younger. Sarojini's self-deprecation, thus, need not be taken at face value.

The best contrast to Sarojini within Indian English poetry is Sri Aurobindo, though modernist critics tend to club them together and also dismiss them with almost identically facile gestures. Sri Aurobindo was an intellectual and philosophical poet who tried to use his poetry as a vehicle for an incredibly well-thought-out ideological and spiritual project. He wrote several books of poems, capping his achievement with *Savitri*, a poem of over 24,000 lines. Sarojini, in contrast, wrote very little, and mostly in the lyric mode. While Sri Aurobindo, obviously, had so much to say through his poetry, Sarojini, ostensibly, had so little. Nor did she feel the need to write grand or profound poems meant to be classics.

But this does not mean that she was superficial or had no philosophy to convey through her poetry. On the contrary, the very refusal to philosophise was itself a part of her philosophy. Nowhere is her celebration of the fleeting present more evident than in her Spring poems, the second most important group of poems in her oeuvre after her love songs. The spontaneous and cyclic renewal of vegetal life to Sarojini seemed to contain the answer to the riddle of life. Actually, transience was not the problem, but the *solution* for Sarojini. Once accepted, it makes us free. Transience, paradoxically, is the proof of immortality. Because, even death is transient. This the recurrence of Spring proves again and again. As she says in 'The Poet to Death':

> Tarry a while, O Death, I cannot die
> With all my blossoming hopes unharvested,
> My joys ungarnered, all my songs unsung,
> And all my tears unshed. (123)

Spring, thus, is not just renewal and regeneration, but the proof of the continuity and persistence of life. Sarojini would have us believe that even if we grow old and die, as long as a single flower blooms, life endures and, through it, so do we. That is because though apparently atomised and individualised, all life is actually one, a sort of *élan vital* or force that informs and animates all living organisms.

'In the Forest' is an interesting composition that expresses what could be the poet's manifesto. The first two of the three stanzas recount the end of dreams: 'Here, O my heart, let us burn the dear dreams that are dead,/ Here in this wood let us fashion a funeral pyre' (139-140). There is recognition not just of pain, heartbreak, and the sorrow that comes from broken things, but also the realisation that these experiences must be cremated, like the dead bodies of Hindus, and laid to rest. But the Sarojini does not stop there. The last stanza ends with a reaffirmation that life must go on, again we must face the pain and strife of the world, not giving up, even if it means that what we experience will be sorrow, not joy: 'Let us rise, O my heart, let us gather the dreams that remain,/ We will conquer the sorrow of life with the sorrow of song' (116). It is art that can, even if it is sad, counter and cope with the more primal sorrow of life. Here, art is seen as a palliative, a salve to human suffering; even if it conveys sadness. Art leads not so much to escape or expression but through active combat with pain to victory; the utility of art is not just to offer catharsis or therapy, but to lead us to the mastery and conquest of life. It is art that takes us from being victims to victors.

In Sarojini's view, life is a tension or balance of opposites and diversities. There can be no laughter without sorrow, no love without death. But she would revel in the entire process, not just embrace the pleasure and eschew the pain. Unlike many of the male poets, salvation for Sarojini is here and now, in life on earth, not in renunciation or denial of this world of senses. The dissolution of the centre or detached ego through a keen sensual experience is her idea of emancipation. In this she is not just romantic, but sensualist. Sense to her is, ultimately, sensibility. The capacity to feel, to experience, to be one with life is crucial to her. And she seeks a heightening of this capacity repeatedly, feverishly, and compulsively—almost like an addict. Hence, the element of exaggeration and excess in her poetry. Her senses are her source of ecstasy and life is the stimulant; often, she forces both the stimulants and the senses beyond their capacities in her attempt to reach her 'high.'

Overall, Sarojini, like the aesthetes and symbolists, was an idealist; she did believe in the soul, but a soul which worked through the senses, not one which was transcendental and which could only be reached through repression or denial of what we experience through our senses. Thus, while her poetry downplays the intellectual aspects of the human personality and celebrates the life of emotion and sensuality, it is not totally devoid of a philosophical content and foundation. Perhaps, no poem sums up her idealist-aesthetic manifesto as much as 'Guerdon' (152) in which she declares that her chosen gifts from life, which express her true calling, are 'The Rapture of Love,' 'The Rapture of Truth!' and 'The Rapture of Song.'

As a writer of prose, Sarojini was never well known. Except for a few booklets, including a moving and biographically rich memorial to Gokhale, she never published sustained prose in her lifetime. Her collected speeches are uneven in quality and lacking in well-developed or original thinking. In fact, most of the thousands of speeches she delivered were extempore. There is therefore no record of them. Especially from 1925 (when the third edition of her speeches and writings was published) to 1947 (when she became Governor of U.P.), I have been almost unable to find any prose by her. 'Mah Rukh Begum,' 'Women's Education and the Unity of India,' and 'Remarks While Conferring Honorary Degrees at the Silver Jubilee Convocation of Lucknow

University,' were published for the first time when this collection came first came out in 1993.

The two sketches, 'Mah Rukh Begum: A Romance of Fate' and 'Nilambuja,' though early texts, are of great interest because they are the only examples of her literary prose. Thus, they show a continuity with her poetry. The rest of her prose consists of political speeches and biographical sketches.

The manuscript of 'Mah Rukh Begum' dated 6 May 1897 in the National Archives shows it to be, like 'Nilambuja,' an early work, which also remained unpublished. It is thus the earliest available example of Sarojini's prose. Written when she was in England and only eighteen, it is a remarkable work, in a highly ornate and stylised poetic prose. The period and atmosphere are evoked with graphic particularity and effectiveness. It is, moreover, replete with symbolic import despite the hackneyed ending. The piece shows that Sarojini certainly had the makings of a fine writer of fiction.

The situation in the piece is typical of the dilemma in Sarojini's work, and by extension, in her life. The rebellious adolescent, Mah Rukh Begum, is a kind of self-representation of the poet. She is poised between two worlds—one offers her security and identity, the other freedom and, in a sense, death. But the conflict between the two never comes to a head because Mah Rukh finds both security and freedom of choice where she is, thus being saved from making a life-threatening choice. The man she falls in love with, turns out to be her husband in the arranged marriage into which circumstances force her.

Mah Rukh has the makings of a rebel, but her rebellion is forestalled by her getting what she wants within the system which she thinks of as oppressive. This is the significance of the sub-title, 'A Romance of Fate.' But, surely, this turn of events is purely fortuitous, though it does seem to endorse, in a roundabout manner, the closed and repressive society in which she lives. What if the man, her betrothed, had happened to be someone else?

Such a question is never asked, but left to the readers to mull over. The resolution of the story is, thus, no resolution at all. It is merely an apology for the status quo. The implication is that at its very best, the system into which Mah Rukh is born, will suffice in giving her, by some quirk of fate, the man she loves.

In her own life, though, Sarojini had to rebel. Her marriage to M. Govindarajulu Naidu was an inter-caste marriage which had to be solemnised according to Brahmo rites under the provisions of the Special Marriage Act of 1872 in Madras. This was an act of rebellion on Sarojini's part, yet it was supported by the pillars of the social reform movement of her time. We must not also forget that her parents had a Brahmo background. Varada Sundari studied and resided at a Brahmo home for girls while her husband, Aghorenath, was working for his D. Sc. at Edinburgh. At Sarojini's wedding, the officiating priest was a well-known social reformer. The couple were received in society without major impediments. Sarojini, in other words, never broke with her class or faced serious repercussions for her rebellion. In Mah Rukh we see both Sarojini's attraction and repulsion to the conservative Hyderabadi society into which she was born. Like Mah Rukh, Sarojini had an ambivalent relationship to it. She was neither able to accept it completely, nor reject it altogether.

Nilambuja: The Fantasy of a Poet's Mood was first published in *The Indian Ladies' Magazine,* December 1902, and reprinted in the *Speeches and Writings of Sarojini Naidu.* Nilambuja (literally, born of the blue lotus) is a version of Sarojini herself (Sarojini means 'lotus born'). Padmaja, which also means lotus born incidentally, says as much: 'Nilambuja could well be Sarojini herself just stepping out of her world' (38). The piece is fascinating for its dense texture of dreamlike imagery, which can well be interpreted in psychoanalytic terms as a young woman's discovery of her sexuality. There is a touch of the occult in it too, which adds to its tantalising appeal. For instance, she recalls her childhood self-recognition, when was probably too young even to articulate it:

A lyric child standing in the desert of her own lonely temperament, watching the stars, till she had caught from their inaccessible fires the soaring flame of a manifold enthusiasm, a myriad-hearted passion for humanity, for knowledge, for life, above all, for the eternal beauty of the universe. (204)

Now, the young poet's sexual awakening is viewed as something of a loss of that profound innocence and vast possibility. Incidentally, Sarojini's own motto, printed on her first stationary, before she even went to England, was the Latin, '*Excelsior ad astra,*' to excel and aspire unto the very stars. But now, a young woman, Nilambuja's world is closing in, even as she is sexually awakened. In Sarojini's own life, her falling in love at fifteen triggered a crisis in her life, leading to her confinement and then to her being sent to England. In England, too, she projected herself at Girton as a silken-robed, waiflike 'Indian princess,' in contrast to the healthy and robust British girls, who were being trained for nursing or teaching in the only women's college at Cambridge. Later, in her poetry, too, we find a similar languid, seductive sexuality almost as in response to Orientalist expectations.

'Nilambuja' shows, once again, a protagonist at a threshold, unable to decide which way to go. The narrative movement outlines a journey from the freedom of vast spaces outside to the enclosed and secure world of the woman's quarters. The hesitating heroine chafes at the closing in of her world, but is unable to decide to abandon it. The piece ends on an uncertain and indecisive note. Sarojini faced a similar choice, not just before, but after she was married. Before, it was whether to be so bold as to marry the man she loved; after whether to remain a hausfrau or break out of a world of sequestered comfort to join the rough and tumble of national life. With four children and a comfortable home, she could have sunk into obscure and easy domesticity, but chose, instead, to enter public life. As in 'Mah Rukh Begum,' the choices in real-life were more radical than in her writing.

The rest of Sarojini's prose is of interest not so much for its literary qualities but for its place in the archive of the Indian freedom movement. The bulk of it, at any rate, consists of the speeches she delivered all over India and abroad on various topics relating to national life. In those that are available, we see some common thematic and formal preoccupations.

Chief among these is clearly her concern with 'women's issues.' For instance, 'Women's Education and the Unity of India' 206-208). This is a speech Sarojini gave at a function to celebrate the fiftieth anniversary of a Gujarati reformist journal, *Stree Bodh*, in March 1908, Bombay (Padmini Sengupta 69). The first part of the speech tries to compare the Indian renaissance with the European and, more recent, transformations in Ireland and Japan. Sarojini was very perspicacious in recognising the tremendous achievements of Japan even as early as 1908. She argues that the Indian renaissance is slower, but sure and far-reaching. To her, both the issues of women's education and the unity of India are seen as a part of this ongoing transformation of Indian society. Sarojini is, thus a feminist-nationalist, seeing the amelioration of women as part of the larger agenda of national regeneration. On women's education, Sarojini advocates a gradual, reformist programme, especially as regards the removal of *purdah*. She is, hence, somewhat conservative in her position. She does not want women's issues to become too threatening or divisive. Solidarity across different special interest groups is, thus, a prerequisite for a succession national struggle. The key to such a unity of India, for Sarojini, is education. Upon the realisation of such a unity will be predicated a larger unity of the human race. Thus, like Tagore, Aurobindo, and Gandhi, Sarojini sees the national as integral to the cosmopolitan, not opposed to it. Besides its content, the speech has an unmistakable eloquence and literariness, characteristic of much of Sarojini's oratory.

One of the most important speeches that Sarojini gave was her Presidential Address to Indian National Congress, delivered at its 40th annual session on 26 December 1925, at Kanpur. As mentioned earlier, Sarojini was the first Indian woman to become the President of the Congress and the second woman ever, after Annie Besant, to do so. This is, perhaps, her most important public statement because here she speaks her own mind more than reflecting the dominant ideas of her time. Sarojini emphasises and foregrounds her gender throughout the address. There is a deliberate attempt to use her difference as a woman strategically and rhetorically. While she invokes traditional and even retrogressive stereotypes of the role of women in Indian society, she is doing so, perhaps, out of a sense of trying to represent her constituency. Certainly, Sarojini herself was very far from being an ignorant, unskilled, and subservient housewife and mother as she makes her position out to be. In her policy perspective for the Congress, she stresses the Gandhian programme of village reconstruction as a solution to the problems of poverty and colonialism:

> we must try to enlist a large band of missionary patriots of burning zeal who set free from material wants by the pious charity of the householders of the country as in ancient times, should carry through the length and breadth of the land the beneficent evangel of self-reliance and self-respect, taking the immemorial twin symbols of the plough and the spinning-wheel as the central text of the teaching that shall liberate our unhappy peasantry from the crushing misery and terror of hunger, ignorance and disease. (270)

Unfortunately, the very poetry in her turn of phrase seems quite inappropriate to what she describes. Only more hardy and less dreamy-eyed grassroots workers could do the job she recommends. Phrases such as 'missionary patriots,' 'burning zeal,' 'pious charity,' 'beneficent evangel,' and so on sound cloyingly affected, if not sanctimonious, to contemporary ears. She goes on emphasises her two pet themes, education and Hindu-Muslim unity, before ending on a characteristically 'sublime' note with a translation of a well-known prayer from the Upanishads.

Like her poetry, Sarojini's speeches were primarily emotional. They do not usually embody original ideas or theories, but reflect current, politically correct notions. She was a nationalist and a Congress worker to the core, a follower first of Gokhale and then of Gandhi. Most of what she voiced were, thus, the vetted opinions of the Congress Party. She was, in other words, a faithful espouser of the party line. But there were some issues which were dear to her heart. These she went back to again and again. One was education, especially the education of women. For Sarojini education was much more than book learning. It was, in essence, the realisation of the equality and fraternity of all human beings which followed upon the extirpation of all prejudices and chauvinisms. She also believed in the cultural and political unity of India, in its great past, and even more glorious future as an independent country. She believed that this would only be possible through a national uprising in which the consciousness of the masses was raised by a responsible elite. And this could be done, in turn, through educating that elite to fulfil the role of *noblesse oblige* that history had given it.

In this sense, she was a diehard bourgeois liberal. All the causes that she championed, including her life-long advocacy of Hindu-Muslim unity and of the rights of women, were premised upon this liberalism. In the first instance, history proved her to be naïve, as Gokhale had predicted. She made lofty appeals to the higher sentiments in her audiences and moved them as few other orators did. But she often ignored the real motives of people and seemed to have a dim grasp of how central the struggle for power and dominance was in politics. As far as her role in the women's movement is concerned, she similarly believed in the benevolence of the patriarchy in India. When abroad, she often clarified that she was not a feminist because India did not need

Western-style feminism. She believed that conflicts between the sexes could be resolved through cooperation and not through confrontation. This was not so much a liberal feminism as a belief in Sarvodaya or commonweal. She considered society to be a totality and did not believe in the salvation of any single group or faction by itself. Nor did she, who had preached against narrow sectarianism, wish to be identified with anyone special interest group. She rejected the exceptionalism of the group just as she did bit subscribe to the solipsism of the individual.

The appeal of Sarojini's rhetoric lay in her ability to strike the sublime key. It was Gandhi who gave her the title 'Bharat Kokila,' or the Nightingale of India. But this was as much because of her speeches as of her poetry. As Harindranath Chattopadhyaya, her brother, observed:

> Sarojini came to be called Bulbul-i-Hind, the Nightingale of India, not, I am convinced, because of her verse, but because of her extraordinary oratory which poured through her like music, silver shot with gold, cataracting from summits of sheer inspiration.
> (Quoted by Izzat Yar Khan 17)

In his tribute to her in Parliament, Nehru observed how she 'infused artistry and poetry into the national struggle' (Baig 163). It is as a practitioner of the sublime that she is memorable as a prose writer. It was her gift to shift the attention from the nitty-gritty of politics to the solace of some eternal ideals and principles. Her prose is, thus, more poetic than some of her nationalistic poetry, which is prosaic. Throughout, her sense of humour remained unfazed. Regarding her high office as Governor of U.P., she often quipped that she was less a Governor than a governess. In her 'Remarks' during the Convocation Address of Allahabad University, delivered just a month before she died, she made several light hearted comments on the eminent personalities, including the Prime Minister, who had been conferred honorary doctorates. This shows what an original personality she was, witty, vain, irreverent, boisterous, and utterly engaging.

V
Conclusion

All told, Sarojini's writings offer us a vivid portrait of her multi-faceted personality. They reveal a woman who had a fragile physique but an indomitable spirit, who could stand great pain and suffering but yet emerge from it unscarred, who could laugh at herself and at others, who had immense panache and presence of mind, who loved society and got along with a wide variety of people, who was broadminded and open to new ideas, who had the capacity to enjoy herself even under adverse circumstances, who had patience and fortitude, who could and often did offer solace and comfort to others around her, who was aware of the important role she was playing in India's national life, who was confident and self-assured, who was both a great wag and a wit, who had the discipline to make her personal life subservient to her public obligations, who was essentially optimistic and forward looking, who had an inner faith which gave her strength, who was utterly free from prejudice of caste, race, gender, nation, or religion, who was not a feminist but worked for the cause of Indian women, who though bourgeois in sensibility, values, beliefs, was yet an anti-imperialist, who loved spring and the bounties of nature, who tried to be a loyal wife and conscientious mother, who worked tirelessly for Hindu-Muslim unity, who until the last days of her life showed rare solicitude for others, who, in short, managed the ambivalences and contrary pulls of her character and her times in such a manner as to make her life both worthwhile and memorable.

Ultimately, the source of her strength was a deep and abiding inner faith. In her letter of 2 September 1920 to Gandhi she explained:

> Immediate or apparent failure leaves me undismayed or even [un]disturbed in my inmost self because I am so certain of ultimate and real success. For I believe all thoughts and endeavours that are born of intense conviction are the guarantee of their own abiding triumph. (*Selected Letters* 152)

Such confidence was unusual and remarkable even in the optimistic times she lived in. That Sarojini had intimations of a higher certitudes is clear from several letters and poems, but the fullest and plainest description of a transcendental experience is found in her letter of 2 August 1932 to Padmaja. Written from jail, the letter is also a statement of her most intimate beliefs. Sarojini realises that it is 'the lovely lyric' Shravan, the month of festivals, the month of Janmashtami, Nag Panchami, and Raksha Bandhan:

> The world outside will be engrossed in commemorations and ceremonials with pageantry, music, crowds, and all the colour and tumult of mass adoration. . . . And yet . . . I wonder, if all the millions of worshippers in the sombre and splendid temples, steeped and drowned in the symbolism and gorgeous rituals of prayer and praise can ever 'realise God' as the phrase goes so intimately and deeply, with so keen and sweet a consciousness of communion as one prisoner in a high-walled prison garden standing in the magic hour between sunset and sunrise in a shining sea of lilies. . . . lilies, lilies, lilies, foam-white, pearl-white as clouds and the breasts of swans, white as manna and milk and the miracle of silver filigree beaten out on fairy anvils into chalices of incense and nectar. Truly, Beauty is the Face of God and the perfume of Beauty his breath . . . And who needs to go on a longer pilgrimage than to step down from a roofed and walled chamber into the green and fragrant place where the Beauty of

all Beauty exalts the Soul of the Seeker and Love, the
Singer, the Dreamer whose vision knows no barriers and
horizons . . . (Unpublished MS in the Nehru Memorial
Library)

Not unexpectedly, this passage reaches its climax in an almost mystical celebration of flowers. But in the beauty of the lilies, Sarojini sees a fusion of God as Beauty and God as Love. Poet, lover, seeker, dreamer—all coalesce in this passage, creating a rare luminosity. This was the core of Sarojini's life, this fusion of reality and imagination, beauty and truth, love and God. This vision of the fundamental unity of the most cherished values of her life gave direction and substance to her various endeavours.

My work on Sarojini Naidu was hard and time-consuming. Not the least of the difficulties was deciphering her handwriting. I was on the verge of giving up several times. Luckily, I didn't lose heart. The progress was tortured and slow, but over a period of several years, I managed to decipher most of her available letters and manuscripts. In some cases, I had unexpected luck: Padmaja had already prepared typescripts of some important letters, having realised their historical value. After my two books on Sarojini were published, I found a colleague and advanced PhD student, willing to do an independent study and compilation of the nearly 1300 letters Sarojini had written to Padmaja, her eldest daughter.

My prolonged labours, which had seemed masochistic and utterly pointless to many, were at last yielding rewards, not just to me, but to others, and not just professionally, but personally too. There is, as Nehru once said, something magical about the whole struggle for independence:

> What a strange period this has been in India's history, and the story, with all its ups and downs and triumphs and defeats, has the quality of a ballad or a romance. Even our trivial lives were touched by a halo of romance,

because we lived through this period and were actors in greater or lesser degree, in the great drama of India. (Mahadevan 4)

I think I too, though vicariously, was touched by this romance while working on Sarojini. Though she may not have been the most important, interesting, or significant of the several charismatic personalities that emerged during the freedom movement, she opened up a whole world for me. Through her I found a way or reading and accessing the rest of the major figures of that era. I am convinced that Indian academics, if it is to be meaningful, must locate itself in the larger tradition of modern Indian intellectual life, which begins with India's response to the west in the early nineteenth century, and reaches its apogee during the anti-imperial struggle in the first half of this century. The writings of Sarojini Naidu constitute one additional and not insignificant set of documents in this still ongoing and unfolding 'grand' narrative.

Poetry

JUVENILIA

Mehir Muneer

CANTO I

    What power, ah! what power often lies
    In th' magic e'en of a fakir's crude word!
    As upward he doth turn his holy eyes,
    Or gently bends them on the grassy sod
5   In low tones breathing th' name of God,
    What wonders he performs with that great pow'r!
    Can raise a palace on the open sward,
    Can change a desert to a fairy bow'r,
    Or on unequalled grief bright peerless joys can show'r.

I

10 In Persia's land long, long ago,
    In that fair land where roses blow
    In dewy fragrance, hung in bow'rs,
    Perfuming aye the tranquil hours;
    And where the bulbul pours her lay
15 At lovely close of glowing day—
    In that fair land where flows the wine
    Of which did sing that bard divine,
    That guardian spirit on whose tomb
    Perennial garlands ever bloom,

20   And where the incense ever burns,
      And ev'ry eye in rev'rence turns—
      In that bright land, choice throne of Spring,
      There lived in splendour great, a king.

II

      A monarch he, renowned and great,
25   Of mighty pow'r and grand estate,
      Of boundless wealth; upon his head
      Rare Fortune, brightest smiles, had shed;
      And God did show'r with lib'ral hand,
      Upon this king of Iran's land,—
30   Full many a blessing, many a friend,
      And countless favours Heav'n did send.
      His courtiers loved him as they ought;
      And sages wise his presence sought;
      And took this monarch endless pains
35   To wisely rule his vast domains—
      Oft times did send relief to Need,
      The bare did clothe, the hungry feed—
      In all a perfect model he
      Of what a monarch ought to be.

III

40   But on his gen'rous heart a grief
      Did rest to which no, no relief
      Could be administered; and he
      Did guard it with great secrecy.
      Ah! who could tell! ah! who could know
45   How it did eat him sure tho' slow!
      That mighty man, that monarch great
      On whom th' world's rev'rence sate,
      To whom each vassal king did bow,
      Who wore upon his noble brow

50　　The victor's wreath of myrtle flow'rs
　　　By fair hands wove in virgin bow'rs—
　　　What grief was his—his, who did own
　　　Pure, choicest bliss! He had no son!

IV

　　　Ah! this the secret that did bide
55　　Within his breast. It did he hide—
　　　From friend and slave, from sage and bard,
　　　This secret sorrow, he did guard.
　　　Ah! this upon him darkly sate
　　　And ev'ry pleasure made him hate;
60　　And in his chambers watch would keep,
　　　And this high monarch sad would weep.
　　　Ah! what is grief till man's proud head
　　　Is bow'd, and man, sad tears, doth shed!
　　　Ah! who can talk of grief till when
65　　He sees the tears of gallant men!

V

　　　But God is good and He is Love,
　　　And Sorrow's bitter tears him move
　　　His listens to the mournful cry
　　　The breezes waft beyond the sky;
70　　And He who made his creatures all
　　　Doth gracious hearken to the call,
　　　And sendeth joy like evening dew
　　　That bathes the fragrant violets blue,
　　　And cools their thirsty, panting hearts
75　　When glare with heat from daylight parts.
　　　And He did send to him, like balm,
　　　A joy to heal his heart, and calm
　　　The throbbing of his breaking breast.
　　　And give to him sweet, tranquil rest.

VI

80 It chanced one day, at break of morn,
While the bright heavens, did adorn
The rosy cloudlets streaked with gold
That Phoebus' coming reign foretold—
And myriad birds from leafy bow'rs
85 Did pour, upon the summer hours,
Their joyous notes in tuneful lays
To welcome forth the genial rays—
The sorrowing king all brooding stood
Where sunlight streamed in golden flood.
90 Thro' the gemmed casement passing grand,
Pride of the king of Iran's land,
It chanced that he a form did spy
As he did gaze with a strained eye;
And faster in his royal breast
95 Did throb his manly heart opprest
And why? A still, small peaceful voice
To him, it whispered: "O, rejoice!
For Heav'n to thee sends yonder sage,
The mighty prophet of his age.
100 Speak, speak to him of this, thy grief,
His counsel shall bring sweet relief.
And what advice to thee doth give
Receive, and human heart! still live."

VII

He hearkened to that still small voice
105 That bid his grief-fill'd heart rejoice:
And with quick footsteps he did wend
His way to meet the sage, did blend
With veneration, kingly grace
In which the eye could plainly trace

110 That though in rev'rence bow'd to man
   Forget himself he never can.
   His sorrow deep he did confide;
   And in his halls extending wide,
   Did beg the holy man to share
115 The kingly rooms, the regal fare,
   And pray among you flow'ry vales
   Lives with the lays of nightingales.

VIII

   A venerable man the sage,
   His flowing beard grown white with age;
120 And Time with gentle hand did show'r
   Upon his head a snowy dow'r.
   His dark eyes filled with holy fire
   Seemed as tho' God did them inspire
   To punish wrong, to stop a sigh,
125 To grant a pray'r, to soothe a cry.
   His flowing robes, his solemn mien,
   His hoary locks—in them were seen
   A saint, a prophet, man of God
   As slow upon the plain he trod
130 With eyes bent on the fragrant sod.
   And when the monarch to him brake
   His mournful tale 'twas thus he spake:
   "O! King, I a fakir, to pray,
   It is my duty night and day:
135 Last night God unto me long spoke
   To me thy grief-fill'd tale he broke
   And hither did I bend my way,
   O! King, to give relief this day.
   Conduct me to thy palace fair,
140 Bring 'fore mine eyes thy wife of rare
   And passing loveliness and mien,

Of such a king a worthy queen;
And I o'er thee will read a pray'r,
And thou shalt be free from thy care!"

IX

145 In trembling haste the king did bear
The sage-fakir to his high palace, fair;
And unto him a slave he hailed
To bid the queen come forth unveiled.
Thrice soon she came unveiled and prest
150 Her hand against her snowy breast
And lowly did her king salute
In language eloquent but mute.
But th' sage did fondly to her hie;
And gazed he into her gazelle-like eye
155 As trembling by him she did stand,
The beauteous queen of Iran's land.
Ah! fairer was she than a dream,
Her beauty, poet's darling theme!
But ah! no poet saw that face,
160 So lovely, fraught with seraph grace,
No bard had seen that peerless eye
Whose lustre did with di'monds vie,
Those fragrant hyacinthine curls,
Those glitt'ring rows of orient pearls.
165 None, none had heard that voice divine
So softly sweet, and sweetly fine,
Which, like god Israfili's lyre,
With poetry did the heart inspire.
None but her king did her behold,
170 But O! to them 'twas bliss untold—
For he adored his consort fair,
And she loved him with love so rare.

X

  Then the fakir from his girdle took
  A leaflet from his vellum book,
175 And, lifting up his eyes to Heav'n,
  Prayed that to him the pow'r be giv'n.
  And with a reed pen did inscribe—
  May Allah e'er increase his tribe!—
  A sacred charm in words of fire
180 With which his God did him inspire,
  And gazed upon the royal pair
  The noble king, his consort fair,
  With hands outstretched a pray'r did breathe,
  And round their hands the charm did wreathe
185 And the dead silence he did brake,
  And thus the holy man, he spake:
  "In Allah's name and by the pow'r
  He grants to me in this same hour.
  By Mahomet's, prophet of our creed.
190 O'er ye this holy pray'r I read.
  O! king, take thou this charm and throw
  In a rose-liquid of clear flow,
  And when the charm's dissolved, thy wife
  And thou must quaff the liquid life.
195 Then thou shalt have a son so fair
  And brave and gallant, debonair.
  O! give to him to learn each art
  And educate him to his heart.
  Thou'lt have a son," so said the seer,
200 "And let his name be Mehir Muneer."

XI

  The holy man, he strolled away,
  Thro' Persia's land, that summer day.

And the glad king did cull the flow'rs
That clust'ring hung, in fragrant bow'rs
205 Round the gemmed window, passing grand,
Pride of the king of Iran's land—
Press'd their sweet juice to vases bright
That sparkled in the golden light,
And cooled the drink with mountain snow,
210 And into it the charm did throw;
When 'twas dissolved, and twilight's face
Did smile around in pensive grace,
And stars did gem the heavens blue,
And softly fell the evening dew,
215 The royal pair, in Allah's name,
Did quaff the draught of widespread fame.
And by God's grace within a year
They had a son—Our Mehir Muneer.

XII

The infant babe to boyhood grew,
220 His blessings many, sorrows few.
He was his father's life and joy.
He was his mother's darling boy.
And Iran's people him did love.
He, of the beauty from above,
225 He had his father's kingly mien,
The features of his mother queen—
Strong was his frame, and bright his eye,
As cloudless as the summer sky.
And manly was he, gentle, kind,
230 And gracious, of a noble mind.
And all did love this princely heir—
The noble, manly Mehir Muneer.

XIII

Each useful science was him taught,
And Art with splendid beauties fraught.
235 And education full, complete,
To him was given as was meet.
Quick was he e'er to learn, to know,
And with him did this quickness grow.
E'er thirsting after Wisdom, Truth,
240 With all the fiery zeal of youth.
And Poesy was his chiefest theme.
And weaved he many a bright dream.
He freely took from learning's store
And had a treasure-mine of lore.
245 And thus did thrive in Wisdom's ways
This worthy theme of minstrel lays.

CANTO II

'Tis but a little cause that oft doth bring
To pass thrice great events. It oft doth seem
That darkness doth its frightful shadows fling
Upon our heads, when Heaven sends a gleam
5 To light our path with thrice celestial beam,
And realized before our dazzled eyes
We then behold the ideal of our dream,
The radiant peerless form of Paradise,
That seraph-form that oft, in dream, hath waked our sighs!

I

10 The youthful Prince, in plenty, thrived,
And unto manhood's years arrived.
One morrow he and his followers true—
He had a gallant retinue—
Set forth to 'joy a sportive chase

15. Of timid deer in woodland place.
    The mighty sun's refulgent eye
    Shone in the dreamy-clouded sky,
    And gilded every tree and bough,
    And danced on rills of crystal flow
20. Upon whose banks the violets blue,
    Their fragrant hearts yet wet with dew,
    Did from their lowly bowers peep
    Like lovely maidens waked from sleep,
    And, kissed by Phoebus' golden light,
25. Turned to the Eastern portals bright.
    The roses fair beside the streams,
    Rejoicing in the sun-lit beams,
    In blushing sweetness raised their heads
    Like virgins pure from velvet beds.
30. The stately date with creamy flowers
    That crown her lovely head that towers
    'Bove all th' rest, like a Princess proud
    That gazes on th' heads low bow'd
    To her high grandeur, rose in grace
35. To welcome Sol with smiling face.
    And gladness reigned thro' woods and bow'rs
    As flew morn's fairy-footed hours.

II

Such was the scene that met his eyes
Rejoicing 'neath the summer skies—
40. And fairer than my pen can trace
    Was, in the woodland, Nature's face,
    As Mehir Muneer with gallant band
    Did ride, that morn, thro' th' wooded land.
    With joyous mien and happy hearts,
45. Their golden quivers filled with darts—
    As bounding on their steeds thro' shade

They cantered, or thro' sunny glade,
Each looked around with eager face
For deer to 'gin the nimble chase.
50. Long did they gaze with strained sight
To 'gin the chase in earnest might.

III

'Fore long there bounded by the streams
Where danced the lovely golden beams,
A beauteous fawn so wondrous fair,
55 A young gazelle of beauty rare,
Whose timid glance from matchless eye
If human, had waked poet's sigh.
Around its slender neck, of gold
A well-wrought collar, did behold
60 The hunters who on it did gaze
With admiration all ablaze.
So spake the Prince: "My men to me
Now hark. This fawn so wild and free
Surround and catch—if living then
65 So much the better gallant men.
But if the fawn escape with leap—
Now followers my command must keep—
He o'er whose head she bounding fleets
And shelter seeks in wild retreats,
70 Must spur his steed and swiftly ride,
And seek the place where it doth hide,
And seize the young gazelle and hie
Soon to our band, nor let it fly.
My men, this fawn is passing fair,
75 Its matchless eyes of lustre rare;
So gentle be your touch, and light—
O, hurt it not, that gaz'lle so bright."
So spake the Prince to his brave men,
And then began the chase—O then!

IV

80 With hasty move they did surround
    The young gazelle which gazed around
    In tim'rous wonder and surprise;
    Then brightly flashed its beauteous eyes,
    And desperation courage lent,
85 And with its nimbleness well blent,
    In sheer despair it looked around.
    And lo! on every side the ground
    By pawing steeds and eager glance
    Surrounded was; and every lance
90 Was pointed to the young gazelle—
    To mercy and to ruth farewell!
    No longer did she linger there
    But bounded to the silent air
    With agile leap—each horse did rear—.
95. Leapt o'er the head of Mehir Muneer!
    "O! what is this?"—his courtiers cry
    In voices distressed, with many a sigh—
    "O! what is this? Why this, by Fate,
    Was writ that he, Prince of our State,
100 Should headlong fall in peril's way?
    And should we lose him? Summer's day
    Is not more fair than he! O Heaven!
    Guard him, guard him! to him be given
    To find the fawn, his fancy's whim,
105 And keep him safe e'en him, e'en him!"
    "Adieu my men," he gaily cried
    As gallantly forth he did ride
    To track th' refuge of th' deer,
    His bright eye glancing without fear.
110 Most anxiously his form did watch
    His courtiers, till they did catch

The latest glimpses hid between
Tall, giant trees of ancient mien.
To follow him their wish, but word
115 Of firm command of him, their lord,
Forbade their breaking plighted troth
E'en tho' he rode in peril's path.

VI

Prince Mehir Muneer did wend his way,
Alone that dreamy summer's day,
120 Thro' woodland paths, and sunny glades,
'Mong deepest beds, 'mid friendly shades.
In ev'ry depth, in each retreat
He searched for th' fawn so agile, fleet.
Thus unattended and alone,
125 Heir to the king of Iran's throne,
He wandered seeking for a deer—
The poet Prince, our Mehir Muneer!

VII

The day was spent in fruitless chase,
And Mehir Muneer with downcast face
130 All wearied, did his good steed rest,
And fondly stroked his Kaukab's crest.
"Good steed, forgive," he murmured low,
"To thee thrice cruel proved I now.
I rest thee Kaukab. Vain the chase,
135 Nor the refuge of th' fawn could trace.
Alone I wander thro' the wood,
Since morn not tasted any food,
Since morn have ridden like a fool.
But drink thee Kaukab at this pool."

VIII

140 The sun did kiss a bright farewell
    To tree and flow'r, o'er hill and dell.
    The heav'ns were all transformed to gold
    And crimson as, with pow'r untold,
    Did Sol in glory sink to rest
145 Upon the mountain's glowing breast.
    Each bird did seek its leafy nest
    Each beast to its night's shelter prest.
    And twilight veiled the peaceful earth,
    And twinkling stars then had their birth,
150 And gleamed from their pavilions blue;
    While softly fell the evening dew
    O'er fairy dells and flow'r-starred trees,
    And balmy blew the evening breeze
    O'er wreaths of rosy lotus blooming,
155 And th' blossoms sweet perfuming,
    With fragrant breath, far rare and sweet,
    The woodland place, that dear retreat.

IX

    Soon did the shades of night dispel
    The twilight charms bade "farewell."
160 And darker, darker grew the place,
    And o'er its fragrance-breathing face
    Did Darkness frightful shadows throw.
    O! where is now the sunset glow?
    "Mad fool!"—cried Mehir Muneer distresst,
165 And closer round his form he prest
    His mantle. "Fool! this young gazelle
    Did fire my thoughts and robbed as well
    My senses, for its bright, black eye
    I love—for such I oft did sigh.

170 All day I've roved alone, alone,
    To find th' fawn's wild shelt'ring throne;
    'Tis night, too late to turn to home,
    Still thro' the forest I must roam
    Alone. Heir to my father's crown
175 And kingdom of bright, pure renown,
    I am o'er-ta'en by shades of Night
    With ne'er a spark my path to light.
    Where shall I lay my wearied head?
    Must dewy grass be my low bed?
180 My curtains darkest folds of Night?
    My roof the heav'ns of gloomy light?
    But let that pass. Shall my good horse
    Here stand by morn to turn a corpse—
    My Kaukab, matchless star of steeds,
185 O Heav'n! for shelter, earnest pleads
    This heart perplexed. O! guide my feet
    To some roofed cavern, some retreat.
    Oh Allah! in thy name I go,
    Preserve thou me from ev'ry woe!"

X

190 And thro' the darkness groped his way
    Perplexed and troubled. At last a ray
    He sees across his vision gleam—
    It shines 'fore him with heav'nly beam.
    "My prayer is answered, God"—he cried
195 As that sweet lustre he espied.
    His limbs were freshed with vigour new
    And his quick breath he quickly drew;
    In its direction did proceed
    Prince Mehir Muneer with his good steed.
200 At length he reached a dwelling place,
    And joy did light his noble face

As knocked he at its ancient gate
With hope and gladness all elate.

XI

Opened were the portals by a sage
205 In mien, bent low his head with age.
"O! holy man,"—the Prince began
As him the ancient sage did scan—
"Benighted am I, shelter me;
And God will bless O! hermit, thee."
210 "Thrice welcome son,"—the hermit said—
"In my cell shall all things be made
To suit thee and thy wearied steed.
Now to my cell let us proceed."
The holy sage looked on his face;
215 And by his gracious Allah's grace
'Twas given to know unto th' seer,
That this young man was Mehir Muneer—
Who to his blessing owed his birth,
The heir of glorious Iran's earth.
220 In silence 'gan he to prepare
A lowly bed, a frugal fare,
For his young guest; and his proud steed
With plenteous grain and hay did feed;
And feigning ignorance the seer
225 Asked questions of Prince Mehir Muneer—
Asked who he was and what his name,
And what disaster to him came
To make him seek this poor abode
Of this old hermit, man of God.

XII

230 The unsuspecting Prince replied
To queries all without e'er pride—

Related his parentage, birth,
Dwelt on the holy sage of worth,
To whom his birth the prince, he owed,
235 And gratefully his bosom glowed
While of that sage he spoke with praise
Unconscious that his eyes did raise
He unto that same sage's face—
He knew not that his host was he,
240 The mighty prophet, old and free.
And spoke he of the beauteous fawn
That met his eyes at break of dawn,
That robbed him of his wits so well
With its bright eye, that young gazelle.

XIII

245 But sudden did a marvellous light
Flash dazzlingly across his sight;
And softly did a blazing seat
Of diamonds fall before his feet;
And decked in richest cloths of gold
250 Half hid by gems of price untold,
He saw four fairy queens of rare
And splendid beauty, wondrous fair,
Alight from, 'bove their jewelled throne,
And 'fore the holy man bow down
255 In low obeisance, deep, profound,
And sate themselves upon the ground
In presence of that man of God—
Four fairy queens in that abode!

XIV

"Why come ye all to-night? Why here?
260 Not this your day"—remarked the seer.
"Nay, holy saint,"—the fairies said,

And many low salutes they made—
"We're on our way to see that rare
And beauteous maiden, passing fair,
265 The lovely, sweet Badar Muneer.
Our road lies this way, holy seer,
And O! within our minds we thought
To seek thy blessing; and we sought
Thy presence our respects to pay
270 Tho' this is not our happy day."

XV

"Well," said the sage, "ye fairies bright!
Ye children of a land of light!
Unto your princess him, too, bear,
And be he judge if far more fair
275 Be she, or ladies of his halls
Shut in between the harem walls—
Those maidens with the gazelle eye
As cloudless as the summer sky.
Depart to bless prince Mehir Muneer!"
280 So kindly spake the ancient seer.

XVI

The fairies sate him on their throne;
And in a moment they had flown
With him into the outer air.
Now shone the moon with lustre rare;
285 And th' heavens, a space since full of gloom,
As black as is a raven's plume,
Now smiled in splendour, studded bright
With myriad torches, filled with light.
But Mehir Muneer, he little saw—
290 His soul was filled with joyful awe
As sat he by these fairy queens,

Of graceful forms and lovely miens,
Borne far away into the skies—
Now past the stars, those heaven's eyes—
295 O! wither, wither do him bear?
O! higher, higher in the air!
And faster faster than my rhymes,
Did fly that throne to fairy climes.
O! hearken to those tinkling chimes!

XVII

300 At length they reached her fragrant bower
Where music of enchanting power
Did float upon the perfumed breeze,
And lingered o'er the flow'r-gemmed trees.
And wilder beat Mehir Muneer's heart
305 To hear those glorious strains impart
Such melting tenderness that he
Said to himself: "What *she* must be
Who thus the guitar's strings inspires
With notes that breathe in living fires!"
310 The gentle wind the throne did waft
With perfumed breath, so sweet and soft,
Thro' the oped casement of her bower
Rich with the sigh of many a flower.

XVIII

Why stood Mehir Muneer transfix'd,
315 His face with joy and wonder mix'd?
Why rooted thus? Why doth he seem
As tho' he saw a heav'nly dream?
Lo! on a glitt'ring, golden throne
With sparkling gems and priceless gown,
320 Reclined, a form, a form more fair,
A face of beauty far more rare

Than seraphs e'en by Allah's seat;
In highest heaven, that loved retreat!
Zuhura's dewy lustre bright.
325 The young fawn's eye of tender light—
O! what were they before her glance
Whose ev'ry gleam was pure romance?
The wreaths of starry river-buds
That tumble o'er the wavy floods,
330 Lost their bright colour washed with dew
Before her passing brilliant hue.
The Gul-i-susan, snowy white,
Was not more fair, more dazzling bright
Than hands of her—so rosy painted
335 Were their fingertips untainted;
More exquisite and more blooming
Than a lovely rose perfuming
The ev'ning air, her fragrant mouth;
As glowing as the sunny south;
340 And not more sweet the bow of heaven
Than her brows, all pencilled even;
More resplendent and more fair
Her dream-sweet brow than Dian's rare;
Her breath like flowers whose gentle fan
345 Is balmy breeze of Peristan;
Her tresses flowed in seraph curls;
Hid 'tween rose-buds, were matchless pearls.
Who could describe such radiant grace,
Transcending fairness, mien and face?
350 For realized 'fore him did beam
The pure ideal of his dream—
There, 'fore him, there without peer
Did she recline, Badar Muneer!

XIX

    And she, the matchless Beauty-Queen—
355 And in her glance, O! what was seen?
    Love-lit became those dream-bright eyes,
    And softly trembled balmy sighs
    Upon those rosy lips—'twas bliss
    To press on them one glowing kiss!
360 High beat her heart beneath its vest,
    Close unto it her hand she prest;
    And brighter, brighter grew her gaze
    With wondering surprise all 'blaze—
    Ne'er had she seen so fair a face,
365 So passing grand, in which could trace
    High royal birth; whose ev'ry glance
    Did virgin spirits quite entrance
    Thrice radiant was her smile and sweet
    With which the poet-prince did meet,
370 For Cupid with his feath'ry dart
    Had shot his fire into her heart!

XX

    She softly rose from her gemm'd seat,
    And her fair stranger-guest did greet.
    "Welcome!"—so tremulous she breathed
375 And ev'ry word his heart, it wreathed—
    "Welcome O! stranger to my bower,
    And blissful be this self-same hour!"
    He knelt before Badar Muneer,
    That lovely form without e'er peer,
380 And prest upon her glowing hand
    A kiss—he, heir of Iran's land,
    Felt low and mean before this fay
    More radiant than a summer's day.
    "Badar Muneer!"—he cried so soft

385 'Twas music that the breeze did waft
   To her loved ear—"me thought that
   Could be so fair; but there is one;
   And thou art she who now dost beam
   Far fairer than the poet's theme—
390 Ideal of my wildest dream!"

XXI

   She set him on her Masnad grand,
   Him heir t'the throne of Iran's land;
   And unseen hands hid by rich screens,—
   Her handmaid's hands of gorgeous miens—
395 Did string the harp and the guitar;
   And music pealed sweet as from far.
   O! far. beyond the azure seas
   The strains were wafted by the breeze
   Enliv'ning thus the banquet hour
400 At midnight, in that lovely bower
   While moon and stars did brightly gleam,
   Sent thro' the lattice their soft beam;
   The myrtle shed its snowy bloom
   Upon the fruits of ripe perfume;
405 Th' pomegranate shining bright;
   The orange glowed with golden light;
   Blossoming limes their fragrance sent,
   And to the rest their power lent
   To bind the senses, charm the eye
410 With mellow odours, various dye;
   And sherbets cooled with purest snow
   In jewelled vases bright did glow
   And sparkled in their crystal flow.

XXII

   The banquet o'er, Badar Muneer

415 Placed rosy wreaths with hands so dear
　　Upon her lover's brow and neck,
　　His form with garlands sweet did deck;
　　And taking up her lute, did blend
　　Her glorious strains with its, did lend
420 Such melting tenderness and power,
　　As rose the notes within her bower,
　　As bore him to th' enchanted Isles
　　Where summer beauty ever smiles,
　　Whose queen was fair Badar Muneer,
425 His beauteous love without e'er peer,
　　And he the slave of her so dear!

XXIII

　　In rapture harked he to the lay—
　　So wild and varied sang this fay—
　　As o'er her lute her fingers flew,
430 And these the strains that 'neath them grew:—

(i)

What is your language, lovely flow'rs
In blushing sweetness bloom,
And load the fairy-footed hours
With breathing of perfume?

(ii)

435 *What is your language, roses fair,*
With fiery hearts of gold
That fill the e'er ambrosial air
With scent of pow'r untold?

(iii)

Why doth my bosom brightly glow
440 *As on you fall mine eyes,*

  And softly, softly ye do blow
  Beneath the dreamy skies?

(iv)

  What language is the one ye breathe
  Unto me as my glance
445 *Doth rest on you, and ye do wreathe*
  My soil with bright romance?

(v)

  Yes roses, why to ye I sing
  These wild and varied notes,
  And on the gentle Zephyr fling
450 *My lay in fragrance floats?*

(vi)

  O whisper flow'rs, ye rosy flow'rs,
  What language do you own,
  As ye do blush in ev'ning hours
  Upon your em'rald throne?

(vii)

455 *So spake the flow'rs as from above*
  The silver stars did shine:
  Our language sweet, O maid, is Lore—
  'Tis Love, that flame divine.

(viii)

  "When softly fell the ev'ning dew
460 *Within our fragrant breasts,*
  We blushed in joy, the self-same hue
  Upon our face yet rests!"

(ix)

"*Our hearts are gold, for in that hour*
They glowed with fire from 'bove
465 *And gave to us this charmer's pow'r—*
Our language sweet, is Lore!"

XXIV

Three watches of the night did fleet
In harmony and music sweet
And soul-inspiring melody
470 The breezes wafted to the sky;
Each moment stronger grew their love
And burnt with fire from above;
They gazed at one another—this
To them was tasting cup of bliss;
475 And rapt'rous joy their breasts did light,
And brighter shone their glance, more bright:
And softer, tend'rer grew their tone,
And glorious love was all their own.

XXV

"'Tis waxing late," the fairies said,
480 "Prince Mehir Muneer, 'tis time for bed;
Now let us hie back to the cell
Where he, the holy man doth dwell.
Come Mehir Muneer we're homeward bound,
For mortals 'tis time to sleep sound."
485 "Go, if you will," the prince, he cried.
"And on your homeward journey ride.
But I will stay with her I love.
Badar Muneer, and gaily rove
By murm'ring rills and dancing streams
490 Send forth the music, as in dreams
And with my lute in fragrant bowers

    Beguile the tranquil, ev'ning hours.
    And when sweet Cynthia lights the skies—
    Soft, beauteous lamp of Paradise!"—
495 With many a charming tale will I
    Fill with bright Rapture's light her eye
    And I for ever will abide
    Near her, my own, loved, peerless bride

XXVI

    "What shall we do?" the fairies thought,
500 And they each other's counsel sought.
    "If we but bear him from her bower
    Rich with the sigh of many a flower,
    Offended will she be, nay grief
    Will pierce her soul, and no relief—
505 Could it be giv'n; to her most dear
    Has grown this handsome Mehir Muneer!
    But if we leave him here and fly
    How shall we meet the hermit's eye?
    What shall we do? Ah! wait, but wait,
510 Too long they have thus joyful sate.
    Let Morpheus spread his gentle hand
    And bind them with his rosy band."

XXVII

    They waited all, and before long
    Charmed into sleep by fairy song,
515 Both fell to nodding; and the fays
    The form of Mehir Muneer did raise
    With gentle touch from his bright throne,
    And softly placed him on their own.
    The sleeping prince unconscious lay;
520 And at the lovely break of day
    The fairy queens away did fly

And to the hermit's cell did hie,
And gave unto the holy seer
The slumb'ring form of Mehir Muneer.

CANTO III

Love! O what matchless power thou dost own!
And undisputed e'er that pow'r shall be,
And thou wilt reign for ever on thy throne—
In but one moment thou canst bind the force
5 And fearless fancies of a youthful breast
O Love! divinest love, for e'er shall be
Of ev'ry minstrel theme the purest, best
Thy hallowing influences make each bosom blest!

I

'Twas noon when Mehir Muneer his eyes
10 Did ope. "Alas! alas!" he cries
As he did view the hermit's cell
And bitter tears from him they fell.
"Oh! where is now her lovely bower?
Where is her lute of magic power?
15 And where am I? Oh! where am I?
Far from the influence of her eye?
Oh! where is she the one so dear,
The one adored without peer,
Badar Muneer, Badar Muneer."
20 And thus he raved in fever high;
And sat the sage his pallet nigh.
"Badar Muneer!"—so wild did rave,
And sought her hand his brow to have
"Badar Muneer!"—he sought the bliss
25 Would be imparted by one kiss
Of her loved lips upon his form

To still the raging of the storm.
The burning fever within him burned,
Restless upon his bed he turned;
30 He sought the one so passing dear,
"Badar Muneer! Badar Muneer!"

III

At length as thus the Prince, he cried,
The watchful hermit, he espied
A gallant party who drew near
35 The dwelling where did live the seer.
"What seek ye here!" the hermit said
As low salutes to him they made.
"O holy man! but yester morn
Did we set out with hounds and horn
40 With our loved prince to join the chase.
A young gazelle of matchless grace
His fancy caught; he bade us stay
Behind him, and so fearless, gay
After her rode, nor found we him,
45 Nor traces of his Fancy's whim.
Benighted were we in the wood
Without e'er tasting any food,
And seeking for him wended here—
Knowest thou aught of Mehir Muneer?"

IV

50 The sage them bore into his cell
Their bosoms with surprise did swell
As they did gaze on Mehir Muneer.
Then quest'ning turned upon the seer
Who did relate all he did know
55 In accents hurried, soft and low.
Prince Mehir Muneer then oped his eye

And heaved profound and baleful sighs.
"O Royal prince! O Iran's heir!
Of warriors the flow'r most fair!
60 O what is this? O tell us now,
Why thus beside thy self art thou?"

V

"Badar Muneer! Badar Muneer!"—
Was all he spoke. In trembling fear
His courtiers stood beside their lord,
65 Their idol-prince whose ev'ry word
To them was law. By Iran's heir
They silent stood—by him most fair.
How now? With what sad tidings now
Were they before the king to bow?
70 Had they like trusted courtiers true
Performed their duties—they were few?
Toward their idolised prince,
Did they aught loyalty evince?

VI

Back through the woodland him they bore
75 Nature the self-same aspect wore
As yester morn; but for the grace
And beauties of fair Nature's face
No eyes had they; on Mehir Muneer
Their thoughts and glance in anxious fear
80 Were fixed, for he did wildly rave.
"Badar Muneer," was all did crave
This love-born Prince—'twas but her name
Unto his burning lips it came;
In high delirium he tost
85 And his young life was all but lost!

VII

    They reached His Majesty's proud halls
    And entered in the golden walls,
    And laid the burning fevered head
    Of Mehir Muneer upon his bed;
90 In haste did seek the Persian King
    And to his son's loved side did bring
    The sorrowing father; did relate
    All that thus far had been his fate—
    Told of that fawn of matchless eye
95 And how unattended he did hie
    To seize her; and the hermit's tale
    To tell to him they did not fail.
    And standing by they did bewail.

VIII

    Ah! who could understand the grief
100 That filled his heart without relief!
    He wept, he wept; like drops of blood
    Wrenched from his inmost heart in flood
    Seemed the large tear-drops of the youth
    Ah! who could view them without ruth?
105 Who but a poet knows full well
    The joys and sorrows that do dwell
    Within a poet's heart? Ah! who
    Can interpret, can read more true?
    A poet he, Prince Mehir Muneer
110 To him was beauty ever dear.
    O brother bards! but ye do know
    If this dire grief be common woe!
    A poet, 'fore his eyes did beam—
    Ah! realized 'fore him did gleam
115 A form more beauteous and more rare

Than seraph's e'en, surpassing fair,
Before him smiled; that face did seem
Far fairer than the poet's theme—
Ideal of his wildest dream!
120 And she did bear for him pure love
That fire divine seat from above;
And soft upon his manly breast
Her peerless head in sleep did rest;
And he had prest a glowing kiss
125 Upon her lips to find it bliss;
And now was wrenched from her loved side
From her, his own dear, lovely bride!
And in a moment all was gone!
Reason had well nigh left her throne—
130 His youthful hopes all blasted were
His glorious future, passing rare,
Would be as naught; his proud career,
Illustrious, did close Mehir Muneer.
What cared he now? But for a while
135 Fortune had shed on him a smile
Of wondrous lustre. He had seen
But for an hour his heart's sole queen
What cared he now for life apart
From her, the idol of his heart,
140 That form ideal, without peer,
Transcending fair, Badar Muneer?

IX

The king, his loving arms, did wreathe
Around his son, and soft did breathe:
"Loved boy, tell us of this, thy woe;
145 Of this, thy grief let us but know.
Look up, my son, for I am near."—
His sole reply: "Badar Muneer!"

The royal father sorrowed o'er,
O'er his loved son he did adore;
150 The queen,—who knows a mother's love,
Divinest flame, from God above?—
Her mother heart did bleed full sore,
For he was her fond bosom's core.
They wrung their hands, they smote their breast;
155 And fled from them was ev'ry rest.
They watched in tender, anxious fear
O'er the loved form of Mehir Muneer!
The Vizier of the Shah-in-Shah,
A wise man, he discreetly saw
160 That all affairs to ruin ran;
And summoned courage like a man,
And to the grief-filled king did go
And lowly 'fore his seat did bow.
"O king of kings! Shrine of all climes!
165 For ever live thou thro' all times!
Be not distressed! I am thy slave.
Sent couriers all o'er, I have.
She, whose proud name he doth repeat
To him must be thrice loved and sweet—
170 The name of one he loves full well,
The one that in his heart doth dwell—
If we but find where she doth stay,
O! royal king, the self same day,
Will wed her to thy noble heir—
175 And happiness be their glad share!
Now 'gain affairs, take them in hand,
Else ruin waits for Iran's land!"

X

'Twas long before the men arrived
Where Badar Muneer's sire lived

180 A mighty king was he and great
Of vast domains and splendid state.
The couriers did his presence seek,
And in respectful tones and meek,
Did the proud king fully acquaint
185 With real facts. Nor did they paint
In livelier colours what befell,
And told their story passing well.
The spoke of Mehir Muneer's state
Unto the mighty monarch great
190 And sought for him without e'er peer,
The hand of loved Badar Muneer.

XI

The king did hark unto the tale,
In rapt attention ne'er did fail;
And at its conclusion he did sigh—
195 'Twas in relief. And his proud eye
Did light with pleasure, and he spoke:
"Take her, my child, take her, O take!
These weary days naught but the name
Of Mehir Muneer unto her came.
200 The lustre of her cheek doth pale,
Her matchless form's becoming frail
'Tis him she longs for, Mehir Muneer,
Take her my daughter without peer!
No preparations must be made"—
205 'Twas thus the royal king, he said—
"No rich brocade, no priceless gem,
No radiant, brilliant diadem.
But haste ye to your sov'reign great,
Nor for a moment must ye wait;
210 But bid him hie with Mehir Muneer,
To take my daughter without peer."

XII

It was a bright, resplendent day—
The sun did shine all laughing, gay;
And strains of music filled the air,
215 And pealed thro' heav'n in notes most rare;
And gorgeous flags and pennants
Did gaily flutter; tinkling bells
Did blithely chime with merry ring,
And thousand voices glad did sing;
220 And rich caparisoned steeds did prance
E'en elephants, sedate, did dance;
And myriad rockets in gold showers
Did fall on earth like starry flowers.
And countless voices did proclaim,
225 "It was a marriage of fame,
It was an hour of dear delight
Each bosom did with joy excite."
In matchless pomp and splendour great,
Magnificence and full in state,
230 With charming harmony and song
The proud procession moved along
This day did see Prince Mehir Muneer
United to his bride whose peer
Nor flow'ry earth, nor starry heaven
235 In any hour birth had given—
It was the one so passing dear
To him, his own Badar Muneer!"

XIII

Prince Mehir Muneer's poet heart
Had found its lovelier, better part.
240 The true ideal of his dream
Now realized by him did beam,

His own to love, revere, adore
Each day to love her more and more.
His own, the idol of his breast
245 Upon his bosom now did rest.
Their meeting—it was pure romance
That steepeth one into a trance,
But more romantic still their love
Shed on their hearts by Him above.
250 May Heaven grant pure joys most rare!
May happiness e'er be their share!
And blessings on the loving pair!

From THE GOLDEN THRESHOLD

PALANQUIN-BEARERS

Lightly, O lightly, we bear her along,
She sways like a flower in the wind of our song;
She skims like a bird on the foam of a stream
She floats like a laugh from the lips of a dream.
5   Gaily, O gaily we glide and we sing,
We bear her along like a pearl on a string.

Softly, O softly we bear her along,
She hangs like a star in the dew of our song;
She springs like a beam on the brow of the tide,
10 She falls like a tear from the eyes of a bride
Lightly, O lightly we glide and we sing,
We bear her along like a pearl on a string.

WANDERING SINGERS
(*Written to one of their tunes*)

Where the voice of the wind calls our wandering feet,
Through echoing forest and echoing street,
With lutes in our hands ever-singing we roam,
All men are our kindred, the world is our home.

5   Our lays are of cities whose lustre is shed,
    The laughter and beauty of women long dead;
    The sword of old battles, the crown of old kings,
    And happy and simple and sorrowful things.

    What hope shall we gather, what dreams shall we sow?
10 Where the wind calls our wandering footsteps we go.
    No love bids us tarry, no joy bids us wait:
    The voice of the wind is the voice of our fate.

∽

INDIAN WEAVERS

    Weavers, weaving at break of day,
    Why do you weave a garment so gay? . . .
    Blue as the wing of a falcon wild,
    We weave the robes of a new-born child.
5   Weavers, weaving at fall of night,
    Why do you weave a garment so bright? . . .
    Like the plumes of a peacock, purple and green,
    We weave the marriage-veils of a queen.

    Weavers, weaving solemn and still,
10 What do you weave in the moonlight chill? . . .
    White as a feather and white as a cloud,
    We weave a dead man's funeral shroud.

∽

CORN-GRINDERS

O little, mouse, why dost thou cry
While merry stars laugh in the sky?

Alas! alas! my lord is dead!
Ah, who will ease my bitter pain?
5 He went to seek a millet-grain
In the rich farmer's granary shed;
They caught him in a baited snare,
And slew my lover unaware . . .
Alas! alas! my lord is dead.

10 *O little deer, why dost thou moan,*
Hid in thy forest-bower alone?

Alas! alas! my lord is dead!
Ah! who will quiet my lament?
At fall of eventide he went
15 To drink beside the river-head;
A waiting hunter threw his dart
And struck my lover through the heart.
Alas! alas! my lord is dead . . .

O little bride, why dost thou weep
20 *With all the happy world asleep?*
Alas! alas! my lord is dead!
Ah, who will stay these hungry tears,
Or still the want of famished years,
And crown with love my marriage-bed?
25 My soul burns with the quenchless fire
That lit my lover's funeral pyre . . .
Alas! alas! my lord is dead.

VILLAGE-SONG

Honey, child, honey, child, whither are you going?
Would you cast your jewels all to the breezes blowing?

Would you leave the mother who on golden grain has fed you?
Would you grieve the lover who is riding forth to wed you?
5   Mother mine, to the wild forest I am going,
Where upon the *champa* boughs the *champa* buds are blowing;
To the koil-haunted river-isles where lotus lilies glisten,
The voices of the fairy-folk are calling me, O listen!

Honey, child, honey, child, the world is full of pleasure,
10   Of bridal-songs and cradle-songs and sandal-scented leisure.
Your bridal robes are in the loom, silver and saffron glowing,
Your bridal cakes are on the hearth: O whither are you going?

The bridal-songs and cradle-songs have cadences of sorrow,
The laughter of the sun today, the wind of death tomorrow.
15   Far sweeter sound the forest-notes where forest-streams are falling;
O mother mine, I cannot stay, the fairy-folk are calling.

INDIAN LOVE-SONG

She

Like a serpent to the calling voice of flutes,
Glides my heart into thy fingers, O my Love!

Where the night-wind, like a lover, leans above
His jasmine-gardens and *sirisha*-bowers;
5 And on ripe boughs of many-coloured fruits
Bright parrots cluster like vermilion flowers.

❧

He

Like the perfume in the petals of a rose,
Hides thy heart within my bosom, O my love!
Like a garland, like a jewel, like a dove
10 That hangs its nest in the *asoka*-tree.
Lie still, O love, until the morning sows
Her tents of gold on fields of ivory.

❧

SUTTEE

Lamp of my life, the lips of Death
Hath blown thee out with their sudden breath;
Naught shall revive thy vanished spark . . .
Love, must I dwell in the living dark?

5 Tree of my life, Death's cruel foot
Hath crushed thee down to thy hidden root;
Nought shall restore thy glory fled . . .
Shall the blossom live when the tree is dead?

Life of my life, Death's bitter sword
10 Hath severed us like a broken word,
Rent us in twain who are but one . . .
Shall the flesh survive when the soul is gone?

❧

AUTUMN SONG

Like a joy on the heart of a sorrow,
The sunset hangs on a cloud;
A golden storm of glittering sheaves,
Of fair and frail and fluttering leaves
5   The wild wind blows in a cloud.

Hark to a voice that is calling
To my heart in the voice of the wind:
My heart is weary and sad and alone,
For its dreams like the fluttering leaves have gone,
10 And why should I stay behind?

∾

ALABASTER

Like this alabaster box whose art
Is frail as a cassia-flower, is my heart,
Carven with delicate dreams and wrought
With many a subtle and exquisite thought.

5   Therein I treasure the spice and scent
Of rich and passionate memories blent
Like odours of cinnamon, sandal and clove,
Of song and sorrow and life and love.

∾

ECSTASY

Cover mine eyes, O my Love!
Mine eyes that are weary of bliss

As of light that is poignant and strong,
O silence my lips with a kiss,
5   My lips that are weary of song!

Shelter my soul, O my Love!
My soul is bent low with the pain
And the burden of love like the grace
Of a flower that is smitten with rain:
10   O shelter my soul from thy face!

ODE TO H.H. THE NIZAM OF HYDERABAD
(Presented at the Ramzan Durbar)

Deign, Prince, my tribute to receive,
This lyric offering to your name,
Who round your jewelled sceptre bind
The lilies of a poet's fame;

5   Beneath whose sway concordant dwell
The peoples whom your laws embrace,
In brotherhood of diverse creeds,
And harmony of diverse race:

The votaries of the Prophet's faith,
10   Of whom you are the crown and chief
And they, who bear on Vedic brows
Their mystic symbols of belief;
And they, who worshipping the sun,
Fled o'er the old Iranian sea;
15   And they, who bow to Him who trod
The midnight waves of Galilee.

Sweet, sumptuous fables of Baghdad
The splendours of your court recall,
The torches of a *Thousand Nights*
20 Blaze through a single festival;
And Saki-singers down the streets,
Pour for us, in a stream divine,
From goblets of your love-*ghazals*
The rapture of your Sufi wine.

25 Prince, where your radiant cities smile,
Grim hills their sombre vigils keep,
Your ancient forests hoard and hold
The legends of their centuried sleep;
Your birds of peace white-pinioned float
30 O'er ruined fort and storied plain,
Your faithful stewards sleepless guard
The harvests of your gold and grain.

God give you joy, God give you grace
To shield the truth and smite the wrong,
35 To honour Virtue, Valour, Worth.
To cherish faith and foster song.
So may the lustre of your days
Outshine the deeds Firdusi sung,
Your name within a nation's prayer,
40 Your music on a nation's tongue.

ଓ

LEILI

The serpents are asleep among the poppies,
The fireflies light the soundless panther's way
To tangled paths where shy gazelles are straying,

And parrot-plumes outshine the dying day.
5　O soft! the lotus-buds upon the stream
Are stirring like sweet maidens when they dream.
A caste-mark on the azure brows of Heaven,
The golden moon burns sacred, solemn, bright
The winds are dancing in the forest-temple,
10　And swooning at the holy feet of Night,
Hush! in the silence mystic voices sing
And make the gods their incense-offering.

IN THE FOREST

Here, O my heart, let us burn the dear dreams that are dead,
Here in this wood let us fashion a funeral pyre
Of fallen white petals and leaves that are mellow and red,
Here let us burn them in noon's flaming torches of fire.
5　We are weary, my heart, we are weary, so long we have borne
The heavy loved burden of dreams that are dead, let us rest,
Let us scatter their ashes away, for a while let us mourn;
We will rest, O my heart, till the shadows are grey in the west.

But soon we must rise, O my heart, we must wander again
10　Into the war of the world and the strife of the throng;
Let us rise, O my heart, let us gather the dreams that remain,
We will conquer the sorrow of life with the sorrow of song.

PAST AND FUTURE

The new hath come and now the old retires:
And so the past becomes a mountain-cell,
Where lone, apart, old hermit-memories dwell
In consecrated calm, forgotten yet
5 Of the keen heart that hastens to forget
Old longings in fulfilling new desires.

And now the Soul stands in a vague, intense
Expectancy and anguish of suspense,
On the dim chamber-threshold . . . lo! he sees
10 Like a strange, fated bride as yet unknown,
His timid future shrinking there alone,
Beneath her marriage-veil of mysteries.

TO THE GOD OF PAIN

Unwilling priestess in thy cruel fane,
Long hast thou held me, pitiless god of Pain
Bound to thy worship by reluctant vows,
My tired breast girt with suffering, and my brows
5 Anointed with perpetual weariness.
Long have I borne thy service, through the stress
Of rigorous years, sad days and slumberless nights,
Performing thine inexorable rites.

For thy dark altars, balm nor milk nor rice,
10 But mine own soul thou'st ta'en for sacrifice:
All the rich honey of my youth's desire,
And all the sweet oils from my crushed life drawn
And all my flower-like dreams and gem-like fire
Of hopes up-leaping like the light of dawn.

15 I have no more to give, all that was mine
Is laid, a wrested tribute, at thy shrine;
Let me depart, for my whole soul is wrung,
And all my cheerless orisons are sung;
Let me depart, with faint limbs let me creep
20 To some dim shade and sink me down to sleep.

INDIAN DANCERS

Eyes ravished with rapture, celestially panting,
what passionate bosoms aflaming with fire
Drink deep of the hush of the hyacinth heavens
that glimmer around them in fountains of light;
5 O wild and entrancing the strain of keen music
that cleaveth the stars like a wail of desire,
And beautiful dancers with houri-like faces
bewitch the voluptuous watches of night.

The scents of red roses and sandalwood flutter and
10 die in the maze of their gem-tangled hair,
And smiles are entwining like magical serpents the
poppies of lips that are opiate-sweet;
Their glittering garments of purple are burning
like tremulous dawns in the quivering air,
15 And exquisite, subtle and slow are the tinkle and
tread of their rhythmical, slumber-soft feet.

Now silent, now singing and swaying and swinging
like blossoms that bend to the breezes or showers,
Now wantonly winding, they flash, now they falter,
20 and, lingering, languish in radiant choir;
Their jewel-girt arms and warm, wavering, lily-

long fingers enchant through melodious hours,
Eyes ravished with rapture, celestially panting,
what passionate bosoms aflaming with fire!

∽

MY DEAD DREAM

Have you found me, at last, O my Dream? Seven aeons ago
You died and I buried you deep under forests of snow.
Why have you come hither? Who bade you awake from your sleep
And track me beyond the cerulean foam of the deep?

5   Would you tear from my lintels these sacred green garlands of leaves?
Would you scare the white, nested, wild pigeons of joy from my caves?
Would you touch and defile with dead fingers the robes of my priest?
Would you weave your dim moan with the chantings of love at my feast?

Go back to your grave, O my Dream, under forests of snow,
10 Where a heart-riven child hid you once, seven aeons ago.
Who bade you arise from your darkness? I bid you depart!
Profane not the shrines I raised in the clefts of my heart.

∽

DAMAYANTI TO NALA IN THE HOUR OF EXILE
(A Fragment)

Shalt thou be conquered of a human fate
My liege, my lover, whose imperial head
Hath never bent in sorrow of defeat?
Shalt thou be vanquished, whose imperial feet
5   Have shattered armies and stamped empires dead?
Who shall unking thee, husband of a queen?
Wear thou thy majesty inviolate.
Earth's glories flee of human eyes unseen,
Earth's kingdoms fade to a remembered dream,
10 But thine henceforth shall be a power supreme,
Dazzling command and rich dominion,
The winds thy heralds and thy vassals all
The silver-belted planets and the sun.
Where'er the radiance of thy coming fall,
15 Shall dawn for thee her saffron footcloths spread,
Sunset her purple canopies and red,
In serried splendour, and the night unfold
Her velvet darkness wrought with starry gold
For kingly raiment, soft as cygnet-down.
20 My hair shall braid thy temples like a crown
Of sapphires, and my kiss upon thy brows
Like cithara-music lull thee to repose,
Till the sun yield thee homage of his light.

O king, thy kingdom who from thee can wrest?
25 What fate shall dare uncrown thee from this breast,
O god-born lover, whom my love doth gird
And armour with impregnable delight
Of Hope's triumphant keen flame-carven sword?

THE QUEEN'S RIVAL

I

Queen Gulnaar sat on her ivory bed,
Around her countless treasures were spread;

Her chamber walls were richly inlaid
With agate, porphyry, onyx and jade;

5   The tissues that veiled her delicate breast
Glowed with the hues of a lapwing's crest;

But still she gazed in her mirror and sighed
"O King, my heart is unsatisfied."

King Feroz bent from his ebony seat:
10 "Is thy least desire unfulfilled, O Sweet?
"Let thy mouth speak and my life be spent
To clear the sky of thy discontent."

"I tire of my beauty, I tire of this
Empty splendour and shadowless bliss;

15 "With none to envy and none gainsay,
No savour or salt hath my dream or day."

Queen Gulnaar sighed like a murmuring rose:
"Give me a rival, O King Feroz."

II

King Feroz spoke to his Chief Vizier:
20 "Lo! ere to-morrow's dawn be here,

"Send forth my messengers over the sea,
To seek seven beautiful brides for me;

"Radiant of feature and regal of mien,
Seven handmaids meet for the Persian Queen."

25 Seven new moon tides at the Vesper call,
King Feroz led to Queen Gulnaar's hall

A young queen eyed like the morning star:
"I bring thee a rival, O Queen Gulnaar."

But still she gazed in her mirror and sighed:
30 "O King, my heart is unsatisfied."

Seven queens shone round her ivory bed,
Like seven soft gems on a silken thread

Like seven fair lamps in a royal tower,
Like seven bright petals of Beauty's flower.

35 Queen Gulnaar sighed like a murmuring rose
"Where is my rival, O King Feroz?"

III

When spring winds wakened the mountain floods.
And kindled the flame of the tulip buds,

When bees grew loud and the days grew long,
40 And the peach groves thrilled to the oriole's song.

Queen Gulnaar sat on her ivory bed,

Decking with jewels her exquisite head;

And still she gazed in her mirror and sighed:
"O King, my heart is unsatisfied."

45 Queen Gulnaar's daughter two spring times old,
In blue robes bordered with tassels of gold,

Ran to her knee like a wildwood fay,
And plucked from her hand the mirror away.

Quickly she set on her own light curls
50 Her mother's fillet with fringes of pearls;

Quickly she turned with a child's caprice
And pressed on the mirror a swift, glad kiss.

Queen Gulnaar laughed like a tremulous rose:
"Here is my rival, O King Feroz."

∾

THE POET TO DEATH

Tarry a while, O Death, I cannot die
While yet my sweet life burgeons with its spring;
Fair is my youth, and rich the echoing boughs
Where *dhadikulas* sing.

5 Tarry a while, O Death, I cannot die
With all my blossoming hopes unharvested,
My joys ungarnered, all my songs unsung,
And all my tears unshed.

Tarry a while, till I am satisfied
10 Of love and grief, of earth and altering sky;
Till all my human hungers are fulfilled,
O Death, I cannot die!

THE INDIAN GIPSY

In tattered robes that hoard a glittering trace
Of bygone colours, broidered to the knee,
Behold her, daughter of a wandering race,
Tameless, with the bold falcon's agile grace,
5 And the lithe tiger's sinuous majesty.

With frugal skill her simple wants she tends,
She folds her tawny heifers and her sheep
On lonely meadows when the daylight ends,
Ere the quick night upon her flock descends
10 Like a black panther from the caves of sleep.

Time's river winds in foaming centuries
Its changing, swift, irrevocable course
To far off and incalculable seas;
She is twin-born with primal mysteries,
15 And drinks of life at Time's forgotten source.

THE PARDAH NASHIN

Her life is a revolving dream
Of languid and sequestered ease;
Her girdles and her fillets gleam

Like changing fires on sunset seas;
5 Her raiment is like morning mist,
   Shot opal, gold and amethyst.

   From thieving light of eyes impure.
   From coveting sun or wind's caress,
   Her days are guarded and secure
10 Behind her carven lattices,
   Like jewels in a turbaned crest,
   Like secrets in a lover's breast.

   But though no hand unsanctioned dares
   Unveil the mysteries of her grace,
15 Time lifts the curtain unawares,
   And Sorrow looks into her face . . .
   Who shall prevent the subtle years,
   Or shield a woman's eyes from tears?

∽

NIGHTFALL IN THE CITY OF HYDERABAD

See how the speckled sky burns like a pigeon's throat,
Jewelled with embers of opal and peridote.

See the white river that flashes and scintillates,
Curved like a tusk from the mouth of the. city-gates.

5 Hark, from the minaret, how the *muezzin's* call
Floats like a battle-flag over the city wall.

From trellised balconies, languid and luminous
Faces gleam, veiled in a splendour voluminous.

Leisurely elephants wind through the winding lanes,
10 Swinging their silver bells hung from their silver chains.

Round the high Char Minar sounds of gay cavalcades
Blend with the music of cymbals and serenades.

Over the city bridge Night comes majestical,
Borne like a queen to a sumptuous festival.

∽

STREET CRIES

When dawn's first cymbals beat upon the sky,
Rousing the world to labour's various cry,
To tend the flock, to bind the mellowing grain,
From ardent toil to forge a little gain,
5 And fasting men go forth on hurrying feet,
Buy bread, buy bread, rings down the eager street.

When the earth falters and the waters swoon
With the implacable radiance of noon,
And in dim shelters koels hush their notes,

10 And the faint, thirsting blood in languid throats
Craves liquid succour from the cruel heat,
Buy fruit, buy fruit, steals down the panting street.
When twilight twinkling o'er the gay bazaars,
Unfurls a sudden canopy of stars,

15 When lutes are strung and fragrant torches lit
On white roof-terraces where lovers sit
Drinking together of life's poignant sweet,
Buy flowers, buy flowers, floats down the singing street.

TO INDIA

O young through all thy immemorial years!
Rise, Mother, rise, regenerate from thy gloom,
And, like a bride high-mated with the spheres,
Beget new glories from thine ageless womb!

5   The nations that in fettered darkness weep
Crave thee to lead them where great mornings break . . .
Mother, O Mother, wherefore dost thou sleep?
Arise and answer for thy children's sake!

Thy Future calls thee with a manifold sound
10 To crescent honours, splendours, victories vast;
Waken, O slumbering Mother, and be crowned,
Who once wert empress of the sovereign Past.

THE ROYAL TOMBS OF GOLCONDA

I muse among these silent fanes
Whose spacious darkness guards your dust;
Around me sleep the hoary plains
That hold your ancient wars in trust.
5 I pause, my dreaming spirit hears,
Across the wind's unquiet tides,
The laughter of your royal brides.

In vain, O Kings, doth time aspire
To make your names oblivion's sport,
10 While yonder hill wears like a tiara
The ruined grandeur of your fort.
Though centuries falter and decline,
Your proven strongholds shall remain

　　　　Embodied memories of your line,
15　　Incarnate legends of your reign.

　　　　O Queens, in vain old Fate decreed
　　　　Your flower-like bodies to the tomb;
　　　　Death is in truth the vital seed
　　　　Of your imperishable bloom.
20　　Each new-born year the bulbuls sing
　　　　Their songs of your renascent loves;
　　　　Your beauty wakens with the spring
　　　　To kindle these pomegranate groves.

TO A BUDDHA SEATED ON A LOTUS

　　　　Lord Buddha, on thy Lotus-throne,
　　　　With praying eyes and hands elate,
　　　　What mystic rapture dost thou own,
　　　　Immutable and ultimate?
5　　　What peace, unravished of our ken,
　　　　Annihilate from the world of men?

　　　　The wind of change for ever blows
　　　　Across the tumult of our way,
　　　　To-morrow's unborn griefs depose
10　　The sorrows of our yesterday.
　　　　Dream yields to dream, strife follows strife,
　　　　And Death unweaves the webs of Life.

　　　　For us the travail and the heat,
　　　　The broken secrets of our pride,
15　　The strenuous lessons of defeat,
　　　　The flower deferred, the fruit denied;

But not the peace, supremely won,
Lord Buddha, of thy Lotus-throne,

With futile hands we seek to gain
20 Our inaccessible desire,
Diviner summits to attain,
With faith that sinks and feet that tire;
But nought shall conquer or control
The heavenward hunger of our soul.

25 The end, elusive and afar,
Still lures us with its beckoning flight,
And all our mortal moments are
A session of the Infinite.
How shall we reach the great, unknown
30 Nirvana of thy Lotus-throne?

From THE BIRD OF TIME
SONGS OF LIFE, DEATH & THE SPRING

THE BIRD OF TIME

    O Bird of Time on your fruitful bough
What are the songs you sing? . . .
Songs of the glory and gladness of life,
Of poignant sorrow and passionate strife,
5   And the lilting joy of the spring;
Of hope that sows for the years unborn,
And faith that dreams of a tarrying morn,
The fragrant peace of the twilight's breath,
10 And the mystic silence that men call death.

    O Bird of Time, say where did you learn
The changing measures you sing? . . .
In blowing forests and breaking tides,
In the happy laughter of new-made brides,
15 And the nests of the new-born spring;
In the dawn that thrills to a mother's prayer,
And the night that shelters a heart's despair,
In the sigh of pity, the sob of hate,
And the pride of a soul that has conquered fate.

DIRGE
(In sorrow of her bereavement)

What longer need hath she of loveliness
Whom Death has parted from her lord's caress?
Of glimmering robes like rainbow-tangled mist,
Of gleaming glass or jewels on her wrist,
5   Blossoms or fillet-pearls to deck her head,
Or jasmine garlands to adorn her bed?

Put by the mirror or her bridal days . . .
Why needs she now its counsel or its praise,
Or happy symbol of the henna leaf
10 For hands that know the comradeship of grief,
Red spices for her lips that drink of sighs,
Or black collyrium for her weeping eyes?

Shatter her shining bracelets, break the string
Threading the mystic marriage-beads that cling
15 Loth to desert a sobbing throat so sweet,
Unbind the golden anklets on her feet,
Divest her of her azure veils and cloud
Her living beauty in a living shroud.

Nay, let her be! . . . what comfort can we give
20 For joy so frail, for hope so fugitive?
The yearning pain of unfulfilled delight,
The moonless vigils of her lonely night,
For the abysmal anguish of her tears,
And flowering springs that mock her empty years?

AN INDIAN LOVE SONG
(Written to an Indian tune)

He

Lift up the veils that darken the delicate moon of thy
 glory and grace,
Withhold not, O Love, from the night of my longing the
 joy of thy luminous face,
Give me a spear of the scented *keora* guarding thy pinioned
 curls,
Or a silken thread from the fringes that trouble the dream
 of thy glimmering pearls;
5 Faint grows my soul with thy tresses' perfume and the
 song of thy anklet's caprice,
Revive me, I pray, with the magical nectar that dwells in
 the flower of thy kiss.

She

How shall I yield to the voice of thy pleading, how shall I
 grant thy prayer,
Or give thee a rose-red silken tassel, a scented leaf from
 my hair?
Or fling in the flame of thy heart's desire the veils that
 cover my face.
10 Profane the law of my father's creed for a foe of my
 father's race?
Thy kinsmen have broken our sacred altars and
 slaughtered our sacred kine,
The feud of old faiths and the blood of old battles sever
 thy people and mine.

He

What are the sins of my race, Beloved, what are my people
 to thee?

And what are thy shrine, and kin and kindred, what are
    thy gods to me?
15 Love recks not of feuds and bitter follies, of stranger,
    comrade or kin,
Alike in his ear sound the temple bells and the cry of the
    muezzin.
For Love shall cancel the ancient wrong and conquer the
    ancient rage,
Redeem with his tears the memoried sorrow that sullied a
    bygone age.

LOVE AND DEATH

I dreamed my love had set thy spirit free,
Enfranchised thee from Fate's o'ermastering power,
And girt thy being with a scatheless dower
Of rich and joyous immortality;
5 Of Love, I dreamed my soul had ransomed thee,
In thy lone, dread, incalculable hour
From those pale hands at which all mortals cower,
And conquered Death by Love, like Savitri.
When I awoke, alas, my love was vain
10 E'en to annul one throe of destined pain,
Or by one heart-beat to prolong thy breath;
O Love, alas, that love could not assuage
The burden of thy human heritage,
Or save thee from the swift decrees of Death.

AT TWILIGHT
(On the way to Golconda)

Weary, I sought kind Death among the rills
That drink of purple twilight where the plain
Broods in the shadow of untroubled hills:
I cried, "High dreams and hope and love are vain,
5   Absolve my spirit of its poignant ills,
And cleanse me from the bondage of my pain!

"Shall hope prevail where clamorous hate is rife,
Shall sweet love prosper or high dreams find place
Amid the tumult of reverberant strife
10   'Twixt ancient creeds, 'twixt race and ancient race,
That mars the grave, glad purposes of life,
Leaving no refuge save thy succouring face?"

E'en as I spake, a mournful wind drew near,
Heavy with scent of drooping roses shed,
15   And incense scattered from the passing bier
Of some loved woman canopied in red,
Borne with slow chant and swift-remembering tear,
To the blind, ultimate silence of the dead. . . .

O lost, O quenched in unawakening sleep
20   The glory of her dear, reluctant eyes!
O hushed the eager feet that knew the steep
And intricate ways of ecstasy and sighs!
And dumb with alien slumber, dim and deep,
The living heart that was love's paradise!

25   Quick with the sense of joys she hath foregone,
Returned my soul to beckoning joys that wait,
Laughter of children and the lyric dawn,

And love's delight, profound and passionate,
Winged dreams that blow their golden clarion,
30 And hope that conquers immemorial hate.

∾

A Rajput Love Song

(Parvati *at her lattice*)

O Love! were you a basil-wreath to twine among my tresses,
A jewelled clasp of shining gold to bind around my sleeve,
O Love! were you the *keora's* soul that haunts my silken raiment,
A bright, vermilion tassel in the girdles that I weave;

5   O Love! were you the scented fan that lies upon my pillow,
A sandal lute, or silver lamp that burns before my shrine,
Why should I fear the jealous dawn that spreads with cruel laughter,
Sad veils of separation between your face and mine?

Haste, O wild-bee hours, to the gardens of the sunset!
10   *Fly, wild-parrot day, to the orchards of the West!*
Come, O tender night, with your sweet, consoling darkness,
And bring me my Beloved to the shelter of my breast!

(Amar Singh *in the saddle*)

O Love! were you the hooded hawk upon my hand that flutters,
Its collar-band of gleaming bells atinkle as I ride,
15   O Love! were you a turban-spray or floating heron-feather,
The radiant, swift, unconquered sword that swingeth at my side;

O Love! were you a shield against the arrows of my
    foemen,
An amulet of jade against the perils of the way,
How should the drum-beats of the dawn divide me from
    your bosom,
20 Or the union of the midnight be ended with the day?

Haste, O wild-deer hours, to the meadows of the sunset!
Fly, wild-stallion day, to the pastures of the West!
Come, O tranquil night, with your soft, consenting darkness,
And bear me to the fragrance of my Beloved's breast!

∽

A SONG IN SPRING

Wild bees that rifle the mango blossom,
Set free awhile from the love-god's string,
Wild birds that sway in the citron branches,
Drunk with the rich, red honey of spring,

5 Fireflies weaving ethereal dances
In fragile rhythms of flickering gold,
What do you know in your blithe, brief season
Of dreams deferred and a heart grown old?

But the wise winds know, as they pause to slacken
10 The speed of their subtle, omniscient flight,
Divining the magic of unblown lilies,
Foretelling the stars of the unborn night.

They have followed the hurrying feet of pilgrims,
Tracking swift prayers to their utmost goals,
15 They have spied on Love's old and changeless secret,
And the changing sorrow of human souls.

They have tarried with Death in her parleying-places,
And issued the word of her high decree,
Their wings have winnowed the garnered sunlight,
20 Their lips have tasted the purple sea.

∽

VASANT PANCHAMI*
(Lilavati's *lament at the feast of Spring*)

Go, dragon-fly, fold up your purple wing,
Why will you bring me tidings of the spring?
O lilting *koels*, hush your rapturous notes,
O *dhadikulas*, still your passionate throats,
5 Or seek some further garden for your nest . . .
Your songs are poisoned arrows in my breast.

O quench your flame, ye crimson *gulmohurs*,
That flaunt your dazzling bloom across my doors,
Furl your white bells, sweet *champa* buds that call
10 Wild bees to your ambrosial festival,
And hold your breath, O dear *sirisha* trees . . .
You slay my heart with bitter memories.

O joyous girls who rise at break of morn
With sandal-soil your threshold to adorn,
15 Ye brides who streamward bear on jewelled feet
Your gifts of silver lamps and new-blown wheat,
I pray you dim your voices when you sing
Your radiant salutations to the spring.

---

*The Vasant Panchami is the spring festival when Hindu girls and married women carry gifts of lighted lamps and new-grown corn as offerings to the goddess of the spring and set them afloat on the face of the waters. Hindu widows cannot take part in any festive ceremonials. Their portion is sorrow and austerity.

>   *Hai!* what have I to do with nesting birds,
> 20 With lotus-honey, corn and ivory curds,
>   With plantain blossom and pomegranate fruit,
>   Or rose-wreathed lintels and rose-scented lute,
>   With lighted shrines and fragrant altar fires,
>   Where happy women breathe their hearts' desires?
>
> 25 For my sad life is doomed to be, alas,
>   Ruined and sere like sorrow-trodden grass,
>   My heart hath grown, plucked by the wind of grief,
>   Akin to fallen flower and faded leaf,
>   Akin to every lone and withered thing
> 30 That hath foregone the kisses of the spring.

IN A TIME OF FLOWERS

>   O Love! do you know the spring is here
>   With the lure of her magic flute? . . .
>   The old earth breaks into passionate bloom
>   At the kiss of her fleet, gay foot.
> 5   The burgeoning leaves on the almond boughs,
>   And the leaves on the blue wave's breast
>   Are crowned with the limpid and delicate light
>   Of the gems in your turban-crest.
>   The bright pomegranate buds unfold,
> 10 The frail wild lilies appear,
>   Like the blood-red jewels you used to fling
>   O'er the maidens that danced at the feast of spring
>   To welcome the new-born year.
>
>   O Love! do you know the spring is here? . . .
> 15 The dawn and the dusk grow rife

With scent and song and tremulous mirth,
The blind, rich travail of life.
The winds are drunk with the odorous breath
Of *henna, sarisha,* and *neem* . . .

20 Do they ruffle your cold, strange, tranquil sleep,
Or trouble your changeless dream
With poignant thoughts of the world you loved,
And the beauty you held so dear?
Do you long for a brief, glad hour to wake
25 From your lonely slumber for sweet love's sake,
To welcome the new-born year?

∽

IN PRAISE OF GULMOHUR BLOSSOMS

What can rival your lovely hue
O gorgeous boon of the spring?
The glimmering red of a bridal robe,
Rich red of a wild bird's wing?
5 Or the mystic blaze of the gem that burns
On the brow of a serpent-king?

What can rival the valiant joy
Of your dazzling, fugitive sheen?
The limpid clouds of the lustrous dawn
10 That colour the ocean's mien?
Or the blood that poured from a thousand breasts
To succour a Rajput queen?

What can rival the radiant pride
Of your frail, victorious fire?
15 The flame of hope or the flame of hate,
Quick flame of my heart's desire?

Or the rapturous light leaps to heaven
From a true wife's funeral pyre?

❀

NASTURTIUMS

Poignant and subtle and bitter perfume
Exquisite, luminous, passionate bloom,
Your leaves interwoven of fragrance and fire
Are Savitri's sorrow and Sita's desire,
5   Draupadi's longing, Damayanti's fears,
And sweetest Shakuntala's magical tears.*

❀

GOLDEN CASSIA

O Brilliant blossoms that strew my way,
You are only woodland flowers they say.

But, I sometimes think that perchance you are
Fragments of some new-fallen star;

5   Or golden lamps for a fairy shrine,
Or golden pitchers for fairy wine.

Perchance you are, O frail and sweet!
Bright anklet-bells from the wild spring's feet,

---

*These are the immortal women of Sanskrit legend and song, whose poignant sorrows and radiant virtues still break the heart and inspire the lives of Indian women.

Or the gleaming tears that some fair bride shed
10 Remembering her lost maidenhead.

But now, in the memoried dusk you seem
The glimmering ghosts of a bygone dream.

∽

CHAMPAK BLOSSOMS

Amber petals, ivory petals,
Petals of carven jade,
Charming with your ambrosial sweetness
Forest and field and glade,
5 Foredoomed in your hour of transient glory
To shrivel and shrink and fade!

Tho' mango blossoms have long since vanished,
And orange blossoms be shed,
They live anew in the luscious harvests
10 Of ripening yellow and red;
But you, when your delicate bloom is over,
Will reckon amongst the dead.
Only to girdle a girl's dark tresses
Your fragrant hearts are uncurled:
15 Only to garland the vernal breezes
Your fragile stars are unfurled.
You make no boast in your purposeless beauty
To serve or profit the world.

Yet, 'tis of you thro' the moonlit ages
20 That maidens and minstrels sing,
And lay your buds on the great god's altar,
O radiant blossoms that fling

Your rich, voluptuous, magical perfume
To ravish the winds of spring.

ECSTASY

Heart, O my heart! lo, the springtime is waking
   In meadow and grove.
Lo, the mellifluous *koels* are making
   Their paeans of love.
5 Behold the bright rivers and rills in their glancing,
Melodious flight,
Behold how the sumptuous peacocks are dancing
   In rhythmic delight.
Shall we in the midst of life's exquisite chorus
10 Remember our grief,
O heart, when the rapturous season is o'er us
   Of blossom and leaf?
Their joy from the birds and the streams let us borrow,
   O heart! let us sing,
15 The years are before us for weeping and sorrow . . .
   Today it is spring!

VILLAGE SONGS

Full are my pitchers and far to carry,
Lone is the way and long,
Why, O why was I tempted to tarry
Lured by the boatmen's song?
5 Swiftly the shadows of night are falling,
Hear, O hear, is the white crane calling,

Is it the wild owl's cry?
There are no tender moonbeams to light me,
If in the darkness a serpent should bite me,
10 Or if an evil spirit should smite me,
Rām re Rām! I shall die.

My brother will murmur, "Why doth she linger?"
My mother will wait and weep,
Saying, "O safe may the great gods bring her,
15 The Jamuna's waters are deep." . . .
The Jamuna's waters rush by so quickly,
The shadows of evening gather so thickly,
Like black birds in the sky . . .
O! if the storm breaks, what will betide me?
20 Safe from the lightning where shall I hide me?
Unless Thou succour my footsteps and guide me,
Rām re Rām! I shall die.

∾

SONGS OF MY CITY

I. In A Latticed Balcony

How shall I feed thee, Beloved?
On golden-red honey and fruit.
How shall I please thee, Beloved?
With th' voice of the cymbal and lute.
5 How shall I garland thy tresses?
With pearls from the jessamine close.
How shall I perfume thy fingers?
With th' soul of the keora and rose.

How shall I deck thee, O Dearest?

10 *In hues of the peacock and dove.*
How shall I woo thee, O Dearest?
With the delicate silence of love.

II. In the Bazaars of Hyderabad
(To a tune of the Bazaars)

What do you sell, O ye merchants?
Richly your wares are displayed.
Turbans of crimson and silver,
Tunics of purple brocade,
5 *Mirrors with panels of amber,*
Daggers with handles of jade.

What do you weigh, O ye vendors?
Saffron and lentil and rice.
What do you grind, O ye maidens?
10 *Sandalwood, henna, and spice.*
What do you call, O ye peddlers?
Chessmen and ivory dice.

What do you make, O ye goldsmiths?
Wristlet and anklet and ring,
15 *Bells for the feet of blue pigeons,*
Frail as a dragon-fly's wing,
Girdles of gold for the dancers,
Scabbards of gold for the king.

What do you cry, O ye fruitmen?
20 *Citron, pomegranate, and plum.*
What do you play, O musicians?
Sithār, sarangi, and drum.
What do you chant, O magicians?
Spells for the aeons to come.

25 What do you weave, O ye flower-girls
   With tassels of azure and red?
   Crowns for the brow of a bridegroom,
   Chaplets to garland his bed,
   Sheets of white blossoms new-gathered
30 *To perfume the sleep of the dead.*

∽

SONG OF RADHA, THE MILKMAID

I carried my curds to the Mathura* fair . . .
How softly the heifers were lowing . . .
I wanted to cry, "Who will buy
These curds that are white as the clouds in the sky
5 When the breezes of *shrawan* are blowing?"
But my heart was so full of your beauty, Beloved,
They laughed as I cried without knowing:
      Govinda! Govinda!
      Govinda! Govinda! . . .
10 How softly the river was flowing!

I carried my pots to the Mathura tide . . .
How gaily the rowers were rowing! . . .
My comrades called, "Ho! let us dance, let us sing
And wear saffron garments to welcome the spring.
15 And pluck the new buds that are blowing."
But my heart was so full of your music, Beloved,
They mocked when I cried without knowing:

---

*Mathura is the chief centre of the mystic worship of Krishna, the Divine Cowherd and Musician—the 'Divine Beloved' of every Hindu heart. He is also called Govinda.

> *Govinda! Govinda!*
> *Govinda! Govinda! . . .*
20 How gaily the river was flowing!

I carried my gifts to the Mathura shrine . . .
How brightly the torches were glowing! . . .
I folded my hands at the altars to pray
"O shining ones guard us by night and by day"—
25 And loudly the conch shells were blowing.
But my heart was so lost in your worship, Beloved,
They were wroth when I cried without knowing:
> *Govinda! Govinda!*
> *Govinda! Govinda! . . .*
30 How brightly the river was flowing!

∽

SPINNING SONG

PAMDINI:
My sisters plucked green leaves at morn

To deck the garden swing,
And donned their shining golden veils
5 For the Festival of Spring . . .
But sweeter than the new-blown vines,
And the call of nesting birds
Are the tendrils of your hair, Beloved,
And the music of your words.

10 MAYURA:
My sisters sat beside the hearth
Kneading the saffron cakes,
They gathered honey from the hives

For the Festival of Snakes . . .
15 Why should I wake the jewelled lords
With offerings or vows,
Who wear the glory of your love
Like a jewel on my brows?

SARASVATI:
20 My sisters sang at evenfall
A hymn of ancient rites,
And kindled rows of silver lamps
For the Festival* of Lights . . .
But I leaned against the lattice-door
25 To watch the kindling skies,
And praised the gracious gods, Beloved,
For the beauty of your eyes.

THE HUSSAIN SAGAR

The young dawn woos thee with his amorous grace,
The journeying clouds of sunset pause and hover,
Drinking the beauty of thy luminous face,
But none thine inmost glory may discover,
5 For thine evasive silver doth enclose
What secret purple and what subtle rose
Responsive only to the wind, thy lover.
Only for him thy shining waves unfold
Translucent music answering his control;

10 Thou dost, like me, to one allegiance hold,
O lake, O living image of my soul.

---

*The Festivals are known respectively as the Vasant Panchami, Nagpanchami, and Deepavali. (Sarojini's note)

THE FAERY ISLE OF JANJIRA
(To Her Highness Nazli Raffia, Begum of Janjira)

Fain would I dwell in your faery kingdom,
O faery queen of a flowering clime,
Where life glides by to a delicate measure,
With the glamour and grace of a far-off time.

5   Fain would I dwell where your wild doves wander,
Your palm-woods burgeon and sea-winds sing . . .
Lulled by the rune of the rhythmic waters,
In your Island of Bliss it is always spring.

Yet must I go where the loud world beckons,
10 And the urgent drum-beat of destiny calls,
Far from your white dome's luminous slumber,
Far from the dream of your fortress walls,

Into the strife of the throng and the tumult,
The war of sweet Love against folly and wrong;
15 Where brave hearts carry the sword of battle,
'Tis mine to carry the banner of song,

The solace of faith to the lips that falter,
The succour of hope to the hands that fail,
The tidings of joy when Peace shall triumph,
20 When Truth shall conquer and Love prevail.

THE SOUL'S PRAYER

In childhood's pride I said to Thee:
"O Thou, who mad'st me of Thy breath,

Speak, Master, and reveal to me
Thine inmost laws of life and death.

5 "Give me to drink each joy and pain
Which Thine eternal hand can mete,
For my insatiate soul would drain
Earth's utmost bitter, utmost sweet.

"Spare me no bliss, no pang of strife,
10 Withhold no gift or grief I crave,
The intricate lore of love and life
And mystic knowledge of the grave."

Lord, Thou didst answer stern and low:
"Child, I will hearken to thy prayer,
15 And thy unconquered soul shall know
All passionate rapture and despair.

"Thou shalt drink deep of joy and fame,
And love shall burn thee like a fire,
And pain shall cleanse thee like a flame,
20 To purge the dross from thy desire.

"So shall thy chastened spirit yearn
To seek from its blind prayer release,
And spent and pardoned, sue to learn
The simple secret of My peace.

25 "I, bending from my sevenfold height
Will teach thee of My quickening grace,
Life is a prism of My light,
And Death the shadow of My face."

THE OLD WOMAN

A lonely old woman sits out in the street
'Neath the boughs of a banyan tree,
And hears the bright echo of hurrying feet,
The pageant of life going blithely and fleet
To the feast of eternity.
5   Her tremulous hand holds a battered white bowl,
If perchance in your pity you fling her a dole;
She is poor, she is bent, she is blind,
But she lifts a brave heart to the jest of the days,
And her withered, brave voice croons its paean of praise,
10 Be the gay world kind or unkind:
"La ilaha illa-l-Allah,
La ilaha illa-l-Allah,
Muhammad-ar-Rasul-Allah."

In hope of your succour, how often in vain,
15 So patient she sits at my gates,
In the face of the sun and the wind and the rain,
Holding converse with poverty, hunger and pain,
And the ultimate sleep that awaits . . .
In her youth she hath comforted lover and son,
20 In her weary old age, O dear God, is there none
To bless her tired eyelids to rest? . . .
Tho' the world may not tarry to help her or heed.
More clear than the cry of her sorrow and need
Is the faith that doth solace her breast:
25 *"La ilaha illa-l-Allah,*
La ilaha illa-l-Allah,
Muhammad-ar-Rasul-Allah."

AN ANTHEM OF LOVE

Two hands are we to serve thee, O our Mother,
To strive and succour, cherish and unite;
Two feet are we to cleave the waning darkness,
And gain the pathways of the dawning light.

5   Two years are we to catch the nearing echo,
The sounding cheer of Time's prophetic horn;
Two eyes are we to reap the crescent glory,
The radiant promise of renascent morn.

One heart are we to love thee, O our Mother,
10 One undivided, indivisible soul,
Bound by one hope, one purpose, one devotion
Towards a great, divinely-destined goal.

∾

THE CALL TO EVENING PRAYER

Allah O Akbar! Allah O Akbar!
From mosque and minar the *muezzins* are calling;
Pour forth your praises, O Chosen of Islam;
Swiftly the shadows of sunset are falling:
5 *Allah O Akbar! Allah O Akbar!*

Ave Maria! Ave Maria!
Devoutly the priests at the altars are singing,
O ye who worship the Son of the Virgin,
Kneel soft at your prayers for the vespers are ringing:
10 *Ave Maria! Ave Maria!*

Ahura Mazda! Ahura Mazda!
How the sonorous Avesta is flowing!

Ye, who to Flame and the Light make obeisance,
Bend low where the quenchless blue torches are glowing!
15 *Ahura Mazda! Ahura Mazda!*

Naray'yana! Naray'yana!
Hark to the ageless, divine invocation!
Lift up your hands, O ye children of Brahma,
Lift up your voices in rapt adoration:
20 *Naray'yana! Naray'yana!*

GUERDON

To field and forest
The gifts of the spring,
To hawk and to heron
The pride of their wing;
5 Her grace to the panther,
Her tints to the dove . . .
For me, O my Master,
The rapture of Love!

To the hand of the diver
10 The gems of the tide,
To the eyes of the bridegroom
The face of his bride;
To the heart of a dreamer
The dreams of his youth . . .
15 For me, O my Master,
The rapture of Truth!

To priests and to prophets
The joy of their creeds
To kings and their cohorts
20 The glory of deeds;

And peace to the vanquished
And hope to the strong . . .
For me, O my Master,
The rapture of Song!

From THE BROKEN WING

'Why should a song-bird like you have a broken wing?'
                                        —G.K. Gokhale

Question

    The great dawn breaks, the mournful night is past,
    From her deep age-long sleep she wakes at last!
    Sweet and long-slumbering buds of gladness ope
    Fresh lips to the returning winds of hope,
5   Our eager hearts renew their radiant flight
    Towards the glory renascent light,
    Life and our land await their destined spring . . .
    Song-bird why dost *thou* bear a broken wing?

Answer

    Shall spring that wakes mine ancient land again
10 Call to my wild and suffering heart in vain?
    Or Fate's blind arrows still the pulsing note
    Of my far-reaching, frail, unconquered throat?
    Or a weak bleeding pinion daunt or tire
    My flight to the high realms of my desire?
15 Behold! I rise to meet the destined spring
    And scale the stars upon my broken wing!

THE GIFT OF INDIA

Is there aught you need that my hands withhold,
Rich gifts of raiment or grain or gold?
Lo! I have flung to the East and West
Priceless treasures torn from my breast,
5   And yielded the sons of my stricken womb
To the drum-beats of duty, the sabres of doom.

Gathered like pearls in their alien graves
Silent they sleep by the Persian waves,
Scattered like shells on Egyptian sands,
10 They lie with pale brows and brave, broken hands,
They are strewn like blossoms mown down by chance
On the blood-brown meadows of Flanders and France.

Can ye measure the grief of the tears I weep
Or compass the woe of the watch I keep?
15 Or the pride that thrills thro' my heart's despair
And the hope that comforts the anguish of prayer?
And the far sad glorious vision I see
Of the torn red banners of Victory?

When the terror and tumult of hate shall cease
20 And life be refashioned on anvils of peace,
And your love shall offer memorial thanks
To the comrades who fought in your dauntless ranks,
And you honour the deeds of the deathless ones,
Remember the blood of my martyred sons!

THE TEMPLE

Priest

Awake, it is Love's radiant hour of praise!
Bring new-blown leaves his temple to adorn,
Pomegranate-buds and ripe *sirisha*-sprays,
Wet sheaves of shining corn.

Pilgrim

5   *O priest! only my broken lute I bring*
    For Love's praise-offering!

Priest

Behold! the hour of sacrifice draws near.
Pile high the gleaming altar-stones of Love
With delicate burdens of slain woodland deer
10 And frail white mountain dove.

Pilgrim

O priest! only my wounded heart I bring
For Love's blood-offering!

Priest

Lo! now it strikes Lover's solemn hour of prayer,
Kindle with fragrant boughs his blazing shrine,
15 Feed the sweet flame with spice and incense rare,
    Curds of rose-pastured kine.

Pilgrim

O priest! only my stricken soul I bring
For Love's burnt-offering!

THE IMAM BARA
(Of Lucknow)

I

    Out of the sombre shadows,
    Over the sunlit grass,
    Slow in a sad procession
    The shadowy pageants pass
5 Mournful, majestic, and solemn,
    Stricken and pale and dumb,
    Crowned in their peerless anguish
    The sacred martyrs come.
    Hark, from the brooding silence
10 Breaks the wild cry of pain
    Wrung from the heart of the ages
    Ali! Hassan! Hussain!

II

    Come from this tomb of shadows,
    Come from this tragic shrine
15 That throbs with the deathless sorrow
    Of a long-dead martyr line.
    Love! let the living sunlight
    Kindle your splendid eyes
    Ablaze with the steadfast triumph
20 Of the spirit that never dies.
    So may the hope of new ages
    Comfort the mystic pain
    That cries from the ancient silence
    Ali! Hassan! Hussain!*

---

*The Imam Bara is a Chapel of Lamentation where Mussulmans of the Shia community celebrate the tragic martyrdom of Ali, Hassan, and Hussain during the mourning month of Moharram. A sort of passion-play takes place to the accompaniment of the refrain, *Ali! Hassan! Hussain*

A SONG FROM SHIRAZ

The singers of Shiraz are feasting afar
To greet the Nauroz with sarang and cithar. . . .
But what is their music that calleth to me,
From glimmering garden and glowing minar?
5   The stars shall be scattered like jewels of glass,
And Beauty be tossed like a shell in the sea,
Ere the lutes of their magical laughter surpass
The lute, of thy tears, O Mohamed Ali!

From the Mosque-towers of Shiraz ere daylight begin
10 My heart is disturbed by the loud muezzin,
But what is the voice of his warning to me,
That waketh the world to atonement of sin?

The stars shall be broken like mirrors of brass,
And Rapture be sunk like a stone in the sea,
15 Ere the carpet of prayer or of penance surpass
Thy carpet of dreams, O Mohamed Ali!

In the silence of Shiraz my soul shall await,
Untroubled, the wandering Angel of Fate . . .
What terror or joy shall his hands hold for me,
20 Who bringeth the goblet of guerdon too late?

The stars shall be mown and uprooted like grass,
And Glory be flung like a weed in the sea,
Ere the goblet of doom or salvation surpass
Thy goblet of love, O Mohamed Ali!

MEMORIAL VERSES

I. YA MAHBUB!*

Are these the streets that I used to know—
Was it yesterday or aeons ago?
Where are the armies that used to wait—
The pilgrims of Love—at your palace gate?
5   The joyous paeans that thrilled the air
The pageants that shone thro' your palace square?
And the minstrel music that used to ring
Thro' your magic kingdom . . . when you were king?

O hands that succoured a people's need
10 With the splendour of Haroun-al-Rasheed!
O heart that solaced a sad world's cry
With the sumptuous bounty of Hatim tai!
Where are the days that were winged and clad
In the fabulous glamour of old Baghdad.
15 And the bird of glory used to sing
In your magic kingdom . . . when you were king?

O king, in your kingdom there is no change.
'Tis only my soul that hath grown so strange,
So faint with sorrow it cannot hear
20 Aught save the chant at your rose-crowned bier.
My grieving bosom hath grown too cold
To clasp the beauty it treasured of old,
The grace of life and the gifts of spring,
And the dreams I cherished . . . when you were king!

---

*'Ya Mahbub,' which means O Beloved, was the device on the State banner of the late Nizam of Hyderabad, Mir Mahbub Ali Khan, the beloved of his people.

II. GOKHALE*

Heroic Heart! lost hope of all our days!
Need'st thou the homage of our love or praise?
Lo! let the mournful millions round thy pyre
Kindle their souls with consecrated fire
5   Caught from the brave torch fallen from thy hand,
To succour and to serve our suffering land,

And in a daily worship taught by thee
Upbuild the temple of her Unity.

WANDERING BEGGARS

From the threshold of the Dawn
On we wander, always on
Till the friendly light be gone
   Y' Allah! Y' Allah!

5   We are free-born sons of Fate,
What care we for wealth or state
Or the glory of the great?
   Y' Allah! Y' Allah!

Life may grant us or withhold
10 Roof or raiment, bread or gold,
But our hearts are gay and bold.
   Y' Allah! Y Allah!

---

*Gopal Krishna Gokhale, the great saint and soldier of our national righteousness. His life was a sacrament, and his death was a sacrifice in the cause of Indian unity. (Sarojini's note)

Time is like a wind that blows,
The future is a folded rose,
15 Who shall pluck it no man knows.
   Y' Allah! Y Allah!

So we go a fearless band,
The staff of freedom in our hand
Wandering from land to land,
20 *Y' Allah! Y' Allah!*

Till we meet the Night that brings
Both to beggars and to kings
The end of all their journeyings
   Y' Allah! Y' Allah!

∽

THE LOTUS

(To M.K. Gandhi)

O mystic Lotus, sacred and sublime,
In myriad-petalled grace inviolate,
Supreme o'er transient storms of tragic Fate,
Deep-rooted in the waters of all Time,
5 What legions loosed from many a far-off clime
Of wild-bee hordes with lips insatiate,
And hungry winds with wings of hope or hate,
Have thronged and pressed round thy miraculous prime
To devastate thy loveliness, to drain
10 The midmost rapture of thy glorious heart . . .
But who could win thy secret, who attain
Thine ageless beauty born of Brahma's breath,
Or pluck thine immortality, who art

Coeval with the Lords of Life and Death?

THE PRAYER OF ISLAM

We praise Thee, O Compassionate!
Master of Life and Time and Fate,
Lord of the labouring winds and seas,
 Ya Hameed! Ya Hafeez!

5 Thou art the Radiance of our ways,
Thou art the Pardon of our days,
Whose name is known from star to star,
 Ya Ghani! Ya Ghaffar!

Thou art the Goal for which we long,
10 Thou art our Silence and our Song,
Life of the sunbeam and the seed—
 Ya Wahab! Ya Waheed!

Thou dost transmute from hour to hour
Our mortal weakness into power
15 Our bondage into liberty,
 Ya Quadeer! Ya Quavi!

We are the shadows of Thy light,
We are the secrets of Thy might,
The visions of thy primal dream,
20 *Ya Rahman! Ya Raheem!**

---

*These are some of the ninety-nine beautiful Arabic names of God as used by followers of Islam.

BELLS

Anklet-bells

Anklet-bells! frail anklet-bells!
That hold Love's ancient mystery
As hide the lips of limpid shells
Faint tones of the remembered sea,
5   You murmur of enchanted rites,
Of sobbing breath and broken speech,
Sweet anguish of rose-scented nights
And wild mouths calling each to each
Or mute with yearning ecstasy.

Cattle-bells

10 Cattle-bells! soft cattle-bells!
What gracious memories you bring
Of drowsy fields and dreaming wells,
And weary labour's folded wing,
Of frugal mirth round festal fires,
15 Brief trysts that youth and beauty keep,
Of flowering roofs and fragrant byres
White heifers gathered in for sleep,
Old songs the wandering women sing.

Temple-bells

Temple-bells! deep temple-bells!
20 Whose urgent voices wreck the sky!
In your importance music dwells
Man's sad and immemorial cry
That cleaves the dawn with wings of praise,
That cleaves the dark with wings of prayer,
25 Craves pity for our mortal ways,

Seeks solace for our life's despair,
And peace for suffering hearts that die!

THE PEARL

How long shall it suffice
   Merely to hoard in thine unequalled rays
   The bright sequestered colours of the sun,
O pearl above all price,
5 And beautiful beyond all need of praise,
World-coveted but yet possessed of none,
Content in thy proud self-dominion?

Shall not some ultimate
   And unknown hour deliver thee, an attest
10 Life's urgent and inviolable claim
To bind and consecrate
   The glory on some pure and bridal breast,
Or set thee to enhance with flawless flame
A new-born nation's coronal of fame?

15 Or wilt thou self-denied
   Forgo such sweet and sacramental ties
As weld Love's delicate bonds of ecstasy,
And in a barren pride
   Of cold, unfruitful freedom that belies
20 The inmost secret of fine liberty
Return unblest into the primal sea?

KALI THE MOTHER

All Voices:	O terrible and tender and divine!
	O mystic mother of all sacrifice,
	We deck the sombre altars of thy shrine
	With sacred basil leaves and saffron rice;
	All gifts of life and death we bring to thee,
	Uma Haimavati!
Maidens:	We bring thee buds and berries from the wood!
Brides:	We bring the rapture of our bridal prayer!
Mothers:	And we the sweet travail of motherhood!
Widows:	And we the bitter vigils of despair!
All Voices:	All gladness and all grief we bring to thee,
	Ambika! Parvati!
Artisans:	We bring the lowly tribute of our toil!
Peasants:	We bring our new-born goats and budded wheat!
Victors:	And we the swords and symbols of our spoil!
Vanquished:	And we the shame and sorrow of defeat!
All Voices:	All triumph and all tears we bring to thee,
	Girija! Shambhavi!
Scholars:	We bring the secrets of our ancient arts.
Priests:	We bring the treasures of our ageless creeds.
poets:	And we the subtle music of our hearts.
Patriots:	And we the sleepless worship of our deeds.
All Voices:	All glory and all grace we bring to thee,
	Kali! Maheshwari!*

∾

---

*These are some of the many names of Eternal Mother of Hindu worship. (Sarojini's note)

AWAKE!*

(To Mohamed Ali Jinnah)

Waken, O mother! thy children implore thee,
Who kneel in thy presence to serve and adore thee!
The night is aflush with a dream of the morrow,
Why still dost thou sleep in thy bondage of sorrow?
5 Awaken and sever the woes that enthrall us,
And hallow our hands for the triumphs that call us!

Are we not thine, O Belov'd, to inherit
The manifold pride and power of thy spirit?
Ne'er shall we fail thee, forsake thee or falter,
10 Whose hearts are thy home and thy shield and thine altar.
Lo! we would thrill the high stars with thy story,
And set thee again in the forefront of glory.

Hindus:	Mother! the flowers of our worship have crowned thee!
Parsees:	Mother! the flame of our hope shall surround thee!
15 *Mussulmans:*	Mother! the sword of our love shall defend thee!
Christians:	Mother! the song of our faith shall attend thee!
All Creeds:	Shall not our dauntless devotion avail thee? Hearken! O queen and O goddess, we hail thee!

---

*Recited at the Indian National Congress, 1915.

THE MAGIC OF SPRING

    I buried my heart so deep, so deep,
    Under a secret hill of pain,
    And said: "O broken pitiful thing
    Even the magic spring
5   Shall ne'er wake thee to life again,
    Tho' March woods glimmer with opal rain
    And passionate koels sing."

    The *kimshuks* burst into dazzling flower,
    The *seemuls* burgeoned in crimson pride,
10 The palm-groves shone with the oriole's wing,
    The koels began to sing,
    The soft clouds broke in a twinkling tide . . .
    My heart leapt up in its grave and cried,
    "Is it the spring, the spring?"

JUNE SUNSET

    Here shall my heart find its haven of calm,
    By rush-fringed rivers and rain-fed streams
    That glimmer thro' meadows of lily and palm.
    Here shall my soul find its true repose
5   Under a sunset sky of dreams
    Diaphanous, amber and rose.
    The air is aglow with the glint and whirl
    Of swift wild wings in their homeward flight,
    Sapphire, emerald, topaz, and pearl.
10 Afloat in the evening light.
    A brown quail cries from the tamarisk bushes,
    A bulbul calls from the cassia-plume,
    And thro' the wet earth the gentian pushes

Her spikes of silvery bloom.
15 Where'er the foot of the bright shower passes
Fragrant and fresh delights unfold;
The wild fawns feed on the scented grasses,
Wild bees on the cactus-gold.

An ox-cart stumbles upon the rocks,
20 And a wistful music pursues the breeze
From a shepherd's pipe as he gathers his flocks
Under the *pipal* trees.
And a young *Banjara* driving her cattle
Lifts up her voice as she glitters by
25 In an ancient ballad of love and battle
Set to the beat of a mystic tune,
And the faint stars gleam in the eastern sky
To herald a rising moon.

∽

THE TIME OF ROSES

Love, it is the time of roses!
In bright fields and garden closes
How they burgeon and unfold!
How they sweep o'er tombs and towers
5 In voluptuous crimson showers
And untrammelled tides of gold!

How they lure wild bees to capture
All the rich mellifluous rapture
Of their magical perfume,
10 And to passing winds surrender
All their frail and dazzling splendour
Rivalling your turban-plume!

    How they cleave the air adorning
    The high rivers of the morning
15 In a blithe, bejewelled fleet!
    How they deck the moonlit grasses
    In thick rainbow-tinted masses
    Like a fair queen's bridal sheet!
    Hide me in a shrine of roses,
20 Drown me in a wine of roses
    Drawn from every fragrant grove!
    Bind me on a pyre of roses,
    Burn me in a fire of roses,
    Crown me with the rose of Love!

∽

CAPRICE

    You held a wild flower in your fingertips,
    Idly you pressed it to indifferent lips,
    Idly you tore its crimson leaves apart . . .
    Alas! it was my heart.

5   You held a wine-cup in your fingertips,
    Lightly you raised it to indifferent lips,
    Lightly you drank and flung away the bowl . . .
    Alas! it was my soul.

∽

DESTINY

    It chanced on the noon of an April day
    A dragon-fly passed in its sunward play
    And furled his flight for a passing hour
    To drain the life of a passion-flower . . .

5   Who cares if a ruined blossom die,
O bright blue wandering dragon-fly?

Love came, with his ivory flute,
His pleading eye, and his winged foot:
"I am weary," he murmured; "O let me rest
10 In the, sheltering joy of your fragrant breast."
At dawn he fled and he left no token . . .
Who cares if a woman's heart be broken?

THE TEMPLE

I. THE GATE OF DELIGHT

1. The Offering

Were beauty mine, beloved, I would bring it
Like a rare blossom to Love's glowing shrine;
Were dear youth mine, beloved, I would fling it
Like a rich pearl into Love's lustrous wine.

5   Were greatness mine, Beloved, I would offer
Such radiant gifts of glory and of fame,
Like camphor and like curds to pour and proffer
Before Love's bright and sacrificial flame.

But I have naught save my heart's deathless passion
10 That craves no recompense divinely sweet,
Content to wait in proud and lowly fashion,
And kiss the shadow of Love's passing feet.

2. The Feast

Bring no fragrant sandal-paste,
Let me gather, Love, instead
15 The entranced and flowering dust
You have honoured with your tread
For mine eyelids and mine head.

Bring no scented lotus-wreath
Moon-awakened, dew-caressed;
20 Love, thro' memory's age-long dream
Sweeter shall my wild heart rest
With your footprints on my breast.

Bring no pearls from ravished seas,
Gems from rifled hemispheres;
25 Grant me, Love, in priceless boon
All the sorrow of your years,
All the secret of your tears.

3. Ecstasy

Let spring illume the western hills with blossoming brands
    of fire,
And wake with rods of budded flame the valleys of the
    south—
30 But I have plucked you, O miraculous Flower of my desire,
And crushed between my lips the burning petals of your
    mouth!

Let spring unbind upon the breeze tresses of rich perfume
To lure the purple honey bees to their enchanted death—
But sweeter madness drives my soul to swift and sweeter
    doom

35   For I have drunk the deep, delicious nectar of your breath!

     Let spring unlock the melodies of fountain and of flood,
     And teach the winged word of man to mock the wild bird's art,
     But wilder music thrilled me when the rivers of your blood
     Swept o'er the floodgates of my life to drown my waiting heart!

4. The Lute-song

40   Why need you a burnished mirror of gold,
     O bright and imperious face?
     Mine eyes be the shadowless wells of desire
     For the sun of your glory and grace!

     Why need you the praises of ivory lutes,
45   O proud and illustrious name?
     My voice be the journeying lute of delight
     For the song of your valour and fame!

     Why need you pavilions and pillows of silk,
     Soft foot-cloths of azure, O Sweet?
50   My heart be your tent and your pillow of rest,
     And a place of repose for your feet!

     Why need you sad penance or pardon or prayer
     For life's passion and folly and fears?
     My soul be your living atonement, O Love,
55   In the flame of immutable years!

5. If You Call Me

     If you call me I will come
     Swifter, O my Love,

Than a trembling forest deer
Or a panting dove,
60 Swifter than a snake that flies
To the charmer's thrall . . .
If you call me I will come
Fearless what befall.
If you call me, I will come
65 Swifter than desire,
Swifter than the lightning's feet
Shod with plumes of fire.
Life's dark tides may roll between,
Or Death's deep chasms divide—
70 If you call me I will come
Fearless what betide.

6. The Sins of Love

Forgive me the sin of mine eyes,
O Love, if they dared for a space
Invade the dear shrine of your face
75 With eager, insistent delight,
Like wild birds intrepid of flight
That raid the high sanctuaried skies—
O pardon the sin of mine eyes!

Forgive me the sin of my hands . . .
80 Perchance they were bold overmuch
In their tremulous longing to touch
Your beautiful flesh, to caress,
To clasp you, O Love, and to bless
With gifts as uncounted as sands—
85 O pardon the sin of my hands!

Forgive me the sin of my mouth,
O Love, if it wrought you a wrong,

With importunate silence or song
Assailed you, encircled, oppress'd,
90 And ravished your lips and your breast
To comfort its anguish of drouth—
O pardon the sin of my mouth!

Forgive me the sin of my heart,
If it trespassed against you and strove
95 To lure or to conquer your love
Its passionate love to appease,
To solace its hunger and ease
The wound of its sorrow or smart—
O pardon the sin of my heart!

7. The Desire of Love

100 O could I brew my Soul like Wine
To make you strong,
O could I carve you Freedom's sword
Out of my song!

Instil into your mortal flesh
105 Immortal breath,
Triumphantly to conquer Life
And trample Death.

What starry height of sacrifice
Were left untrod,
110 So could my true love fashion you
Into a God?

8. The Vision of Love

O Love! my foolish heart and eyes
Have lost all knowledge save of you,
And everywhere—in blowing skies

115 And flowering earth—I find anew
　　The changing glory of your face
　　The myriad symbols of your grace.

　　To my enraptured sight you are
　　Sovereign and sweet reality,
120 The splendour of the morning star,
　　The might and music of the sea,
　　The subtle fragrance of the spring,
　　Rich fruit of all Time's harvesting.

　　O Love! my foolish soul and sense
125 Have lost all vision save of you,
　　My sacred fount of sustenance
　　From which my spirit drinks anew
　　Sorrow and solace, hope and power
　　From life to life and hour to hour.

130 O poignant sword! O priceless crown,
　　O temple of my woe and bliss!
　　All pain is compassed by your frown.
　　All joy is centred in your kiss.
　　You are the substance of my breath
135 And you the mystic pang of Death.

∽

II. THE PATH OF TEARS

1. The Sorrow of Love

Why did you turn your face away?
　Was it for grief or fear
Your strength would fail or your pride grow weak,

If you touched my hand, if you heard me speak,
5   After a life-long year?

Why did you turn your face away?
   Was it for love or hate?
Or the spell of that wild miraculous hour
   That hurled our souls with relentless power
10 In the eddying fires of fate?

Turn not your face from me, O Love!
Shall Sorrow or Death conspire
To set our suffering spirits free
From the passionate bondage of Memory
15 Or the thrall of the old desire?

2. The Silence of Love

Since thus I have endowed you with the whole
Joy of my flesh and treasure of my soul,
And your life debt to me looms so supreme,
Shall my love wax ungenerous as to seem
20 By sign or supplication to demand
An answering gift from your reluctant hand?

Give what you will . . . if aught be yours to give!
But tho' you are the breath by which I live
And all my days are a consuming pyre
25 Of unaccomplished longing and desire,
How shall my love beseech you or beset
Your heart with sad remembrance and regret?

Quenched are the fervent words I yearn to speak
And tho' I die, how shall I claim or seek
30 From your full rivers one reviving shower,
From your resplendent years one single hour?

Still for Love's sake I am foredoomed to bear
A load of passionate silence and despair.

3. The Menace of Love

How long, O Love, shall ruthless pride avail you
35 Or wisdom shield you with her gracious wing,
When the sharp winds of memory shall assail you
In all the poignant malice of the spring?

All the sealed anguish of my blood shall taunt you
In the rich menace of red-flowering trees;
40 The yearning sorrow of my voice shall haunt you
In the low wailing of the midnight seas.

The tumult of your own wild heart shall smite you
With strong and sleepless pinions of desire,
The subtle hunger in your veins shall bite you
45 With swift and unrelenting fangs of fire.

When youth and spring and passion shall betray you
And mock your proud rebellion with defeat,
God knows, O Love, if I shall save or slay you
As you lie spent and broken at my feet!

4. Love's Guerdon

50 Fierce were the wounds you struck me, O My Love,
And bitter were the blows! . . .
Sweeter from your dear hands all suffering
Than rich love-tokens other comrades bring
Of crimson oleander and of rose.

55 Cold was your cruel laughter, O my Love,
And cruel were your words! . . .
Sweeter such harshness on your lips than all

Love-orisons from tender lips that fall,
And soft love-music of *chakora*-birds.

60 You plucked my heart and broke it, O my Love,
And bleeding, flung it down! . . .
Sweeter to die thus trodden of your feet,
Than reign apart upon an ivory seat
Crowned in a lonely rapture of renown.

5. If You Were Dead

65 If you were dead I should not weep!
How sweetly would my sad heart rest
Close-gathered in a dreamless sleep
Among the garlands on your breast,
Happy at last and comforted
70 If you were dead!

For life is like a burning veil
That keeps our yearning souls apart,
Cold Fate a wall no hope may scale,
And pride a severing sword, Sweetheart!
75 And love a wide and troubled sea
'Twixt you and me.

If you were dead I should not weep—
How sweetly would our hearts unite
In a dim, undivided sleep,
80 Locked in Death's deep and narrow night,
All anger fled, all sorrow past,
O Love, at last!

6. Supplication

Love, it were not such deep unmeasured wrong
To wreck my life of youth and all delight,

85   Bereave my days of sweetness and to blight
      My hidden wells of slumber and of song,
      Had your atoning mercy let me keep
      For sole and sad possession to assuage
      The loss of my heart's radiant heritage,
90   Power of such blessed tears as mortals weep.

      But I, O Love, am like a withered leaf
      Burnt in devouring noontides of distress
      And tossed upon dim pools of weariness,
      Mute to the winds of gladness or of grief.
95   The changing glory of the earth and skies
      Kindles no answering tribute in my breast,
      My loving dead go streamwards to their rest
      Unhonoured by the homage of mine eyes.

      Restore me not the rapture that is gone,
100 The hope forbidden and the dream denied,
      The ruined purpose and the broken pride,
      Lost kinship with the starlight and the dawn.
      But you whose proud, predestined hands control
      My springs of sorrow, ecstasy and power,
105 Grant in the brief compassion of an hour
      A gift of tears to save my stricken soul!

7. The Slayer

      Love, if at dawn some passer-by should say,
      "Lo! doth thy garment drip with morning dew?
      Thy face perchance is drenched with cold sea-spray,
110 Thy hair with fallen rain?"
         Make answer: *"Nay,*
*   These be the death-drops from sad eyes I slew*
*   With the quick torch of pain."*

       And if at dusk a reveller should cry,
115 "What rare vermilion vintage hast thou spilled,
       Or is thy robe splashed with the glowing dye
       Of some bruised crimson leaf?"
          O Love reply:
"These be the life-drops of a heart I killed
120 *With the swift spear of grief."*

8. The Secret

       They come, sweet maids and men with shining tribute,
       Garlands and gifts, cymbals and songs of praise. . . .
       How can they know I have been dead, Beloved,
       These many mournful days?

125 Or that my delicate dreaming soul lies trampled
       Like crushed ripe fruit, chance-trodden of your feet,
       And how you flung the throbbing heart that loved you
       To serve wild dogs for meat?
       They bring me saffron veils and silver sandals
130 Rich crowns of honour to adorn my head—
       For none save you may know the tragic secret,
       O Love, that I am dead!

III. THE SANCTUARY

1. The Fear of Love

O could my love devise
A shield for you from envious lips and eyes
That desecrate the sweetness of your days
With tumults of their praise!

5   O could my love design
A secret, sealed, invulnerable shrine
To hide you, happy and inviolate,
From covetous Time and Fate.

Love, I am drenched with fear
10 Lest the uncounted avarice of the year
Add to the triumph of all garnered grace
The rapture of your face!

I tremble with despair
Lest the far-journeying winds and sunbeams bear
15 Bright rumours of your luring brows and breath
Unto the groves of Death.

What sanctuary can I pledge
Whose very love of you is sacrilege?
O I would save you from the ravening fire
20 Of my own heart's desire!

2. The Illusion of Love

Beloved, you may be as all men say
   Only a transient spark
Of flickering flame set in a lamp of clay—
I care not . . . since you kindle all my dark
25 With the immortal lustres of the day.

And as all men deem, dearest, you may be
   Only a common shell
Chance-winnowed by the sea-winds from the sea—
I care not . . . since you make most audible
30 The subtle murmurs of eternity.

And tho' you are, like men of mortal race,

Only a hapless thing
That Death may mar and destiny efface—
I care not . . . since unto my heart you bring
35 The very vision of God's dwelling-place.

3. The Worship of Love

Crush me, O Love, betwixt thy radiant fingers
 Like a frail lemon leaf or basil bloom,
Till aught of me that lives for thee or lingers
 Be but the wraith of memory's perfume,
40 And every sunset wind that wandereth
 Grow sweeter for my death!

Burn me, O Love, as in a glowing censer
 Dies the rich substance of a sandal grain,
Let my soul die till nought but an intenser
45 Fragrance of my deep worship doth remain—
And every twilight star shall hold its breath
 And praise thee for my death!

4. Love Triumphant

If your fair mind were quenched with dark distress,
Your dear hands stained with fierce blood-guiltiness,
50 Or your sweet flesh fell rotting from the bone,
Should not my deep unchanging love atone
And shield you from the sore decree of Fate
And the world's storm of horror and of hate?

What were to me your dire disease or crime,
55 The scorn of men, the cold revenge of Time?
Has life a suffering still I shall not dare,
Love, for your sake to conquer or to bear,
If I might yield you solace, succour, rest,
And hush your awful anguish on my breast?

5. Love Omnipotent

60 O Love, is there aught I should fail to achieve for your sake?
  Your need would invest my frail hands with invincible power
  To tether the dawn and the darkness, to trample and break
  The mountains like sea-shells, and crush the fair moon like a flower,
  And drain the wide rivers as dew-drops and pluck from the skies
65 The sunbeams like arrows, the stars like proud impotent eyes.

  O Love, is there aught I should fear to fulfil at your word?
  Your will my weak hands with such dauntless delight would endow
  To capture and tame the wild tempest to sing like a bird,
  And bend the swift lightning to fashion a crown for your brow,
70 Unfurl the sealed triumph of Time like a foot-cloth outspread,
  And rend the cold silence that conquers the lips of the dead.

6. Love Transcendent

  When Time shall cease and the world be ended
   And Fate unravel the judgment scroll,
  And God shall hear—by His hosts attended—
75   The secret legend of every soul,

  And each shall pass to its place appointed,

And yours to His inmost paradise,
To sit encrowned 'mid the peace-anointed,
O my saint with the sinless eyes!

80 My proud soul shall be unforgiven
For a passionate sin it will ne'er repent,
And I shall be doomed, O Love, and driven
And hurled from Heaven's high battlement,

Down, the deep ages, alone, unfrightened,
85 Flung like a pebble thro' burning space
But the speed of my fall shall be sweet and brightened
By the memoried joy of your radiant face!

Whirled like a leaf from aeon to aeon,
Tossed like a feather from flame to flame
90 Love, I shall chant a glorious paean,
And thrill the dead with your deathless name.
So you be safe in God's mystic garden,
Inclosed like a star in His ageless skies,
My outlawed spirit shall crave no pardon,
95 O my saint with the sinless eyes!

7. Invocation

Stoop not from thy proud, lonely sphere,
Star of my Trust!
But shine implacable and pure,
Serene and just;
100 And bid my struggling spirit rise
Clean from the dust!

Still let thy chastening wrath endure.
O be thou still

A radiant and relentless flame,
105　A crucible
　　　To shatter and to shape anew
　　　My heart and will.

　　　Still be thy scorn the burning height
　　　My feet must tread,
110　Still be thy grief the bitter crown
　　　That bows my head,
　　　Thy stern, arraigning silences
　　　My daily bread!

　　　So shall my yearning love at last
115　Grow sanctified,
　　　Thro' sorrow find deliverance
　　　From mortal pride
　　　So shall my soul, redeemed, re-born,
　　　Attain thy side.

8. Devotion

120　Take my flesh to feed your dogs if you choose,
　　　Water your garden-trees with my blood if you will,
　　　Turn my heart into ashes, my dreams into dust—
　　　Am I not yours, O Love, to cherish or kill?
　　　Strangle my soul and fling it into the fire!
125　Why should my true love falter or fear or rebel?
　　　Love, I am yours to lie in your breast like a flower,
　　　Or burn like a weed for your sake in the flame of hell.

From THE FEATHER OF THE DAWN

THE BIRD SANCTUARY

In your quiet garden wakes a magic tumult
Of winged choristers that keep the Festival of Dawn,
Blithely rise the carols in richly cadenced rapture,
From lyric throats of amber, of ebony and fawn.

5   The bulbul and the oriole, the honey-bird and shama
Flit among high boughs that drip with nectar and with dew,
Upon the grass the wandering gull parades its sea-washed silver,
The hoopoe and the kingfisher their bronze and sapphire blue.

Wild grey pigeons dreaming of a home amid the treetops,
10   Fill their beaks with silken down and slender banyan twigs,
But the jade-green gipsy parrots are only gay marauders,
And pause upon their sunward flight to plunder red ripe figs.

In your gracious garden there is joy and fostering freedom,
Nesting place and singing space for every feathered thing,
15   O Master of the Birds, grant sanctuary and shelter
Also to a homing bird that bears a broken wing.

THE AMULET

Beloved take my eyes with you
Jewel-wise, and set
Their beauty on your heart to be
A living amulet.

5   They shall be your torch to slay
The dark with steadfast beams.
They shall be your stars to keep
Soft vigil o'er your dreams.

They shall be your harvesters
10 To reap for your delight
The amaranth meadows of the dawn,
The hyacinth fields of night.
My eyes shall be your questing birds
Proudly to sally forth
15 For tidings from the rich, red South
And from the fierce, gray North.

They shall be your sheathless swords
With Freedom's rune inscrolled,
Your pure relentless crucibles
20 To test your spirit's gold.
My eyes shall burn like beacon fires
To guard your battle camps,
And light your secret sanctuaries
With quenchless altar lamps.

25 Beloved, take my eyes with you
Jewel-wise, and set
Their beauty on your heart to be
A living amulet.

BLIND

I pray you keep my eyes
Till I return one day to Paradise.
Bereaved of you, Beloved, I am blind,
A broken petal drifting on the wind,
5   A sightless Shama with a broken wing,
Forlornly wandering.

O Love, how shall I know
If Spring has kindled the high limpid snow
Into rich crucibles of amethyst,
10 Or in far meadows lulled in smoke-grey mist
Wild poppies waken to the subtle rune
Of the frail pearl-blue moon.

I shall not see, Alas!
Sumptuous and sweet, Life's bridal pageant pass,
15 Or radiant martyr Youth serenely ride,
In Death's gay cohorts mailed in dazzling pride,
Or Mystic hordes assail like storm-tossed seas
Time's ageless sanctuaries.
No lambent rays retrieve
20 The brooding dark in which I grope and grieve
Exiled, remote from the miraculous grace,
The wise compassionate glory of your face.
When will you call me back to Paradise
Love, to redeem my eyes.

ENTREATY

Come not so near, Heart of my hungering heart.
Stand one winged arrow's length from me apart.

Let one long uncurled tendril of the vine
Measure the space between your face and mine.
5 O Love, I tremble lest my will grow weak,
If your deep honey-breath caress my cheek.
How shall my sacrificial strength compete
Against a foe so deadly and so sweet?

Save me from the keen rapture of your touch,
10 My courage, Love, cannot endure e'en such
Light pressure as the zephyrs' kiss that stirs
The dream of slumbrous moon-kissed nenuphars.

Lower your eyelids, O my heart's delight.
Have mercy on my dimmed and dazzled sight
15 Go farther from me still. I cannot bear
The wandering perfume of your windblown hair.

Leave me, O Love, in God's compassionate name,
Ere once again the old, blind, ravening flame
Smite me and slay in a consuming sea
20 Of dread desire and bitter ecstasy.

RENUNCIATION

With rose-lipped laughter and bright-feathered jest
We meet and part as happy comrades should.
But of my speech I weave a shining hood
To veil the hungers that besiege my breast,
5 Yet wait subservient to my will's behest,
A mute, leashed, patient, poignant multitude,
While my heart gleans the colour of your mood
To dye a leaf of memory's palimpsest.

Give nought to me, but to the world, winged words
10 Of Vision, Valour, Faith—like carrier birds
Bearing your message o'er all lands and seas,
Scatter the lustre of resplendent deeds
O'er journeying world winds like immortal seeds
Of sheaves enriching Freedom's granaries.

IMMUTABLE

Love o'er the rose-white alleys
That flower on pale desert sands,
Love through the rose-red valleys
That burgeon in southern lands,
5   In cities ashine with pleasure
On the edge of a sea-girt clime,
Or mountains whose dim caves treasure
The temples of moon-crowned time,
On errands of joy or duty.
10 Wherever the ways you tread,
A carpet of ageless beauty
Is my heart for your feet outspread.

Love, whether Life betray you
And the malice of black-winged Fate
15 Shatter your dream and slay you
With talons of fear and hate,
Or whether yours the story
Of triumph and loneliest fame,
And the stars inscribe your glory
20 In lyric and legend of flame,
On errands of joy or duty,
Wherever the ways you tread,

A carpet of ageless beauty
Is my heart for your feet outspread.

GHANASHYAM

Thou givest to the shadows on the mountains
The colours of thy glory, Ghanashyam,
Thy laughter to high secret snow-fed fountains,
To forest pines thy healing breath of balm.
5   Thou lendest to the storm's unbridled tresses
The beauty and the blackness of thy hair,
And scatterest the joy of thy caresses
In lustrous rain upon the limpid air.
Thou dost vouchsafe to pilgrim-hearted ages
10 The music of thy mercy, Ghanashyam,
And grantest to thy seekers and thy sages
Mystic sanctuaries of transcendent calm.
O take my yearning soul for thine oblation,
Life of all myriad lives that dwell in thee.
15 Let me be lost, a lamp of adoration,
In thine unfathomed waves of ecstasy.

SONGS OF RADHA

At Dawn

All night my heart its lonely vigil kept
Listening for thee, O Love. All night I wept.
Where went thy wanton footsteps wandering,
  Sweet Ghanashyam, my King?

5   My bridal veils are flung upon the floor,
    My bridal garlands drop across the door.
    The buds that on my bed their fragrance spilt,
        Grief-scattered, wane and wilt.

    O Flute-player, how quickly dost thou tire
10 Of thine own gladness and thine own desire!
    Couldst thou not find upon my sheltering breast
        Thy rapture and thy rest?

    Whose are the fingers that like amorous flocks
    Raid the ambrosial thickets of thy locks?
15 Ah, whose the lips that smite with sudden drouth
        The garden of thy mouth?

    What shall it profit to revile or hate
    Thy fickleness, her beauty or my fate,
    Or strive to tear with black and bitter art
20 Thine image from my heart?

    Without thy loveliness my life is dead,
    Love, like a lamp with golden oils unfed.
    Come back, come back from thy wild wandering.
        Sweet Ghanashyam, my King!

At Dusk

    Krishna Murari, my radiant lover
    Cometh O comrades haste.
    Bring me rich perfumes my limbs to cover.
    Saffron and sandal paste.
5   Bring shining garments for my adorning,
    Blue of the dusk and rose of the morning.
    Gold of the flaming noon.
    Bring me a breastband of gems that shimmer,

Making the lamps of the stars grow dimmer,
10 Fillets and fringes of pearls whose glimmer
Shameth the Shravan moon.

Krishna Murari, my radiant lover
Cometh, O sisters spread
Buds and ripe blossoms his couch to cover,
15 Silver and vermeil red.
With flowering branches the doorways darken,
Is that his flute call? Sisters hearken!
Why tarrieth he so long?
O like a leaf doth my shy heart shiver,
20 O Like a wave do my faint limbs quiver.
Softly, softly, Jamuna river,
Sing thou our bridal song.

The Quest

My foolish love went seeking thee at dawn,
Crying—*O wind where is Kanhaya gone?*

I questioned at noonrise the forest glade,
Rests my sweet lover in thy friendly shade?

5 At dusk I pleaded with the dovegray tides,
O tell me where my Flute-player abides?

Dumb were the waters, dumb the woods, the wind,
They knew not where my playfellow to find.

I bowed my weeping face upon my palm,
10 Moaning—*O where art thou, my Ghanashyam?*

Then, like a boat that rocks from keel to rafter,
My heart was shaken by thy hidden laughter.

>   Then didst thou mock me with thy tender malice,
>   Like nectar bubbling from my own heart's chalice.
>
> 15 Thou saidst,—O faithless one, self-slain with doubt,
>   Why seekest thou my loveliness without,
>
>   And askest wind or wave or flowering dell
>   The secret that within thyself doth dwell?
>
>   I am of thee, as thou of me, a part.
> 20 Look for me in the mirror of thy heart.

PROSE

Blank page

MAH RUKH BEGUM

A Romance of Fate

A long stretch of purple clouds hung over the low range of hills that lie around the corn-fields and palm-groves of Mulakpet. The white pigeons were roosting on the mosque-turrets and a man was leisurely driving a herd of bullocks homeward across a vast plain, where the yellow poppies glimmered pale and bright amid the tall spokes of the spear-like amaranths. A band of chattering peasant women came swaying along in their short red and blue cotton draperies, with bundles of cut grass poised on their well-shaped heads, their bangles and anklets tinkling to the sounds of their gay laughter as they passed the scattered huts of thatch and clay, whence floated the savoury smells of wheaten cakes and lentils.

A sunset hush lay over the landscape, and the air creeping up the valley was sweet with the delicate scent of acacia blossoms.

Suddenly as if by magic, the purple clouds vanished ghost-like behind the hills. A quick lightning of stars flashed into the vivid sky and it was night.

On the terrace at the top of the palatial building at the corner of the street, a young girl stood looking out into the swift starlight. She was dressed in the silk and gauze garments of her people, and her arms and neck were heavily covered with jewels. In her face she carried the meaning of her name: Mah Rukh Begum, the lady of the moon-like cheek. For she had the rich, pale ivory beauty of complexion that is so often to be found in the descendants of the fair Moguls.

There was something a little wistful in the curves of her fresh red mouth, and a puzzled, weary expression in her large black eyes. Unconsciously she sighed, and with a half-impatient movement of her henna-stained fingers she pushed her scarf away from her throat and kneeled down in a corner of the terrace, so as not to be seen, and looked into the lighted bazaars below.

Again she sighed, and then, almost mechanically, began moving her supple body to and from to some haunting Persian melody she half-sang, half-chanted to herself.

All at once she stopped and eagerly leaned her head further over the parapet. A man, evidently a Nawab by his dress, was trying to steady a frightened horse that had backed at the sight of a passing elephant. For a few moments it seemed restive, and then—suddenly the man looked up and met the intense, fascinated gaze of the beautiful girl above him. It was over in a second—Mah Rukh Begum drew back shrinkingly into her corner, her heart beating violently against her side.

'Allah!' she cried, 'What have I done? I have let a man look on my face. Allah!'

So her heart throbbed loud and fast in her breast. For, to this Mohomedan girl, brought up as she had been, in the strict privacy of the zenana, and in rigid observance of the customs and traditions of their social faith, it seemed an outrage, almost a sin, that any man not closely related to her should have looked on her face. And she had brought this shame on herself through her own thoughtless imprudence!

And yet, and yet—she thought with a thrill, how handsome he was, that stranger, and how prince-like he looked in his green and gold tunic and turban, and how his eyes had arrested hers.

'Allah!' she cried again, and drawing her gauze veil over her shoulders, she slowly descended into the courtyard.

II

It was a warm, drowsy afternoon, and the fountain in the courtyard threw up its clear sprays into the hot sunshine, and the peacocks were lazily spreading their plumage in the shadow of the pomegranate trees.

In a large, open hall supported on slender pillars, looking out upon the yard, Mah Rukh Begum lay reclining on velvet cushions among a group of gossiping, idling grandly-dressed Begums, whose bare arms and feet and ears were ablaze with gold and pearl ornaments.

An attendant was sleepily fanning them with a cool, perfumed fan of *khuskhus* grass, another was sitting before an open silver box of spices preparing betel-leaf, while others squatted about around them, some sewing on embroideries and laces on the costly scarves and fragile draperies, and others weaving garlands of roses, or paring vegetables for the evening meal. And all were talking.

Mah Rukh Begum lay with her face half-hidden in the cushions, and her eyes were blind with sad and angry tears.

They were chattering, as usual, of her approaching marriage. One praised her unknown bridegroom to her, and told her of his wealth and estates, and bade her rejoice at her great fortune; another described the jewels and clothes and slaves and eunuchs that should be hers; and yet another reminded her for the hundredth time that on her wedding-day five thousand beggars should receive a rupee each, and that incense should be burnt at the graves of all the saints, that the whole city should be illuminated for the marriage-procession, and that the prince himself—may he live for ever—and all his courtiers should honour the marriage-feast.

She could bear it no longer. Slowly, wearily, she stole up to her favourite rooftop, and leaned her head against the wall, and absently looked down into the street.

Her heart swelled with a passionate sorrow and rebellion as she thought of her coming marriage and the separation from all she loved, and a new life among entire strangers whom she had never even seen—and it seemed to her cruel, cruel, that they should rejoice so exceedingly at what she felt to be almost worse than death.

'I wish I were dead,' she cried. 'I wish I were dead.'

No, she had never even seen any of her future relations. Her mother-in-law and sisters-in-law and aunts had indeed been often to see her on ceremonious visits, but in their presence she had always sat with bent head and closed eyes, and uttered no word. And she had trembled when they lifted up her bowed face to kiss her.

She thought of her bridegroom—she should not look on his face till the marriage was irrevocably sealed. A sudden fear shot into the young girl's breast and her eyes dilated with a vague inexpressible alarm. What was it to be married and live with a man who was a stranger to her?

Her heart stopped still for a moment—then immediately after it began to leap furiously—for the handsome stranger of the day before was looking up at the parapets as he slowly rode by. She saw him, but he could not see her.

A wild thought flashed through her mind. If only this princelike stranger could be her bridegroom. But instantly she covered her face with her veil and muttered, 'Tobah! Tobah! Tobah!' in low, shamed tones. How unmaidenly she was, how wicked to think such an immodest thought!

Then she bowed her head on her knees and wept.

III

The fateful day, the fateful hour has come. What a noise and stir and excitement there is in the women's quarter of the bride's house! The drums beat, the cymbals clash, and the slaves run hither, thither in eager confusion.

The guests crowd into rooms and look out from behind latticed screens—for they are zenana. Only the bride's people and the bridegroom's people are in the large hall surrounding the silver-footed string bed where the sobbing bride lies in a heap of garlands and cloth of gold.

The drums beat faster, the cymbals clang louder, and a breathless expectancy falls on every one. The bridegroom is coming.

His sisters make a canopy of their scarves over his head as they lead him joyously through the courtyard and up the steps to where his unknown bride awaits him like an inexorable fate.

The marriage is over, the knot is inviolably tied, and now the bridegroom shall look on his bride's face while the singers chant their sweetest marriage-songs.

Quickly his mother hands him a mirror and his sister flings a shawl over the heads of the bride and bridegroom. In a very agony of suspense he looks into the mirror for the image of his bride and she, with an involuntary impulse opens her tear-stained eyes and looks also into its magic heart—and the face of the bridegroom is the face of the prince-like stranger and the face of the bride is the face of the beautiful girl on the starlit terrace.

NILAMBUJA: THE FANTASY OF A POET'S MOOD

A woman was walking alone on the shores of a lake that shone like a great fire-opal in its ring of onyx-coloured hills; and her movements were full of a slumberous rhythm, as if they had caught the very cadence of the waters.

A strangely attractive figure, delicate as the stem of a lotus, with an indescribable languor pervading like a dim fragrance, the grace of her flower-like youth. Two unfathomably beautiful eyes flashed from the sensitive oval of a face, not in itself of an extraordinary beauty, but singularly expressive, a subtle revelation, as it were, of the lyric soul within. The heavy hair enfolding in its coils a faint odour of incense-fumes was wound about her head, and wreathed with sprays of newly-opened passion-flowers. The dusky fire of amethysts about her throat and arms, the sombre flame of her purpled draperies embroidered in threads of many-coloured silk and silver, brought out in their perfection, the golden tones, so luminously pale, of her warm, brown flesh. A clinging vapour of dreams hung about her like a veil, investing her with a glamour as of something remote and mystic, and touched with immemorial passion.

Slowly the versatile splendour of the sunset melted into one fleeting moment of twilight that spread itself like a caress over the hills and valleys of acacia and ripening corn. Slowly she left the shore and threaded her way through a garden—herself, a shadowy fantasy among its winding shadows—and entered a courtyard of oleanders and pomegranate trees. On the steps of a long-pillared hall dimly lighted by burning wicks steeped in copper vessels of sandal-oil, she paused, arrested by the vivid charm of the picture before her, and a smile of pure sensuous pleasure pierced through the rapt spirituality of her face. An exquisite picture! A group of girls of her own age were lounging above the chamber like enormous birds or blossoms, in floating raiment of gold and scarlet and green. One, with daintily-jewelled fingers; was embroidering with filmy threads some fabric like auroral mist; another lay back among her pillows, in an attitude of seductive indolence, crushing an aromatic spice between her teeth, one foot audaciously crossed above her knee; a third leaned up against a pillar carved with antique legends, singing to herself vague snatches of a love-song. In a moment, all three suspended their various idleness to welcome the intruder who loitered among them for a second to play with the pigeons that hovered about the ceiling.

Then, she passed up a steep corridor that led her to her own chamber, followed by a murmur of love mingled with a sense of regret, of incomprehension. She was so inexplicably removed and separate from their brilliant, flower-like life that asked for nothing more than the ephemeral dew and the amber sunshine that was so naively content, so frankly enchanted with its own frail purposeless existence.

A wide, latticed chamber with windows that opened to the dawn. Its violet hangings worked with devices, in gold and silver, the garlands of lilac-tinted lotus buds about the doorways, the subdued radiance of the torches on the walls, the cerulean smoke of incense from a brazen censer, the gleam of scattered ornaments of carved ivory and fretted silver, the very detachment of its situation from the rest of the dwelling lent to this room a peculiar significance and fascination, at once austere and sumptuous, as of a shrine dedicated to the goddess of mystery and dreams.

The dreamer stood alone in her temple of dreams, leaning out into the darkness. Her brows were bent as if with the burden of an unknown loneliness, her hands were stretched out as if with the weariness of a futile striving to pluck an unattainable desire. Her mouth was sorrowful as if with the silence of one who cannot render aright the music of inner voices, so importunate in their cry for expression. Memories of her far-off childhood came echoing through the gray desolation of her mood. A lyric child standing in the desert of her own lonely temperament, watching the stars, till she had caught from their inaccessible fires the soaring flame of a manifold enthusiasm, a myriad-hearted passion for humanity, for knowledge, for life, above all, for the eternal beauty of the universe. Thenceforth she had moved in the shadow of a perpetual mystery, consumed with a deep intellectual hunger, an unquenchable spiritual thirst, for ever seeking the ecstasy of Beauty in the voice of the winds and the waters, in the ethereal glory of dawn upon the mountains, in the uttered souls of poets and prophets, the dreamers and teachers, of all ages and every race; but most of all, with a tremulous longing in the touching beauty of human faces and the secret poetry of every human life. Dwelling in the midst of those to whom the opulent loveliness of this earth is an ultimate end, all the sweeter for a knowledge of its perishable charm, and the delights of this material life with its dramatic experiences, a satisfying ideal all the dearer for a consciousness of its evanescent quality, she was for ever possessed by an intolerable desire to penetrate to the hidden eternity at the core of the most trivial accidents of human destiny, the most fleeting moment of this radiant and mutable world.

So the ardent years of her childhood had fled away in one swift flame of aspiration; and the lyric child had grown into the lyric woman. All the instincts of her awakening womanhood for the intoxication of love and the joy of life were deeply interfused with the more urgent and intimate need of the poet-soul for a perfect sympathy with its incommunicable vision, its subtle and inexpressible thought.

A flute-like laughter of delicate revels, a reed-like music of singing voices floated up through the starwrought silence. She paused in the heart of her reminiscence, and smiled a gradual smile that had in it the profound sadness of invisible tears. Ah! how she had lost count of the years, and missed the gracious birthright of her youth, so utterly had she seemed to pass away beyond the measurable shadow of time into the infinite loneliness of her soul's ecstasy for Beauty. And the dreamer so insatiable for immortality, who was a woman full of tender mortal wants, wept bitterly for her unfulfilled inheritance of joy.

WOMEN'S EDUCATION AND THE UNITY OF INDIA

Mrs Muir Mackenzie, ladies and gentlemen, I consider it my good fortune to be present on this happy and I may say historic occasion when the representative men and women of all races and religions in this enlightened capital have united to celebrate the Jubilee of social progress, and in particular to commemorate the fiftieth anniversary of that admirable pioneer journal the *Stree Bodha*, which has rendered such signal service in the cause of the education of women; a cause which I am sure you will all agree with me in thinking the real source and centre of all lasting social reform and national progress.

It has become a favourite commonplace with the advocates of what is generally and I think very vulgarly called 'female education' to recall as an embodied argument a dazzling array of the famous women of antiquity, whose genius and beauty and nobility of character illumine the fairest pages of our annals when India was in the zenith of her civilisation and power. But it is not my purpose to dwell on these radiant yesterdays of our history, for I believe that we are indeed children of tomorrow. But if I ask you to look back upon those great and immortal women whose intellectual gifts and spiritual graces time cannot wither nor custom stale, the records of whose noble lives form at once our proudest inheritance and our brightest inspiration, it is solely to remind you that had it been possible for India to retain that early lofty ideal of the rights and liberties of women unimpaired througli all the changing and chequered vicissitudes of her political history, we should today be rejoicing in an unbroken shining chronicle of twenty centuries of national glory and not be celebrating the mere Jubilee of a tardy renaissance.

But it is a renaissance! A new morning of hope has indeed dawned upon the night of our decadence and apathy. It is not to be compared with that rich and complex renaissance that blossomed like a many-petalled flower of light out of the gloom of the middle ages, and scattered the magic colour and perfume of its beauty over the whole of Europe. Nor can it be compared with that incredibly swift and splendid renaissance which a few years ago transformed a race of artists in a land of cherry blossoms into a nation of indomitable patriots and heroes and in the twinkling of an eye set the little island of Japan foremost amongst the nations of the East and a serious rival to the nations of the West.

But if our awakening is slow, it is sure. It is strong and subtle, and so far-reaching in its influence, that it has even permeated to the heart of that sequestered and dreaming city from where I come—the beautiful and historic city of Hyderabad, which retains with all the glamour of the middle ages much of the implacable conservatism that resents all change.

What then are the features of this renaissance, this awakening on which we have built our hopes? Briefly and essentially I think it consists of two main factors, the education of Indian women, and the union of the Indian races.

So much has been said on the subject of women's education both from public platforms and in the public press that there seems nothing for me to say. Yet, as an Indian woman myself, speaking on behalf of my sisters, I venture to reiterate the urgent necessity for a wide and deep education for those whose high and sacred destiny it is to be the mothers of the Indian nation.

Speaking about a year ago at the Social Conference in Calcutta, I happened to remark that no word in any language was so misunderstood and so deliberately restricted in its significance as the word education. It is generally confused and identified in with that far more limited and mechanical word instruction, the accumulating of knowledge from books. Far be it from me of all persons to deny that instruction, the acquisition of book knowledge is a vital part of education; it is in fact the very foundation on which all true education is founded. But, I go further, and plead for that large and liberal and priceless culture that comes not from books alone but from life itself, from environment, from thought and experience, from the widening of one's material and spiritual horizons by travel and intercourse with diverse and congenial minds. What I plead for is the chance of a full and perfect self-realisation which is the inviolable right of every human being and therefore of every Indian woman! The opportunity to develop all the qualities of the heart and mind and spirit to their utmost capacity so that she may be fitted to fulfil all the noble and versatile duties and responsibilities of her position in every relationship of life; and so that she may adequately and worthily take her place as a distinct and definite unit in the broad scheme of national life.

The subject of women's education in India cannot be fully considered except in its relation to the vexed and delicate problem of the purdah. To be or not to be, that is the question! There are many ardent but not far-seeing social reformers who loudly advocate the immediate and wholesale abolition of the purdah as an initial step towards education. I suppose it is not easy for those whose lives are cast in progressive places where the purdah system is so elastic, to realise that to countless men and women in other parts of India it is dearer than life itself and synonymous with their honour. All my life I have lived in a Mohamedan country which is regarded as the stronghold of the purdah, and I realise what a calamity of incalculably tragic results would follow a premature and total abolition of the system.

Long generations of a rigidly secluded and dependent habit of life have deprived the *purdah-nashin* women of India of the very qualities that are indispensable to those who live in the world! In such, the kindly shelter of the purdah is a safeguard desirable and necessary till they are able to replace it by education which is the spiritual safeguard of the emancipated.

Some of you may ask me how my theory of education is compatible with the keeping of purdah? Why, by a gradual readjustment of the whole system to meet the changed demands of today, by a deft and wise and almost imperceptible relaxing of its rigorous laws day by day as education increases. Indeed I hold that the crowning triumph of education will be the complete emancipation of Indian womanhood. In the fulness of time, like a splendid and full-blown flower, she will emerge from the protecting sheath of her purdah.

The subject of the union of the Indian races is so vast in its scope and so complicated in its details that it calls for more time and knowledge and authority than I have at my command. I can no more than briefly touch on it as pertinent to this occasion which is a successful move in the right direction to bring the races together by the binding charm of a common interest.

It seems to me that there is one power in the world, only one wizard element that can reconcile and harmonize the natural conflict of races and religions. And that is education, aided by Time—and education broad-based upon the fundamental truths of human existence. An education that teaches the unity of a common source that underlies all divisions of race and the central truth that harmonizes all superficial differences of dogma. With prophetic delight I look forward to the day when the Indian races will learn to recognize and glory in that underlying and indestructible brotherhood when they will burn the dross of all deadening prejudice of caste and creed in the purifying flame of patriotism. Then and then only will the races of India become an Indian nation.

Friends, that day is far off as yet. But, as I said, we are the children of tomorrow! I am proud to belong to a generation whose privilege it is to sow the seeds of that ultimate unity. I am more than content to hope that my children's children will live to reap the first fruits of that golden and imperishable harvest.

GOKHALE THE MAN

A Tribute

I

'I wish I had been anywhere near so that I could have gone to see you personally. I do hope your grief will break into songs that will abide.' These beautiful words written on the 12th February, with no apparent premonition of his own fast approaching end, reached me in Calcutta on the sad occasion of my father's *shradh* ceremony. A few days later, Gopal Krishna Gokhale passed away amid the profound sorrow of a nation for once united in the face of an irreparable calamity and loss.

Columns after columns have filled the press with able and eloquent tributes to his manifold and heroic struggles in the cause of India. In every Indian city and remotest centre of Indian interests, men of all creeds and communities, of the most diverse schools of political thought and aspiration, have combined to pay their last offering of reverence and regret for one whose whole life has been a matchless record of selfless devotion to a country for whose welfare he so zealously laboured, in whose dear service he so untimely, so tragically died. And, no poor word of mine is needed to further illumine the story of his noble career or to enhance the value of such universal lamentation and praise. But, I feel, that no chronicle of a great man's work and character can present a complete human document without some of those more personal touches which, however slight and incidental in themselves, may yet act as passing flashlights to reveal the inmost qualities of his mind. In this short sketch, I shall strive to set down a few of my reminiscences of him, not as Gokhale the politician and social reformer, but simply Gokhale the man, as it was my special privilege to know him in his later years.

A Lovely Comradeship

My personal association with Mr Gokhale commenced, as it ended, with a written message. It had fallen to me to propose the resolution on the education of women at the Calcutta sessions of the All-India Social Conference of 1906; and, something in my speech moved him sufficiently to pass me these hurried and cordial sentences which, unworthy as I know myself of such generous appreciation, I venture to transcribe, since they struck the keynote of all our future intercourse. 'May I take the liberty,' he wrote, 'to offer you my most respectful and enthusiastic congratulations? Your speech was more than an intellectual treat of the highest order. It was a perfect piece of art. We all felt for the moment to be lifted to a higher plane.'

An acquaintance, begun on such a happy note of sympathy, grew and ripened at the last into a close and lovely comradeship which I counted among the crowning honours of my life. And, though it was not without its poignant moments of brief and bitter estrangement, our friendship was always radiant both with the joy of spiritual refreshment and the quickening challenge of intellectual discussion and dissent. Above all, there was the ever-deepening bond of our common love for the motherland; and, for a short space, there was also the added tie of a tender dependence, infinitely touching and childlike, on such comfort and companionship as I, with my own broken health, could render him through long weeks of suffering and distress in a foreign land.

Between 1907 and 1911, it was my good fortune to meet him several times, chiefly during my flying visits to Bombay, but also on different occasions, in Madras, Poona and Delhi. After each meeting I would always carry away the memory of some fervent and stirring words of exhortation to yield my life to the service of India. And, even in the midst of the crowded activities of those epoch-making years, he found leisure to send me, now and then, a warm message of approval or encouragement, when any poem or speech or action of mine chanced to please him, or the frequent rumours of my failing health caused him anxiety or alarm.

Paradox of Character

But it was not till the beginning of 1912, when I spent a few weeks in Calcutta with my father, that any real intimacy was established between us. 'Hitherto I have always caught you on the wing,' he said, 'now I will cage you long enough to grasp your true spirit.' It was in the course of the long and delightful conversations of this period that I began to comprehend the intrinsic and versatile greatness of the man, and to marvel by what austere and fruitful process he was able to reconcile and assimilate the complex and often conflicting qualities of his essentially dual personality into so supreme an achievement of single-hearted patriotism. It was to me a valuable lesson in human psychology to study the secret of this rich and paradoxical nature. There was the outer man as the world knew and esteemed him, with his precise and brilliant and subtle intellect, his unrivalled gifts of political analysis and synthesis, his flawless and relentless mastery and use of the consummate logic of coordinated facts and figures, his courteous but inexorable candour in opposition, his patient dignity and courage in honourable compromise, the breadth and restraint, the vigour and veracity of his far-reaching statesmanship, the lofty simplicities and sacrifices of his daily life. And, breaking through the veils of his many self-repressions, was the inner man that revealed himself to me, in all the intense and urgent hunger of his need for human kinship and affection, in all the tumult and longing, the agony of doubt and ecstacy of faith of the born idealist perpetually seeking some unchanging reality in a world full of shifting disillusion and despair. In him, I felt that both the practical, strenuous worker and the mystic dreamer of dreams were harmonised by the age-long discipline of his Brahminical ancestry, which, centuries before, had evolved the spirit of the Bhagavad Gita and defined true Yoga as Wisdom in Action. But even he could not escape the limitations of his inheritance. Wide and just as were his recognitions of all human claims to equality, he had, nevertheless, hidden away, perhaps unsuspected, something of that conservative pride of his Brahminical descent which instinctively resented the least quotation of its ancient monopoly of power. One little instance of this weakness—if I may use the word—occurs to me. At the All-India Social Conference which was held in Calcutta at the end of 1911, in the course of an address on the so-called Depressed Classes, I happened to have remarked that the denial of their equal human rights and opportunities of life was largely due to the tyranny of arrogant Brahmins in the past. My father, who was also present at the meeting, noted and ironically rallied me on the phrase which appealed to both his sense of humour and equity. But, to my surprise, I found that Mr Gokhale regarded the word 'arrogant' almost as a personal affront! 'It was no doubt a brave and beautiful speech,' he said, in a tone of reproach, 'but you sometimes use harsh, bold phrases.' Soon after, discussing an allied topic, he burst out saying, 'You—in spite of yourself—you are typically Hindu in spirit. You begin with a ripple and end in eternity.' 'But,' I answered, a little nettled, 'when have I ever disclaimed my heritage?'

Another conversation of these weeks stands out with special significance in the light of coming events. One morning, a little despondent and sick at heart about national affairs in general, he suddenly asked me, 'What is your outlook for India?' 'One of hope,' I replied. 'What is your vision of the immediate future?' 'The Hindu-Muslim unity in less than five years,' I told him with joyous conviction. 'Child,' he said, with a note of yearning sadness in his voice, 'you are a poet, but you hope too much. It will not come in your lifetime or in mine. But keep your faith and work if you can.'

In the March of the following year, I met him for a few minutes only, at a large party in Bombay given by Sir Pherozeshah Mehta for the members of the Royal Commission. I had recently brought out a new book of verses which just then, happily for me, was attracting some attention and applause. And Mr Gokhale's short conversation with me was very characteristic of his attitude of distrust towards such things. 'Does the flame still burn brightly?' he questioned. 'Brighter than ever,' I answered. But he shook his head doubtfully and a little sternly. 'I wonder,' he murmured, 'I wonder how long it will withstand the storm of such excessive adulation and success.'

The Privilege of Service to India

A week later, it was my unique privilege to attend and address the now historic sessions of the Muslim League which met in Lucknow on the 22nd March to adopt a new constitution which sounded the keynote of loyal cooperation with the sister community in all matters of national welfare and progress. The unanimous acclamation with which it was carried by both the older and younger schools of Mussalman politicians marked a new era and inaugurated a new standard in the history of modern Indian affairs. From Lucknow I travelled, almost without a break direct to Poona, where I was due on the 25th, and on the morning of the 26th, I walked across with the Honourable Mr Paranjpye from Fergusson College to the Servants of India Society. I found the world-famous leader of the Indian National Congress weak and suffering from a relapse of his old illness, but busy scanning the journals that were full of comments and criticisms of the Muslim League and its new ideals. 'Ah,' he cried, with outstretched hands when he saw me, 'have you come to tell me that your vision was true?' And he began to question me over and over again with a breathless eagerness that seemed almost impatient of my words, about the real underlying spirit of the conference. His weary and pain-worn face lighted up with pleasure when I assured him that, so far at least as the younger men were concerned, it was not an instinct of mere political expediency but one of genuine conviction and a growing consciousness of wider and graver national responsibility that had prompted them to stretch out so frankly and generously, the hand of good fellowship to the Hindus, and I hoped that the coming Congress would respond to it with equal, if not even greater, cordiality. 'So far as it lies in my power,' he answered, 'it shall be done.'

After an hour or so I found him exhausted with the excitement of the happy news I had brought him from so far; but he insisted on my returning to complete my visit to him that afternoon. When I went back to the Servants of India Society in the evening, I found a strangely transformed Mr Gokhale, brisk and smiling, a little pale, but without any trace of the morning's languor and depression, 'What,' I almost screamed, as he was preparing to lead the way upstairs, 'Surely you cannot mean to mount all those steps. You are too ill.' He laughed. 'You have put new hope into me,' he said, 'I feel strong enough to face life and work again.'

Presently his sister and two charming daughters joined us for half an hour on the broad terrace with its peaceful view over sunset hills and valleys, and we talked of pleasant and passing things. This was my first and only glimpse and realisation of the personal domestic side of this lonely and impersonal worker.

After their departure we sat quietly in the gathering twilight till his golden voice, stirred by some deep emotion, broke the silence with golden words of counsel and admonition, so grand, so solemn, and so inspiring, that they have never ceased to thrill me. He spoke of the unequalled happiness and privilege of service for India. 'Stand here with me,' he said, 'with the stars and hills for witness and in their presence consecrate your life and your talent, your song and your speech, your thought and your dream to the Motherland. O Poet, see visions from the hilltops and spread abroad the message of hope to the toilers in the valleys.'

As I took my leave of him, he said again to this humble messenger of happy tidings, 'You have given me new hope, new faith, new courage. Tonight I shall rest. I shall sleep with a heart at peace.'

II

In England

Two months later, early in June, after an absence of fifteen years, I found myself in London once more; and, among the many friends who greeted me on my arrival was the familiar figure of Mr Gokhale in wholly unfamiliar European garments and—yes—actually an English top hat. I stared at him for a moment. 'Where,' I asked him, 'is your rebellious turban?' But I soon got accustomed to this new phase of my old friend, to a social Gokhale who attended parties and frequented theatres, played bridge and entertained ladies at dinner on the terrace of the National Liberal Club—a far cry from the terrace of the Servants of India Society.

In spite of his uncertain health, he was very busy throughout the summer with his work on the Royal Commission and his anxious preoccupations with the Indian affairs in South Africa, then threatening an acute crisis. But he would often come to see me where I was staying at the house of Sir Krishna Gupta. Mr Gokhale had a great fancy for cherries and I always took care to provide a liberal supply whenever he was expected. 'Every man has his price,' I would tease him, 'and yours is cherries.'

One day at the end of July, sitting over a dish of ripe red cherries, I broached the subject of a delicate mission which I had undertaken on behalf of the London Indian Association, a new student organization that had been only a few weeks previously founded by Mr M. A. Jinnah with the active and eager support of Indian students in London. It was their earnest endeavour to provide a permanent centre to focus the scattered student life in London and to build up such staunch traditions of cooperation and fellowship, that this young association might eventually grow into a perfect miniature and model of the federated India of the future, the India of their dreams; and, it was their ardent desire to start on their new mission of service with a word of sympathy and blessing from this incomparable friend and servant of India.

At first a firm refusal of my request backed by the strict prohibition of his doctors of all undue strain and fatigue somewhat daunted me. But I had a little rashly more or less pledged my word that he would speak, and I redoubled my persuasions. 'You not only defy all laws of health yourself,' he grumbled, 'but incite me also to disobedieuce and revolt. Besides'—and his eyes flashed for a moment, 'what right had you to pledge your word for me?' 'The right,' I told him, 'to demand from you at all costs a message of hope for the young generation.'

A few days later, on the 2nd August, he delivered a magnificent inaugural address at Caxton Hall in the presence of a large and enthusiastic audience of students, and set before them those sublime lessons of patriotism and self-sacrifice which he alone so signally, among the men of his generation, was competent to teach with authority and grace.

Shortly afterwards he left for India to wage his brave and glorious battle in the cause of his suffering compatriots in South Africa. And though now his health was finally ruined beyond all chance of recovery, it was with the rapture of victorious martyrdom that he wrote from his sick bed, about the end of December, to tell me how prompt and splendid had been the response of a truly united India to the call of her gallant heroes fighting for the eternal laws of right and justice in a far off land.

His Death Warrant

On his return to England in the spring of 1914, his condition was so precarious as to cause his friends and physicians the gravest concern; and at first he was confined entirely to bed. But with his ever-gracious kindness towards me, he paid me a visit on the very day he was permitted to leave his room, as I was then too ill to go and see him. 'Why should a song-bird like you have a broken wing,' he murmured a little sadly; and presently, he told me that he had just received his own death warrant at the hands of his doctors. 'With the utmost care,' he said, 'they think I might perhaps live for three years longer.' But, in his calm and thoughtful manner there was no sign of selfish rebellion or fear—only an infinite regret for his unfinished service to India.

Soon, however, I was well enough to accompany him on the short motor drives that were his sole form of recreation; and on mild days, as we sat in the soft sunshine under the budding trees of Kensington Gardens, he would talk to me with that sure instinct of his for choice and graphic phrases that lent his conversation so much distinction and charm. 'Give me a corner of your brain that I can call my own,' he would say. And in that special corner that was his I treasure many memorable sayings. I learnt to wonder not merely at the range of variety of his culture but at his fastidious preferences for what Charles Lamb has called the delicacies of fine literature. He had too an almost romantic curiosity towards the larger aspects of life and death and destiny and a quick apprehension of the mysterious forces that govern the main springs of human feeling and experience. One day, a little wistfully he said, 'Do you know, I feel that an abiding sadness underlies all that unfailing brightness of yours. Is it because you have come so near death that its shadows still cling to you?' 'No,' I answered, 'I have come so near life that its fires have burnt me.'

But like a homing bird, his heart would always return with swift and certain flight to the one immutable passion of his life, his love for that India, which to him was mistress and mother, goddess and child in one. He would speak of the struggles and disappointments of his early days, the triumphs and failures, the rewards and renunciations of his later years, his vision of India and her ultimate goal, her immediate value as an Imperial asset, her appointed place and purpose in the wider counsels and responsibilities of the Empire.

He spoke too of his work and his colleagues on the Royal Commission, the Viceregal Council and the National Congress; and, though to the end, he remained a better judge of human situations rather than of individuals, I was struck with the essential fairness of his estimates which seemed in one luminous phrase to reveal the true measure of a man. Of one he said that 'He can mould heroes out of common clay,' of another that 'He has fine sincerity a little marred by hasty judgment,' of yet another 'He has true stuff in him and that freedom from all sectarian prejudice which will make him the best ambassador of the Hindu-Muslim unity.' Of a fourth, 'He has made those sacrifices which entitle him to be heard.'

Four Leading Questions

Of the many pressing matters that occupied his mind at that time, there were four which to him were of absorbing interest. His scheme for compulsory education which, he felt, was the only solid basis on which to found any lasting national progress. The Hindu-Mussalman question which, he said, could be most fruitfully solved if the leaders of the sister communities would deal in a spirit of perfect unison with certain fundamental problems of equal and urgent importance to both; the high privilege and heavy responsibility of the young generation whose function it was to grapple with more immense and vital issues than his generation had been called upon to face; and of course, the future of the Servants of India Society which was the actual embodiment of all his dreams and devotion for India.

These open-air conversations, however, came to a speedy end. He suddenly grew worse and was forbidden to leave his room or to receive visitors. But I was fortunate enough to be allowed to see him almost daily for a few hours till his departure to Vichy. In his whimsical way he would call me the best of all his prescriptions. To my usual query on crossing the threshold of his sickroom 'Well, am I to be a stimulant or a sedative today?', his invariable reply was 'both.' And this one word most adequately summed up the need of his sinking heart and overburdened brain through these anxious and critical weeks.

The interval between his first and second visits to Vichy he spent in a quiet little cottage at Twickenham as the guest and neighbour of Mr and Mrs Ratan Tata to whom the nation already owes so many debts of gratitude; and the monotony of the long hours of his temporary and interrupted convalescence was often brightened by the presence of friends whose visits to him were really pilgrimages, and solaced by the devoted attendance of Dr Jivraj Mehta, who has since won such proud academic honours, and of whom Mr Gokhale more than once said, 'He will go far, and be a leader of men.'

From Vichy he wrote, 'Here, in this intense mental solitude, I have come upon the bedrock truths of life and must learn to adjust myself to their demands.' The outbreak of war in August brought him back to England a little prematurely. But though his health had obviously improved, and he was better able to stand the strain of his arduous work on the Royal Commission, he seemed oppressed with a sharp and sudden sense of exile in the midst of an alien civilisation and people, and to be haunted by a deep nostalgia which he himself could not explain, not merely for the wonted physical scenes and surroundings but for the spiritual texts and tongues of his ancestral land. His conversation during these days was steeped in allusion to the old Sanskrit writers whose mighty music was in his very blood.

The Last Occasion

The last occasion on which I saw him was on the 8th October, two days before I sailed for India. Something, maybe, of the autumnal sadness of fallen leaves and growing mists had passed into his mood; or, maybe, he felt the foreshadowing of the wings of Death. But as he bade me farewell, he said, 'I do not think we shall meet again. If you live, remember your life is dedicated to the service of the country. My work is done.'

Early in December, shortly after his arrival from Europe, he wrote to complain of the 'scurvy trick' fate had played him in a renewal of his old trouble; but succeeding letters reported returning strength and ability to work again. In the last letter, written the day before his fatal illness, he spoke of his health being now stationary and of his coming visit to Delhi. But it was otherwise ordained. As the poet says, 'True as the peach to its ripening taste is destiny to her hour.' His predestined hour had already struck. On the 19th February, the selfsame stars that he had invoked two years ago to witness the consecration of a life to the service of India, kept vigil over the passing of this great saint and soldier of the National Righteousness. And, of him surely, in another age and in another land, were the prophetic words uttered—'Greater love hath no man than this, that a man lay down his life for his friends.'

THE SOUL OF INDIA

I

Coeval with earth's oldest empires which are now no more than shadowy myths and memories, and yet contemporary with the youngest world republics in the anguish of their struggle for liberty, India stands supreme amid the marvels of historic survival, and unique among the miracles of historic paradox.

For her earliest record reaching back to periods so remote as to be legendary, holds in a fine perfection of achievement those living principles of national freedom and international federation which we are wont to consider the monopoly of our modern age.

Incomparable too and sublime in its austere, heretic splendour is the tale of her spiritual evolution which, through all the tumult and suffering of centuries of foreign invasion and domination, has kept the inmost Soul of India inaccessible and unconquered, endowed with a perennial vitality and an unmeasured power of ultimate self-renewal, able and ready after each dark epoch of political tribulation to fulfil the prophecy of her own Sri Krishna, and 'be born again and again for the establishing of the national righteousness.'

Today, she—the Immutable, the Immemorial—endures once more the poignant travail of her destined renascence, and her imminent *tomorrow* can seek no lovelier inspiration than the chronicle of her immortal *yesterday*, which offers an ideal so comprehensive and complete in the far-famed efficiency of her elaborate civil and military organisations, her commercial enterprise, her economic prosperity, her matchless learning and her majestic art.

Her old village democracies, self-governing and self-contained, were the living units of an immense imperial commonwealth; her ancient academies and universities were the living temples of the national culture and the national consciousness; her caravan-ways and her sea-ways conveyed to the furthest kingdoms of man not only the precious treasure of her sumptuous merchandise, but the priceless riches of her resplendent thought.

Her civic life was conserved and sustained by that wondrous and versatile caste-system which, now so bitter a source of strife and disunion, represented in that stately era a true division of labour: separate social guilds for united patriotic service. Her priests and her poets were the interpreters and guardians of her transcendent wisdom; her warriors kept alive the tradition of her chivalry and valour as keen and dazzling as their swords; her tillers and her traders, her industrial and her pastoral people were all alike the custodians of the national welfare and the national wealth.

And—highest proof of a country's civilisation—her womanhood enjoyed a freedom and franchise unknown in the modern world. For the woman of ancient India had her lofty and legitimate place and function in the daily life of her race. Not only was it her sweet privilege to tend the hearth-fires and sacrificial fires in the happy and narrow seclusion of her home, but wide as humanity itself were the opportunities and occasions of her compassionate service, her intellectual triumphs and her saintly renunciations. Her agile and brilliant mind had access to the most intricate sciences and occult philosophies. Not seldom in her capacity as queen, regnant or regent, was she called upon to prove the subtlety and sagacity, the breadth and daring of her statecraft. And age after age, she vindicated the fidelity and fortitude, the courage and devotion of her love, on the funeral pyre which was so often the crucible of her purity, on the battlefield which was so frequently the altar of her heroism in defence of the Indian honour of which she was at once the symbol and the shrine.

Shall not the heirs of such illustrious ideals be justified in their belief that in their splendid past lie the promise and guarantee of a splendid future? For, as a great modern thinker has said, 'Not in possessions but in ideals are to be found the seeds of immortality.'

II

The idea of a world-allegiance to a suzerain authority is among the primal dreams of an empire. It is foreshadowed in the *ashvamedha* or quinquennial horse-sacrifice of the Mahabharata. It persists through the changing centuries—a changeless and haunting vision—and flowers, a strange and luminous blossom of spiritual ecstasy in the reign of Ashoka, whose world-wide embassies however were religious rather than political missions to spread afar the gospel of the Buddha and not to enhance his own temporal glory or territorial power.

And it is the time of Jelal-ud-din Akbar, the Moghul Emperor, that first defines and fulfils the central dream and central demand of modern Indian nationalism of 'the Hindu-Moslem unity and a liberal measure of self-government under foreign rule.' So full, so free, and magnificent was the gift of Akbar's superb statesmanship that it survives, not enclosed in the dusty archives of Time, but enshrined in the living folk-song of the people, a beneficent and abiding reality. There is an old folk-song that commemorates the bridals of Akbar's heir with the daughter of a royal Rajput house; and the bride's father says with a touching humility which is the very essence of invincible pride:

> My daughter within thy house shall be a slave and all my kinsfolk thy bondsmen

and Akbar replies:

> Nay, thy daughter within my house shall be a queen and all thy kinsfolk my sirdars.

These exquisite lines lose in translation all their appealing sweetness but none of their deep significance, and serve to express unconsciously, but how perfectly the very soul of that unrivalled political wisdom which built its empire on the spontaneous love of a conquered people by a gracious and magnanimous identification of the alien and indigenous interests and aspirations, and by admitting the subject-race into an equal and generous partnership as common trustees of the national weal.

The paramount powers of administration were entrusted by this Muslim sovereign to his Hindu ministers, comprising the absolute control of the state revenues and armies, of internal legislation and foreign diplomacy. Trust so noble evoked loyal gratitude; political cooperation engendered a deeper social harmony; high responsibility preserved the haughty self-respect of a people conquered indeed but not disinherited and dishonoured in the conquest.

This fusion of ideals, this fellowship of common rights and privileges manifested itself not only in the daily life of the nation, but evolved a new language and a new architecture which kept all the grace and grandeur of their dual descent and symbolised the sympathetic understanding and union between the children of such widely differing origins, faiths and associations.

III

Historic veracity can make no compromises, and it must be confessed that now we come upon a new and melancholy phase of foreign domination. For the first time in the antique palimpsest of India's story under alien rule, the stability and sanctity of her inner life—her only safeguard in the past, her only salvation in the future—were menaced and even partially shaken and destroyed by an adventurous race from the far north which came to expand its trade and stayed to carve an empire; a bold and vigorous race with a glorious literature and a glorious heritage of freedom, which had always given shelter and succour to exiled martyrs of liberty from other lands.

And yet, by some profound and inexplicable enigma or irony of political psychology, the first fruits of England's dominion over India were reaped in a disintegration of the national life and a decadence of the national culture.

Ungrateful and ungracious were it to deny the abundance and variety of the gifts she has bestowed for the convenience and comfort of our existence. But in the inevitable conflict with a material civilisation so antagonistic to her own spiritual ideals, the historic continuity of India's age-long evolution was betrayed and broken, and her ancient landmarks were obliterated. Her marvellous arts and industries, praised in the pages of early Greek writers and Chinese travellers, were ruined, and withered like mown blossoms, and with them the dignity and discipline of patient labour transmuting personality into beauty and art into daily use. Her village republics that for centuries had proved such adequate and effective centres of autonomy perished under a system of foreign government which was no more than a far-off abstraction and which vested the full monopoly of power, hitherto so widely and wisely distributed in a highly-paid and doubtless highly-efficient bureaucracy, usually however ignorant of the tongues and traditions, impatient of the creeds and customs and intolerant of the aims and achievements of a nation whose destinies it controlled.

A deadly policy of distrust insulted, by disarming, the manhood of that epic India of dauntless warriors whose prowess is chanted in the national ballads, whose very steeds and swords had their own heroic names and intrepid histories.

Her immemorial prestige was outraged and trampled under the heel of a young irreverent power, drunk with the pride of material conquest and possession which sought to maintain its political supremacy by an arrogant social aloofness from the people, and with high-handed injustice set up an illogical and arbitrary standard of colour as the only criterion of worth.

But the climax of England's unconscious wrong to India to lay in what was surely meant to be the crown of all her conscious benefactions, embodied in a system of education which, doubtless, flawless and fruitful within its own familiar province, was not merely unsuited but even inimical to the genius of our race. For, education to become the incorruptible living wealth of a nation must be self-evolved and an authentic expression of the national spirit. But this foreign education sold three generations of denationalised Indian youth into a blind intellectual bondage to the West. The old learning that had enriched, the old art that had illumined our daily life were disowned; the old music that had invoked enchantment, the old religious vision that had kindled inspiration were disclaimed and forgotten. The grave and lovely ceremonials and courtesies of our social inheritance were discarded in a lamentable and futile imitation of Western ways; the beautiful Puranic and Qu'ranic names of our children were torn from them in our slavish passion for Western nomenclature.

Could the degradation of a subject race, however temporary and transient, be more sudden, more tragic, more complete? ... to be retrieved, effaced, atoned for by the tears or the blood of her children's sorrow and repentance.

But the high gods that guard the secrets of the future hold the balance true, and the final issues are secure. By some sacred law of recompense or reparation, it is decreed that India which has reached the nadir of her downfall under foreign domination shall rise again swiftly and safely to the zenith of her hope by the willing aid and in the inseparable companionship of the self-same race that has wounded her honour, crushed her pride, challenged her capacity and denied to her for so long the inalienable birthright of individuals and nations liberty, the very breath of life.

IV

Against the background of a starry silence I see the vision of the future, not veiled in the vague glamour of a dream, but lit with the solemn glory of a revelation.

In the great Recension whose appointed hour draws near, when world power shall be revalued and world destinies refashioned, she stands, an India strong and free and fearless with eyes that keep the memory of aeonean wisdom and hands that hold the fourfold gifts of life . . . an equal comrade of mighty modern nations, and queen within her own inviolate lands, administering her own high laws, controlling her own wide wealth, imparting her own rich culture, defending her own vast frontiers. Her old ideals are born again in a myriad-hearted multiform energy, and shine afresh in the revival of her national learning, in the renewal of her national arts, in the restoration of her manifold secular and spiritual activities, in the virile and splendid manhood of her sons, in the brave and radiant womanhood of her daughters, in the confederacy of surpassing love and service which is the united gift to her of every race of which she has been the refuge, of every faith of which she has been the sanctuary.

The dawn of her deliverance is at hand. For imperishable are the prophecies of time and eternal the pledges of the soul.

The soul of India, self-redeemed and victorious, shall become again the mystic temple of humanity, where the pilgrim nations of the earth may sojourn as of yore to share the universal invocation for that ageless peace which is the divinest flower of life's attainment:

Oml Shanti! Shanti! Shanti!

IDEALS OF ISLAM

I thank you for the beautiful words you have uttered welcoming me here today. But even at the risk of being considered egotistical and conceited, I acknowledge that wherever I go to a new city I always look for my special welcome from the Mussalmans of the place. Never have I been disappointed or defrauded of my right. It is my right, because I come from the premier Mussalman city in India. The premier Mussalman state in India rules over the city from which I come, and there the tradition of Islam has truly been carried out for two hundred years, that tradition of democracy that knows how out of its legislation to give equal rights and privileges to all the communities whose destinies it controls. The first accents I heard were in the tongue of Amir Khusru. All my early associations were formed with the Mussalman men and Mussalman women of my city. My first playmates were Mussalman children. Though I stand side by side with you as a Kafir, I am a comrade in all your dreams. I stand beside you in your dreams and aspirations, because the ideals of Islam are so essentially and supremely the progressive human ideals that no human soul that loves progress can refuse allegiance to those ideals. One has to look back to see how the vision of tomorrow may be linked with the vision of the past and, therefore, if in speaking of the ideals of Islam I take you through a long journey into the past, it is only that you may realise, what only the other day it was my privilege to say to the young generation, that it is only in her ideals that we find seeds of immortality and that, if there be today vitality in the Muslim people, it is because the seed was sown into the Desert and the Desert blossomed with rose. Come with me into the Desert where the sun is dazzling, where the people are brave, simple, quick to revenge an insult, strong to defend honour. What is it that the youngest of the religions has given to the world? Of the old religions, some have died and some are still living. When we come to the religion of the Desert, we find that wonderful adjustment between the spiritual and the temporal, for it was the religion of Islam that built up political empires. Comparatively modern as measured by the older civilisations, the civilisation of Islam is young indeed. What does the golden age of Islam represent? What was lacking in the golden age that the modern age has been able to evolve for itself? What was lacking in the intellectual splendour and achievement and what was lacking in the political policies, in its colonising powers? Brotherhood is the fundamental doctrine that Islam taught—brotherhood of civil life, of intellectual life, of spiritual life in the sense of leaving other religions and creeds free to offer their worship. This is what we call modern toleration, the larger outlook, this is what we call civilisation; this is what we call the real understanding of human characteristics, the real understanding of those sources that bind human heart to one another. Ancient Hindu India laid the foundation of her civilisation on the position and responsibility of woman. In modern times, the legal status given to woman is supposed to be a great test of civilisation. Islam, coming centuries later than the Hindu religion, revealed the old world truth in a new language through a new medium and once more asserted the abiding verity that gave woman her responsibility and her place in the national life, by giving her not merely her honour due as wife and mother but as citizen responsible and able to administer her own property, to defend her own property, because it was hers and she was not dependent as mere goods and chattels on husband's and brother's bounty. A sense of justice is one of the most wonderful ideals of Islam, because as I read the Koran, I find those dynamic principles of life, not mystic but practical ethics for the daily conduct of life suited to the whole world. We are fond of saying that we belong to a rational age, that we belong to a practical age. If you belong to a practical and rational age, what more shall you find than those codes of ethics laid down so clearly for your daily conduct? How far-seeing was the wisdom that laid down as religious law those great principles that tended to conserve the brotherhood that the religion taught? What was the meaning of Haj? Did it matter to God that thousands of Mussalmans went to one place or another since he is everywhere? No. The meaning was that streams of pilgrims from various lands, speaking various tongues, having various traditions and customs, should meet together in one common place and one common association and memory to consolidate the brotherhood that Islam preached. The meaning of fast in Muslim religion is that man needs in his busy life some moment to himself when his children might say, 'We have set apart this time to contemplate upon Him who is always with us but we forget that He is always with us.' When we look at the lego-religious law, what is laid down there is the outcome of the prophetic vision that realises that civilisation would tend more and more towards democracy. It was the first religion that preached and practised democracy, for in the mosque when the minaret is sounded and worshippers are gathered together the democracy of Islam is embodied five times a day when the peasant and the king kneel side by side and proclaim, 'God alone is great.' I have been struck over and over again by this indivisible unity of Islam that makes a man instinctively a brother. When you meet.an Egyptian, an Algerian, an Indian and a Turk in London, what matters that Egypt was the motherland of one and India the motherland of another? It was this great feeling of brotherhood, this great sense of human justice that was the gift of Akbar's rule to India, because he was not only Akbar the great Moghul but Akbar the great Mussalman that realised that one might conquer a country but that one must not dishonour those whom one conquered. You may be a king but your subjects are co-partners with you in the defence of the country. It was Akbar who laid down the fruitful policy of unity of that peace which is the greeting of each other. *Salaam*—the national symbol of peace—was the gift of Akbar to the India over which he ruled. The intellectual thought that evolved out of this sense of fundamental oneness formed its beautiful expression in that spiritual Sufism which is blood-kin to Vedantism. What is the teaching of the Sufi doctrine except the Vedanta which we Hindus inherited—the love of mankind, the service to the world, ecstasy in which self is annihilated into the universal life of humanity? Go to the poetry of Islam. What is there so beautiful in all the wide and manifold realms of literature as that immortal lyric of Hafiz, Rumi? . . . there too in its higher manifestation the lyric genius of Islam has been not less than the epic genius of India or of Europe?

When we analyse the evolution of that great literature and when we find the two meeting through one religion, we find, indeed, inheritors of that dual culture—the blending of mysticism with the semetic, dynamic, logical, practical power of life. There, the dreaming and the action become united, because one religion has bound them and we in India are the richer for our Indian descent. When we come to deal in its national aspect with the ideals of Islam, having journeyed first into the Desert and found not the mirage but the revelation, we must always come back home, for, like a lark, we must be true to the kindred bonds of home, and the home of the Indian Mussalman is in India. His endeavour, his destiny, his hope is bound up with the endeavour, destiny, hope of India. How should the ideals of Islam enrich national life? What are the special qualities and gifts that Muslim India has to contribute to united India? I shall always recognise with pride that, what the Hindu Mazzini gives to India, the Muslim Garibaldi gives to India and they make a perfect type to make an Indian patriot. We want the mystic power of dreaming that is the special inheritance of the mystic Hindu, we want the direct, fearless power of action which is the special gift of the children of the sword. It is the spirit of the sword that we want to be brought to this great land. We want that courage that a soldier kept the sword swift in defence of the country, to revenge any insult to the honour of manhood or womanhood that it defended. The young Muslim is to put his contribution—not the sword made of steel but the sword of the Islamic spirit which has been re-tempered in the older fires of Vedic cult—the sword of Muslim love dedicated to the service of Vedic India. That is going to be your contribution to the India of tomorrow. Your poet-laureate Dr Iqbal has done immense service that can never be recompensed adequately, perhaps never even fully recognised by those in other provinces who did not know the national awakening that is coming. It was his patriotic songs that burst like the clarion call when there was strife between two communities. What the poet has done, a poet's race can do.

What a Muslim poet can do, a young Islamite can do in always sending out a clarion call, that cry for unity which has been the one safeguard of Islam in the past and is coming to be the one hope of Islam in the future, because Islam has recognised the fundamental duties of brotherhood. Islam brotherhood must not confine the ideal of brotherhood to those alone that profess their creed but must expand the interpretation of that ideal of brotherhood till every community within this land has learnt the lesson that Muhammad was born to teach in the Desert 1300 years ago. We want to feel today, we who are not merely dreaming the new India but shaping the new India with our hands, we want to be sure of the other manifold substances that are going to mould the great vessel which is to contain the elixir of the hope of the India of tomorrow, what kinds of earth are going to be moulded into a shape to hold the water of life to refresh and regenerate India. That is the clay that came across the seas—the clay from the Desert to be mingled with the Vedic clay—not only the clay that came from Persian Zoroastrians or from the European Christians in the shape of this national life, but we want more than all other clays to be mingled with the Vedic clay—that clay which is the desert clay of Islam—because we feel that unless and until these two great elements are blended together, unified, so that they can never be separated, there can be no vessel of national life that can last for time and centuries. You who are young Muslims—the hope of Muslim India—I speak to you and to you alone tonight, you who have yet to live your lives and hold the destinies to be co-trustees with your Hindu brethren.

The battleground of animosities has become the flower-garden of unity. They in the north who are so eager to unite with the Hindus for national unity are building it up day by day with great sacrifices. I want you, young Muslims in the south, to take your share in that great work here, and that unity will come when you too spend your energies in manifold directions. A group of young men who have the world before them have turned their backs on personal gain, personal joy and personal recognition and made themselves into a band of Muslim volunteers to bring the light of education to their poor Muslim brethren. Nothing is so significant today as the Sultania College where groups of young men have dedicated their lives to the fruitful principle of self-sacrifice which makes Fergusson College the living heart of Maharashtra. I want you to make your southern institution in Vaniambadi the true centre where the ideal of Islam is practised to teach the young Muslim of the south not only the duty of prayer but also to teach the duty of service to the community. Having already embodied the symbol of your ideals in the south, what limit is there to the dream that you can realise within that centre? What limit is there to the ideals of Islam that can be reborn over and over again into a higher and wider life, because you dream true, you dream fine, you dream in accordance with the right to dream what your religion taught you, what your culture has given you, what your truth entitles you in the future, what your strength empowers you to achieve? Do not allow anyone to say to you that for the preservation of the prestige of Islam, there must be separation, sectional difference, aloofness, division. Those are the teachings of those who have forgotten the fundamental ideals of Islam. If you are true to your prophet, if you are true to your land, listen to no voice except the voice within your heart, as a great mystic poet has said, and remember that one of the great duties of those who follow the ideals of Islam is to say to yourself what Muhammed said to himself: 'I am a man even as other men.' There is summed up the entire ideals of Islam. I want you to print that text upon your heart. When one, who was building up a great religion, said to himself: 'I am a man even as other men,' and what one man did in the Desert, shall not the manifold united heart of Islam be able to achieve in this wonderful land? Hindus and Muslims are martyrs for the same liberty, they dream the same dream, they are the deliverers of the same India. We Hindus and Muslims are set out together on the common journey, the common pilgrimage to the combined Benares and Mecca of our lives, and that is Indian unity. Our pilgrim race must carry that ultimate shrine some gift worthy of the goal. The twin comradeship in the pilgrimage will bring unity nearer and nearer to the hearts of pilgrim streams, starting from different associations and creeds, find themselves on the journey's end, even she to whom we go shall not be able to say: 'Was that my Hindu son and that my Muslim daughter?' I want you to revitalise all those ideals in Indian life by those things that enriched the past as the special gift of Islam so that we too with you shall join in praising your God who is our God, and we praise the compassionate Master of life, of time, of faith.

INDIAN WOMEN AND THE FRANCHISE

I

I happen to be here to place before you for your unanimous support a most important resolution of this most important Conference. The actual words of the original resolution on which this resolution is based, I need not repeat at this moment, but the sense of it is this: That the Indian women—in this instance the leading women of Bombay—have sent a requisition—in this instance to the Bombay Provincial Conference—asking that the word 'man' should include, politically speaking, 'woman', in discussing the rights of citizenship—in discussing the political rights and franchises, when the Congress-League scheme comes into existence. Now, with your permission, I would say a word or two as to how this requisition on the part of Indian women came to be placed before the Indian public. Last year the All-India Women's Deputation waited on His Excellency the Viceroy and on Mr Montagu, and among other things, demanded that women should have their rights politically recognised in the coming Reforms. Well, in the course of the conversation afterwards, that is, in the private interview that was granted to some of us, it was the great Mr Montagu who said to me: 'Do you think that the men of India will allow such a thing, or will they oppose it?' I, feeling that my countrymen were still true to their ancient traditions of chivalry and justice, answered in their name, without hesitation, that so far from objecting to the rights being granted to women, they would support them.

Then, at the All-India Congress Committee's meeting in Calcutta, a resolution demanding a very partial franchise was rather half-heartedly drawn up. It was too partial to please me. But taking the circumstances of the moment into thought I decided that it was not a psychological moment to oppose it. I, therefore, withdrew the resolution, meaning thereby that the women of India should not appeal to the chivalry of the men of India but to their sense of justice. Meanwhile, other women of India by the score—by the hundred,—felt awakened to their own responsibilities and to their own privileges in the great reconstruction to come. Their position is this, that so far from demanding the condescension of a partial franchise recommended by men, they are in a position to ask for the full franchise on suitable conditions, whatever the two words may mean. Now, therefore, it is my great privilege to put this resolution before you and to ask you, gentlemen, as responsible citizens, who are demanding large franchises for years, to consider the question of women's franchise from a national point of view. The question is whether in the reconstruction of the national life it will be possible for you to have a rich national life unless and until it is shared and supported by women who are the soul of citizenship and the life of the nation? That really is the point at issue. I understand that the conservative instinct of mankind would consider the new doctrine of life or policy—a devastating one. But look at Europe, where there is the great tradition of comradeship between the sexes. In India, it is not more than a 'Renaissance'. Those of us who are not so far denationalised as to be ashamed of our past, must realise with thrilling pride how far-reaching was the influence of woman in bringing about political and spiritual unity in ancient India. We are always talking of patriotism in the past and for the future, and we must surely recognise that essence of our ancient traditions which was that the woman was given her rightful place as a responsible comrade and co-sharer with man in the trial of his nation, in the victory of his nation, in the sacrifices of his nation and in upholding the honour and the salvation of his nation. Now-a-days we find that almost every day and almost from every platform resolutions are passed meaning to say: 'We are ready to give the last drop of blood for the salvation of our country,' but when you say this, you must remember that you are only a part-possessor, only a co-trustee of that life-blood that you are ready to offer. When you are ready to have the citizen army, when you are ready to send your sons for the defence of the Empire, when you are ready to stake your life and your wealth and all that you hold dear for the freedom of India, you should remember that you are accepting half the responsibilities for India's future in trust. When the Spartan soldier went to fight, it was his mother who said to him: "Come back victorious or touch the shield." Remember that in all great national crises, it is the man that goes out, but it is the woman's hope and woman's prayer that nerves him—nerves his arm to become a successful soldier. I do not think that I need enter into any details of the analysis as to what franchise should there be for women. But I will say this that man ought to share with woman all his rights. He should remember the immutable principle that woman has equal rights with man. Her right is slumbering—is almost in a moribund condition; but it has to be revived. Man must recognise that he and woman come to the door of death to create a nation. Like the right of man, hers is also the right to see how her nation shall live, how her nation shall sacrifice and how her nation shall uphold its honour.

Remember that it is for the honour of the nation that the Indian womanhood day after day comes to the gate of death, so that the Indian people may be born a million times free.

II

Men of India—I shall not address the women of India today; to me has been entrusted a resolution which might seem somewhat controversial. Though it might seem to be premature, the demand made in the resolution I deem to be the primal right of womanhood. This resolution can be treated from the standpoint of national ideals. No matter in which way one deals with the question, I still claim that sex so far from being a disqualification to a primal right of franchise is a human right and not a monopoly of one sex only. I put it before you not from practical consideration, not from economic consideration, but rather from the standpoint of national ideals of India. We Indians have always boasted that we were followers of the Goddesses of our land. Our teachings always inculcated the worship of the mother even before the worship of the father. What is the psychology and interpretation of that inculcation, of that doctrine, of that practice? Woman makes the nation, on her worthiness or unworthiness, weakness or strength, ignorance or enlightenment, her cowardice or courage lies folded in the destiny of her sons. Shall it be said by any law of biology, physiology, psychology or any ology that woman can go down into the valley of eternal shadow and be made irresponsible for the future of a country? Is it possible, is it rational I ask you, that the duty of a woman ends with the physical agony that she endures for the sake of her sons? Are you not aware that in every Indian house, it is the woman that is the centre of life waiting for the dawn? She is the servant of the household, she is the daily sacrifice, every day of her life of her labours, of her love and devotion to the family. Then, being the servant of the family, being the high priestess of the home, being the true legislator of the destinies of India, is it logical I ask you, is it worthy of you to say that she shall face death with no courage to face life, that she shall sacrifice for the sustenance of the family within the wall of her home and yet be not afforded that primal right which is as much hers as it is yours, because she is co-responsible with you for the honour and prosperity of your country? It has been said that to give women franchise would be to rid them of feminine grace. Not long ago, I found myself in the noble, notwithstanding narrow, seclusion of an institution where a child is taken away from the mother at the age of seven and kept from the voice of the woman till the age of twenty-one but mine was the privilege of being admitted to that monastery where the noble guide of this institution quarrelled with me and said: 'Why do you take away the glamour of womanhood by labelling it and defining it?' On the other hand, our young men imbued with the ideals of modern thought say that women must be given franchise because they are comrades of men. But the truth lies in both things. A monastic youth on the banks of the Ganges told me that woman has been true, but if truth be abiding, if truth be fundamental, if truth is one of what a friend calls eternal verities, shall it be less eternal by being acknowledged honestly, squarely, and frankly? I do not think that any male need have apprehension that to extend the horizon of woman's labours is to break all her power in the home. I do not think that there need be any apprehension that in granting franchise to Indian womanhood Indian womanhood will wrench the power belonging to man. Never, never, for we realise that men and women have separate goals and separate destinies and that just as a man can never fulfil the responsibility of a woman, a woman cannot fulfil the responsibility of man. Unless she fulfils the responsibility within her horizon and becomes worthy and strong and brave, there can be no fulness and completeness of national life. We ask for franchise, we ask for vote, not that we might interfere with you in your official functions, your civic duties, your public place and power, but rather that we might lay the foundation of national character in the souls of the children that we hold upon our laps and instil them with the ideas of nationality. We want the franchise for them that we might glorify the dirt, the degradation of civic life, that we might be able by our own implacable ideas of moral purity to cleanse our public life. We want the franchise to wield that power that says that our sons shall not be denationalised. We want the franchise to say that our education shall not be the imitation of unsuitable and alien things but rather that our nationality shall be for enlightening our national traditions and that our national characteristics shall be the outcome of our own needs and capacities. Gentlemen, will you not show your chivalry which is justice, your nobility which is gratitude by saying to them 'You, who within the shelter of our homes are Goddesses, high priestesses, the inspirers of our faith, sustainers of our hopes, the flower of joy upon our breasts, O! mothers, O! sisters, O! wives, we have our feet set upon the path of freedom, we have our own vision, the distant vision of glory; light the torch in your form and then accompany us to that distant goal to be the inspiration of progress and the reward of all our hope.'

III

Not without a due sense of my great privilege do I venture to lay before this Committee, in briefest outline, some of the reasons on which the women of India base their claim to equal franchise in the scheme of reforms to inaugurate responsible self-government for India.

I may observe that my sole title to be regarded as an all-India representative of my sex on a question of such far-reaching importance lies in the fact that I am intimately aware of every shade of orthodox and progressive opinion alike, throughout the country, and I am closely associated with all the larger public movements of the day, especially in relation to the vital and delicate problem of the Hindu-Muslim unity.

There are two reasons why I desire to dwell for a moment on the ancient and historic Indian tradition of woman's place and purpose in the civic and spiritual life of the nation, and to recall the versatile and illustrious record of her contribution to the national achievement by her wit and wisdom, her valour, devotion and self-sacrifice, as scholar and statesman, soldier, saint, queen of her own social kingdom and compassionate servant of suffering humanity.

Firstly, to refute the reiterated argument of the illiberal or uninstructed opponent of women's suffrage as being too premature or too novel and radical a departure from accepted custom likely to offend or alarm a sensitive and stationary prejudice.

Secondly, to demonstrate that the Indian woman is essentially conservative in her impulse and inspiration, and so far from demanding an alien standard of emancipation, she desires that her evolution should be no more than an ample and authentic efflorescence of an age-long ideal of dedicated service whose roots are deep hidden in the past.

I do not for one instant deny that the story of her progressive development has suffered severe interruption and shared in that general decline—I had almost said decadence—that befalls a nation with so continuous a chronicle of subjection to foreign rules but of recent years the woman of the Indian renaissance, largely owing to the stimulus of invigorating Western ideas and influences has once more vindicated herself as not wholly unworthy of her own high social and spiritual inheritance. And already she is beginning to recover her natural place and establish her prerogative as an integral part of the national life.

It is, indeed, a curious and the startling irony of fate that the trend of a doubtless conscientious, but over-cautious official decision is to refuse her a formal legislative sanction for a privilege which is already hers in spirit and substance, tacitly acknowledged and widely exercised; for the power of the Indian woman is supreme and her influence incalculable in the inner life of her own people. I do not exaggerate when I assert that there is no summit to which she might not aspire or attain in any sphere of our national energy or enterprise unhampered save by the limitations of her own personal ambition and ability.

Wherein has her sex disqualified the Indian woman, or disinherited her, from the rich honours she has earned in equal emulation and comradeship with her brother in every field of intellectual or patriotic endeavour?

In our universities she has won brilliant distinction in the arts and sciences, medicine, law and oriental learning. She holds office in the courts and senates of universities, like Bombay University, the Hindu University of Benares and the Women's University of Poona and the National University.

She has evinced her creative talent in literature and music. She has proved her consummate tact and resource in administering vast properties and intricate affairs, and demonstrated beyond all question her marvellous capacity to organise and sustain great educational institutions and large philanthropic missions for social service. She has been pre-eminently associated with the political life of the country, uplifting the voice of her indignation against all measures of unjust and oppressive legislation, like the Partition of Bengal, the Press Act, the Defence of India Bill and the Rowlatt Bill, she has accorded her cordial support to all beneficent, social and economic measures, like Gokhale's Bill for free and compulsory education, the Civil Marriage Bill of Mr Basu, the Inter-Caste Marriage Bill of Mr Patel and the Swadeshi movement inaugurated by my friend and leader, Mahatma Gandhi, and all efforts to ameliorate the condition of the depressed and afflicted members of our society.

Moreover, not only has she participated in the programmes of our great periodic National Assemblies, like the National Congress, the Muslim League, the Social Reform and Social Service Conferences but has not infrequently been called upon to guide their deliberations, direct their policies, harmonise their differences, and unite their ideals towards a common goal of self-realisation.

Where then lies the logic of their refusal of a franchise to Pandita Ramabai, or Swarna Kumari Ghosal? To Ramabai Ranade or Kamala Sathianadhan? To Kamini Sen or Shireenbai Cursetji? To Nagutai Joshi OP Anasuya Sarabhai? To Abola Bose or Cornelia Sorabji? To Indira Devi or Sarala Devi? To Sarala Ray, Faiji Patel,

Uma Nehru or Vidya Ramanbhai? To Mrs Chandrasekhara Aiyar of Mysore or Mrs Sadasiva Aiyar of Madras?

And what of that group of women in the seclusion of the purdah, whose culture and accomplishments rival the golden age of the Saracens? Sultan Jehan of Bhopal and Nazli Raffia of Janjira? Abru Begum, Tyaba Begum, Khujista Sultana Begum; Abadi Banu, the iron-hearted mother of the Ali brothers: to the courageous young wife of the poet Hasrat Mohani; the late Suhaiwardja Begum, who from her sequestered corner set papers in oriental classics for the Calcutta University and Amina Hydari who won the Kaiser-i-Hind decoration for her selfless services in a time of tragic distress in the Hyderabad state?

But it is the purdah which constitutes the chief weapon in the armoury of opposition against franchise for Indian women. I readily concede that it might in its initial stages seriously inconvenience and complicate the electoral system, and perhaps even be attended with temporary danger of fraudulent votes.

Although it is no part of either my mandate or my mission to ask for any concession or preferential treatment for women, I am still constrained to say that I fail to understand, when the interests of small political minorities of men are safeguarded with a scrupulous care, why it might not be possible in course of time to extend a similar chivalrous consideration to the *purdahnashin* in those local and limited areas where this custom is rigidly enforced, for I am sure that her vote would usually be exercised with intelligence and discretion and prove a valuable acquisition to the country.

Without discussing the merits or demerits of this old social custom, I am convinced that, like the other all time-honoured but already obsolete social observances and usages, the purdah system can no longer remain immutable, but must read just itself to the needs and demands of a widespread national re-awakening. And after all, the terrors of the polling booth would scarcely daunt the *purdahnashin* who in the course of her religious pilgrimages habitually encounters immense multitudes and becomes no more than casual unit of a heterogeneous pilgrim-democracy.

What, however, of the unsequestered women of Malabar and Madras, Maharashtra and Gujarat and the Central Provinces? Of the enlightened women of the Parsi, Sikh and Christian communities, of the Arya Samaj of Punjab and the Brahmo Samaj of Bengal? Whether the franchise be one of literacy or of property, their inclusion would in no way disturb or deflect the normal electoral arrangements.

In the name of the women of India, I make my appeal to the statesmen of a glorious country whose cherished freedom is broadbased upon the people's will. There is not one citadel of Hindu civilisation, or one centre of Islamic culture, where I have not scattered broadcast my message of India's duty and destiny among the free nations of the world. I have spoken to the youths in their academies, to the women in their walled gardens, to the merchants in the marketplace, to the peasants in the shade of their fig and banyan trees, but how shall my prophecy be realised and how shall my country take her predestined place worthily in the noble world federation of liberated peoples, until the women of India are themselves free and enfranchised, and stand as the guardians of her national honour and the symbols of her national righteousness?

SPEECH AT TRICHUR

Friends, I have not come to deliver an address, but to lodge a great complaint against three very tyrannical young men, who have kidnapped me! I know when a Brahmin and a Nair and a Christian combine, not even the strongest purpose is inflexible before their joint determination. And you see me here neglecting my duty—I ought to have been at Calicut in another two hours' time—, but I have been brought here forcibly. And you see that you have to stand in the sun, because they thought you might like to hear me speak. But, I feel at this moment like a school-girl who has taken French leave, and has run away from a proper duty! I am just going to have a pleasant time with you, and not going to deliver that kind of serious address which you have heard only two days ago from my friend and colleague, Mr Rajagopalachariar. It is just over one year since I last addressed you in the shade of the same temple and under the shelter of the same banyan tree. How many things have happened in India since last I heard the whisper of the peepal leaves! From Trichur I went straight to Madras and there because I championed the cause of your own tragic/kindred, the suffering Moplahs, the Madras Government threatened me, and I threatened it in return; and I think it was not I who was defeated!

MAHATMAJI'S ARREST

From there I ran to Mahatma Gandhi at Bardoli, because Mahatma Gandhi, that moment, was under the shadow of his impending arrest. And I took to him at Bardoli the message of that tragedy in Malabar. But only a few days after, the whole of India—not merely Malabar—was overshadowed by the incomparable sorrow of its leader imprisoned behind iron bars. You would like to hear a little about just that period of Mahatma Gandhi's arrest. I was in Chitor; the Chitor of Rani Padmini, when the rumour reached me, that in a day or two Mahatma Gandhi was going to be arrested. I went back to Ajmer and made arrangements to leave the next morning for Ahmedabad. But love is a persistent thing, and though I was to have left for Ahmedabad the next morning after my return from Chitor, on the verge of midnight, I felt I must go that same night to Ahmedabad because something threatened my beloved leader. I went straight from the train to the court where Mahatma Gandhi was having his trial. After that I was with him nearly the whole week until finally he was sentenced to six years' imprisonment. The Sabarmati prison became a place of pilgrimage almost as sacred as Rameshwaram and Kashi and hundreds of men and women of all communities came every day for darshan, and women brought their babies to lay at the feet of the great man who was none the less a convict, a felon arraigned by the British law! We talked a great deal about Malabar and how to restore the unity of Malabar. Mahatma Gandhi, who was soon to be shut away from the sight and sound of the love of his people, had time, and had the love of Malabar so great in his heart that we spoke not only how to restore the Hindu-Muslim unity, but how to restore peace among the Christians themselves. You remember that about the time I came to Trichur last year, Mr Andrews had been, a little before me, trying to bring peace among the warring factions and that the relations between the Christians of Cochin and other communities were, at that time, a little strained.

MAHATMA'S MESSAGE

On the 18th March, the judge in a trembling voice, full of pain, felt compelled to do his duty by his own government, and sentenced Mahatmaji to six years' imprisonment. Thousands of people who were waiting in the court and outside were allowed to take their last look of the Master. Leaders had come on behalf of their own provinces from every corner of India. And your own representative from Malabar was not absent from that pilgrim throng. And as men and women passed before him in a mournful procession, to each he gave one word of cheer. To the leaders of Maharashtra he gave a message suitable to the needs and duties of Maharashtra. To the leaders of the Punjab, he gave a message just, needed for unhappy Punjab. To the leaders of Gujarat he gave a message for Gujarat, and for Malabar, he gave the special message for Malabar, the message of reconciliation and reconstruction. But the message to me was not given in the crowd. I was among the two or three privileged to go with him back to the prison to take my leave. I wish that all of you, who love your wives and mothers and sisters, so tenderly, could have seen that tenderness of this great Rishi, and watched his wife as he put his arm around her and took her through the passage into his cell. Just like any ordinary man, just like any of you, this great man, who had made the Empire of Britain tremble, put his arm round his wife to comfort her and said, 'Do not be sad, I shall return to a Free India'!

UNITY AND PEACE

When we went you would like to hear things that nobody else can tell you excepting myself. Because, nobody else had the privilege, besides his own family, of seeing the last of Mahatma Gandhi. As soon as we entered his own block, the jailor came, kind old man, and said, 'Oh Mahatmaji, I was so afraid you might get rigorous imprisonment and therefore with my own hands I washed two sets of prison clothes ready for you.' His black prisoner's blanket was spread in the verandah and his charkha was near the blanket. And we all sat there trying not to shed tears, but Mahatma Gandhi was so happy, he was laughing like one who has received moksha from God! He said, 'I am proud of Devadas, who has not come to see me! He stuck to his post in Allahabad and knew that it would give me more pleasure that he was doing his duty there than that he should leave his post and come to see me.' Then he put his feet out, you know, he always had weakness of the leg that did not enable him to stand when he was speaking. He had some cream in a little tin and said, "I must rub my feet; they are very tired". Then Madan Mohan Malaviya said, "Oh you have been so cruel to your feet carrying your message through the country, give your feet a little peace now." Then Mahatma Gandhi said, "For so many years I have not had time to think or read. Now for six years I shall read, I shall write stories for little children, and I will write my autobiography." Think of this great man who like the Buddha had given a Gospel of Compassion to the world. Think of this great man who like Christ on the Mount of Olives had given his Sermon of Satyagraha to the world. And, think of him writing little stories for little children, stories that have in them all the essence of that love of his, of which he was an incarnate symbol. At 5 o'clock, according to prison regulations, every visitor had to go out of the prison. And as I took leave of my Master he gave a trust into my hands. He said, 'I entrust the unity of India into your hands.' Not national education, not khaddar, not the removal of untouchability—none of these things he gave to me; but. he gave to me that which is the soul of Swaraj, the unity of the Indian nation. And so, since the prison was closed upon Mahatma Gandhi I have been a wanderer throughout the country carrying from corner to corner the message of unity of India. Literally from the shadows of the Himalayas to the very corner where Kanyakumari stands crowned to meet the seas, I have carried this message of unity and peace. From the sands of the sandy desert into the very corner of the temple of Bodh Gaya, I have carried the message across the continent of India. You all know that for weeks and weeks I was in the Punjab trying to bring reconciliation between the Hindus and the Mussalmans, the seed of whose conflict was sown in Malabar itself. Mahatma Gandhi made a mistake when he said, 'Segregate Malabar from India.' The roots of India are in Malabar; and the fruits for good or evil are reaped in the northernmost parts of the Punjab. Therefore the people of Malabar have a special responsibility and a special trust to all India. Hindu-Muslim unity is not enough but there must be unity, harmony, fellowship between Hindus and Mussalmans, Jews and Christians, in this great land of Kerala; and today especially among Christians and Christians, so subdivided, have begun inter-communal factions and conflicts.

SYMBOLISM OF KHADDAR

My friends, I am told that here in Trichur, as in Trivandrum, there is actually a division among Christians themselves. But believe me, you cannot divide the Church of God any more than you can divide the body of St. Paul, whose day you celebrate today, any more than the hundreds of sects and sub-sects of Hinduism can divide the Upanishads and the Shastras, any more than the Shias and the Sunnis can split up Islam, no, any more than the Parsees' sects can divide the Zoroastrian faith; my friends, it is impossible that the Church of Christ can be divided and split up. But it is the common heritage of every Christian, man and woman, no matter of whatever sect or creed. My friends, no matter what your religion may be in this great audience, all of you are like the little seeds within the fig caught together in that one purple skin, each with a minute and different entity indeed, but unable to live apart from that rich sweet, purple skin that enfolds you in a common life. I can think, as I said in Cochin yesterday, I can think of no better place where the fourfold programme of Mahatma Gandhi can be fulfilled so perfectly as in Travancore and Cochin. Nature has been kind to you; history has been kind to you; tradition has been kind to you. Mahatma Gandhi's programme of economic regeneration which, in one word, we call the khadi programme, can be fulfilled because your mountains and your forests are offering you with a generous hand all the things you need for the economic life. Khaddar is not merely spinning and weaving cotton. Khaddar is a movement of the mind as well as the spinning-wheel. The basis of it is, indeed, economic. But its highest achievement is in repatriating the neutrality of the people. Look at your mountains and your forests. They provide all the materials to feed every hungry woman and child in your province. Yesterday at Ernakulam I saw in the museum of a friend a wonderful thing, the basis of a hundred and fifty industries made out of the luxuriant forests, fields and mountainsides. From your plantain tree and your coconut palm, and from the herbs of your fields, from the creepers of your forests, I saw foodstuffs and clothing materials made. Because one Malabar man had the imagination to see whether Malabar could be self-contained and self-supporting, you will hardly believe me when I tell you that out of the ordinary plantain fibre, I saw sewing material like Chinese silk. And made out of that waste product that you throw out when you eat that ordinary thing called "Vendaikai" I saw cloth almost as fine as linen suitable for shirts and coats. Use your imagination, use your mind, use your observation in fulfilling the Khaddar programme; and, believe me, that it is not confined merely to the spinning-wheel but includes the revival of all your arts and crafts, your literatures and music, your philosophies and every type of national self-expression. You will find out ways and means for this economic regeneration; you will lay the foundation of that unity between all communities which I hold so dear and so necessary.

NATIONAL EDUCATION

My friend, Mr Rajagopalachariar, must have spoken to you of education; because one cannot come to Malabar, especially to the native states of Malabar, without thinking of education which is of so high a standard as compared with elsewhere. Culture, both spiritual and secular, is the heritage of Malabar. It was only a simple boy of Malabar who carried that gospel to eleven great centres of India unifying this great Continent by the gospel called the Gospel of Sankaracharya. Even among the snows of Badrinath and the forests of Nepal it is a priest of Malabar who must perform all the rights of the myriads of pilgrims that go to worship. Therefore the people of Malabar are the guardians of the culture that found its highest expressions in Sankaracharya and you must all be the embodiment of that teaching. But what is the use of all philosophy in all religions unless it shapes the national character and gives to our children the true ideals of Indian life and the Indian spirit? Therefore your duty is to use your energies in the shaping of a true ideal of national education that shall unify India even as Sankara unified it by his philosophy. And it is for you like brave and honest men to pay your debts and the debts contracted by generations of your forefathers who robbed and disinherited all human rights of their own kith and kin and called them outcastes and pariahs.

NOT SECTIONAL SWARAJ

The other day at Palghat I was driving near the river and I heard some sounds from the field. I thought it was some people in trouble crying out. Yes, it was a group of people in trouble; but it was an inherited trouble. They were Nayadis, the hunted, not those who hunt with the dog, but those who are hunted worse than wild dogs and wild beasts and kept out of towns and villages. But I am a very determined woman, as even the

Government has found out. And one hundred of these Nayadis, not allowed to walk in your high streets, came to the conference over which I presided, standing by the side of the high-born Brahmin and the Nair. When I talk of liberty and Swaraj, I do not talk of sectional Swaraj or liberty, which is the monopoly of privileged classes. I talk of a Swaraj that is just as the sun that gives his rays alike to the Nambudiri and the Nayadi. I talk of a Swaraj that is as compassionate as rain, that feasts the fields of the king and the peasant alike. And until the people of Malabar remove from the brow of India the curse that they themselves have put upon it, believe me, there cannot be a crown of freedom for those shame-stained brows.

UNITY

And now I come to the fourth item which to me is the first item of what is called the constructive programme. I began with a message of unity; I shall end with a message of unity. There is nothing else that interests me in this life save the unity of India and all that conduce to that unity. Where better than in Cochin can you solve the problem of unity? Yesterday I was looking at the charter granted by the king of Cochin to the Jews who found shelter here after the destruction of Jerusalem. There was no Congress in those days to preach unity. But the king of Cochin gave to those emigrants equal rights and privileges along with his own proper subjects. All the symbols of honour, all the rights of citizenship were conferred upon these Jews whose synagogue I visited yesterday. To the Arab traders, to the Christians who came, equal rights and privileges were granted in Travancore and Cochin. And it was from the shores of Malabar that the cry of the Christian went up to his God and the Iyan or God sounded at the sunset and the voice of the Muezzin sent out Allah-O-Akbar. Surely, the descendants of those liberal and tolerant men who were the hosts and the friends and the comrades of the men of different faiths from Jerusalem and Arabia who came for shelter and help and friendship to this shore, surely, their duty is to extend equal fellowship, equal love and equal harmony to the descendants of the Arabs and the Syrians who came to Cochin and Travancore. Oh! my friends of Cochin, you in Trichur represent the heart of Kerala. So let the heart of Kerala send forth to the rest of India a message of harmony, of harmony but not of diversity, of unity but not of difference, of fellowship but not of division of creeds and communities and focussed together by a common purpose, a common understanding, a common sacrifice, and a common love.

SPEECH AT DURBAN TOWN HALL

Dr Francois, Mrs Gilbert, my European friends, my countrymen, I am so deeply moved tonight by your kindness and by the manifestations of your kindness in the shape of such beautiful flowers and presents that I am hardly able to find words to express my gratitude or to express my deep appreciation of your cordial welcome to me tonight. More than once lately I have been thinking about what to me is a very trying, but to others I believe, apparently a triumphant tour through Africa. I have been thinking of all the valuable and beautiful things that have been showered upon me, the gold and the silver, the ivory, the feathers and the skins of monkeys, blue, white and brown, and many things of other kinds representing birds, beasts and fishes—everything has come to me, and I feel like Alexander Selkirk who said, 'I am monarch of all I survey.' I might almost be deluded in this beautiful subcontinent of South Africa into believing that I am really that monarch and that I am monarch of all I survey, and of the hearts of the women and men of South Africa as well. I said 'women' first. And if tonight I were to make that the standard whereby to judge the response made to my appeal, the answer made to my query, I should say I have succeeded in my mission, but alas, I have lived too long in this world already. I am not going to tell you how old I was a few weeks ago, because you will find it in *Who's Who*, but I have dealt with too many types of men and women—(I put 'men' first in this instance)—to be so easily deluded into the belief that all I desire has been fulfilled.

Had I come on a mission to South Africa, had I come only like those happy mortals to whom life is a prolonged series of *dolce far niente* I should have paused and said to myself that here at least I have found that Garden of Eden for which the whole world has been looking,—here among these green hills and flowering valleys, with the music of the great Indian Ocean reminding me of those epic memories of our far-off land. I should have said here is the paradise for which we have been looking, but without the serpent. But when looking upon the green hills, the blue waters and the smiling land with its fragrant flowers I also see the sons of my comrades, downtrodden and oppressed. I begin to feel something gnawing at my heart and I say to myself what is this in this wonderful paradise. What is it that gnaws at my heart night and day and day and night till there is no hope for me, no rest for me, no peace for me in this Eden by the Indian Ocean? And then I remember that I myself am the heart of my people, and therefore my Garden of Eden as well. I remember also that I came as a stranger into your midst, but you took me at once into the secrets of your heart. When I knocked upon the door of my enemy the door was opened to me and I found behind it the faces of friends. I have nothing in this land to complain of, no grievance for myself in this beautiful land, but when I come here and when I am garlanded and given presents during my mission I realise that my people are indivisible whether born in India and seeking freedom in their own country, or whether they be the children or the grandchildren of the indentured labourers who, coming to this country and choosing this soil to be their mothersoil, lived like helots and outcasts, lived like pariahs and lepers of humanity in your midst. Therefore I must be full of sorrow and of shame because I, too, being of my people, soul of their soul, blood of their blood, bone of their bone, am a helot and slave standing before you, though you garland me and heap upon me what kings and queens of the world have not been able to buy.

When I contemplate this wonderful land where every tree, every bird and every blossom is a parable, a symbol and a sermon and a prophecy as the fulfilment of the miracle of God,—the recurring beauty of love in the world, I wonder how amidst so much beauty and splendour, in the very midst of the living magic of such parables, the heart of man can be so hard, so bitter, so full of hate and conflict. What is it that you are quarrelling about? What is it that makes this conflict in a country where there should be peace? Why is the hand of the white man up against the coloured races in this country? What have my people done to you, my people who did not come as rivals and competitors, but who were brought here poor and uneducated as they were, and brought with promises, with pledges and with hopes held out to them to come and serve the white man in this country, to cut his sugarcane and to serve him, and after a little period he should be free either to go back to his own country or, after a certain period, (mark my words) to live as a free man in this land with a gift of land and freedom to live like the citizens in this country. And in those days when shiploads of the indentured labourers came to this country who could neither read nor write, but could only make thumb-impressions on the documents that made them slaves to the white community; they came, as I said, uneducated, but not uncultured.

They did not know the comparative theology of the world, they did not know history. They did not know the rudiments of such statesmanship as obtained in this Union, but they became children of that Indian soil where every part is impregnated with the call and inspiration of the old Indian lyrics and ballads and philosophies, and though they only came to work, and though they stayed and made their children servants to your need and convenience, none the less they were the Indian people with the culture of India in their very blood, and they stood for loyalty, character and faithfulness to the bond they made, and with that neither friend nor foe might interfere. That is the culture that makes character and that is what has been passed on from the great epics of my country. And because of this, India today, after centuries of class subjection, has sent a new message to a waiting world, and I am the messenger for that message. You all know, whatever may be your ancestry, that the civilisation such as we knew it, such as we accepted it and died to preserve through our children on the battlefields of France and Flanders, the old civilisation is now a thing of ruin and hope has departed from the world, faith has departed from the world.

The young men of India, who were in the trenches because they believed in the idea of brotherhood and peace and justice, have come back saying 'Where is God, where shall we find that dream for which we were willing to die, for which thousands upon thousands of our comrades have died on these battlefields?' They are saying 'We have fought because we believed that when the war was over a new world would be made ready for the younger generation. We have come back wounded not only in our limbs but in our souls only to find the Empire still as it was, where colour is still the test of humanity and where might is still the standard of right.' They say, 'Such is the world for which we fought. What is this imperial greed that statesmen practise that still leads to hatred and conflicts? Shall we live in this world which after all the trial and sacrifice we have endured for well nigh seven years, we find still full of the old hypocrisy, the old juggling, and where there are still the old border quarrels?' That is not the world for which the young men and women of Europe and India sent their beloved to shed their blood, and who are today mourning for those who will never come back. And you in Africa were not free from that, you could not escape the throes and anguish of that conflict. You, too, gave your sacrifice, your young men who died.

But you in Africa, what are you doing to create the new heaven and a new earth which is the heritage of the young who have come back alive in the body, but wounded in their souls—a world divided into what a very distinguished friend of mine in Johannesburg called 'a world of expediency?' Statesmen say 'yes, we recognise the justice of your case; but expediency must come before justice.' Are you in this country building up a heritage of your children on that wicked word 'expediency,' or are you going to build up an undying legacy for your children on the immortal idea of an honest policy with justice for all alike? My friend in the chair has very pertinently asked 'what is equality'? Equality is only another word for justice. And then following up the train of philosophic thought he said equality was only opportunity to do good, opportunity for all to do good alike. Has he lived so long in the world and not realised that even to do good, even to offer a cup of water to a dying person your hands must be free to lift up that cup and offer it to the dying man? You cannot talk of doing good and doing right while you bind with shackles the man to whom you say it. You cannot tell a man of his own degradation and disabilities and yet say 'why don't you fulfil your destiny to humanity as we do.' Oh! had I the tongue of men and angels I would say to you, 'brothers, sisters, white men and women, do not impose upon any section of your fellowmen that disadvantage, that insult, that tyranny, which you ought to recognise as such, because you are full of the passion of self-preservation that you do not stop to analyse the purpose and the implications of your action.'

Let us pause and consider for a moment the question of Natal. I know, and no one knows better, how thorny a problem it is. Africa is like a great red rose set about with thorns, and beset with the problem of privileges and the conflicts of communities. There is this beautiful rose that you have woven with thorn. Let us pull out thorn by thorn and see if we cannot free it to cast its fragrance and beauty upon the world. It is not the ignorant people of Natal, but men and women for whom I have the greatest esteem and affection and who are of just and upright character, following their own creeds faithfully, who have said,

'Yes, you are right, justice in the abstract is the ideal thing, but we live in the world, and how would you advise us statesmen to act when the burden of all these problems is upon us? How shall we satisfactorily solve these problems and yet solve them in accordance with the wishes and the symptoms and threats of the predominant feeling in the country as embodied by the white community?' This in one sentence is the only argument that the most brilliant men in South Africa have been able to advance to me. They say, 'You are right, but we have created this problem and must go on with it.' When, I said, they came to Dalagoa Bay and to you in your hour of need after your representations to the Indian Government that you would be a bankrupt people in South Africa unless India came to your assistance and sent labour to get you out- of your difficulty, they came poor and meek and cheap.

Their highest virtue in the eyes of their employers was not their simplicity or loyalty, but their cheapness, and so, being cheap, it was thought very desirable that these wretched miserable people, who could live on the smell of an oil rag, should be induced to stay in this country, and so they were told they should have land if they stayed over a certain period. I believe some tattered passes are still in existence and I am going to see if I can secure them and have them photographed. What did their employers say? They said, 'You shall go where you like, and when you have the necessary qualifications for a vote you shall become part of the enfranchised community of South Africa.' I want you to remember that these coolies, as you call them, not knowing what 'coolie' means, these coolie nations, you know—and by the way may I digress a little to define what a coolie is? It will surprise many no doubt, I know, that it is a coolie government that today is ruling the Empire. My friends, Mr Clynes, Mr Ramsamy MacDonald, Mr Thomas, Colonel Wedgwood and all the other members of the British government are all coolies, and you are taking your orders, General Smuts and the rest of the government of South

Africa—from a 'coolie' called Thomas who is your Colonial Secretary. And so, I am not ashamed if my people are miscalled by a name that applies literally to the rulers of England today.

Well, these 'coolies', after a period of slavery, were free men. Like the man in Uncle Tom's Cabin they were set free, and how did they use their freedom? They voted for the white man to get him into Parliament, but you cannot ask rivers to flow backwards and the population grew quickly like a passion flower and then the white population said, 'look at the quick growth of this brown population from India.' They said 'this is a menace and therefore although we were very glad of the votes they gave us when we wanted them, they will surely swamp us.' And so the gentleman called Escombe, I think it was, said, 'Oh, this danger must be stopped, let us take away this vote. One stroke of the pen and the few Parliamentary votes of these wretched 'coolies' will no longer be a political menace to us.'

And so stage by stage these people, who were the free citizens of South Africa, had privilege after privilege, right after right, slowly whittled away, and it came to this. They said, 'this brown coolie who lives so cheaply, he is a menace to us and to our trade. We cannot do without tables and chairs and spoons, but this man uses his fingers. He does not want plates at every meal; he lives on banana peel and therefore he is a menace to us. These people do not wear shoes and stockings in their homes and they have no chairs and furniture; they are a menace to us,' Of course we have not got your standard of civilisation, but as I was saying elsewhere today, you cannot judge us by your civilisation, nor we you by yours. For instance in the wilds of Africa I found a tribe wearing a girdle of green leaves only, fresh from the trees, and when I go to Paris I find little more than a girdle of leaves round the waists of the Persian beauties. Each country has its own taste, and the extremes of civilisation and savagery meet in the African forest, but it is not for the Indian, indeed, to judge either. I can only judge my people by my standard, your people by your standard, and you have come into this country—to a country that is not yours—to a heritage not yours by right or blood tradition or by the fair division of ethnological division. It is neither yours nor my people's. You came from those little islands that are so small that they could cradle you but could not give you room to expand.

It was the England of Shakespeare for which your young men died on the field of Flanders, but you, who are the descendants of those traditions, custodians of the ideals and standards of equality instilled through the ages, what are you doing in South Africa to betray the trust that is in your very blood? Shall you say, standing on the very soil of England, that the British shall never be slaves, and saying it for yourselves, shall you give to my people only the legacy of the helots' doom for their children? Is that the British tradition, is that the justice of the British people for which the youth of England died? I know, as you say, there is a menace to you. There is always a menace to you in India. Is that the reason why you are going to turn the Indians out of their own country? Are you going to dare turn the black man out of his heritage, and the coloured man whom you have created? Are you going to deprive this coloured population of their heritage in this land? No, you cannot, and yet their colour is a menace to you. They are in their millions, you in your million and a half. Why do not you speak of the black menace or the coloured menace? Why only of the menace of the 150,000 or 160,000, at the outset 200,000, innocent people, colonists like you and without a home outside Africa?

The rich merchants come and go. They have homes and lands in India, but what home have these children of the indentured labourers who have built up your Garden Colony for you, who have lived here away from kith and kin, excepting here. Their only hope is here, their only breathing space lies here and not across the seas. How can you bring in legislation to hedge them around with hypocritical camouflage which deceives nobody in this world? But your statesmen say, 'We are put into Parliament by the votes of people who have prejudice against colour, therefore we must save ourselves by doing wrong.' Are you freedom-loving people, descendants of Englishmen, descendants of the Scots who with Wallace bled, descendants of those Welshmen who are true to their mountain freedom, and descendants of those Irishmen whose very blood is freedom, are you going to put these people down in the annals of history as murderers and suicides, murderers because you would slay the self-respect and the soul of my people, and suicides because you would wreck the Empire by the loss of India? Why not, without passion or bitterness, call a round table conference of Indian leaders in Natal, colonial leaders and the great leaders of India whose word is law to these people, and put your statements and ours as fair-minded men, whether white or black or yellow does not matter, men who have no stake in the country, no trade policy, nothing but a passion for justice and humanity, put them kindly and with consideration sitting together in a round table conference to discuss these problems in a friendly way, and say to my people, we fear you because you live cheaply, we fear you—from whatever reasons—and tell them they have failed here and therefore you have not done this or that—and let them say to you on the other hand this: 'Where are the promises that brought our people to this land?' We fought and went to prison and struggled and followed our great leader Mahatma Gandhi.

Not only have we endured suffering and insult and every disgrace you would not give a dog, but General Smuts has betrayed that settlement which he arrived at when Mr Gandhi came to South Africa. How many of you have taken the trouble to read what the settlement was, and the correspondence before and after? You must, if you are true, study human documents and not merely official records. Take the correspondence before and after and see where General Smuts said 'It is always the desire of the Government of South Africa to treat the Indians fairly and with justice, and any vested right shall not be challenged or threatened.' And yet in less than ten years that settlement was taken away by the pressure of his constituency. Then began a prolonged whittling away of the liberties and privileges of the Indian people and the curtailment of the settlement by legislation after legislation in Natal under the pressure of the Natal voters against the Indian community, and now the Indians are threatened with the Class Areas Bill. I wonder how many voters know what the Class Areas Bill really means. Oh, says the statesman, 'We deal fairly and justly towards all.' But then the Jewish community runs to him and says, 'Are we going to be included in this Bill?' 'Oh, no, you are not Asiatics, Palestine is not in Asia,' says the statesman. Then the Syrian runs and says, 'My skin is as white as yours, am I to be included,' and the reply is that the Syrian is not a Scandinavian. The native is told that he is protected, and the coloured people also are protected, and who is left to go into segregation? My people, who broke away from home and tradition, kith and kin, for your sakes. Are they to be the only people to pay the penalty because forsooth you come into this tropical climate and have lost some of the moral fibre and firmness and the spirit of fair play,—that ability to play cricket which is the characteristic of the English race.

Therefore, friends, my one appeal to you as white men, as brown men, as men of any colour in the community is to see that you build up the traditions of South Africa on those immutable ideals of justice, liberty, and equality, which form the only abiding place for any republic, any human colony or community. I have come from India to say to you that India will not stand for any injustice to her children any longer. She says to my people, 'You are the children of the soil, be true to Africa. You are citizens of South Africa, use your rights like men, making a splendid contribution to the culture and the character-building and the glory of that country that has given you bread,' but, says India, 'If one hair of your head is touched I, your mother, will remember that citizens of South Africa though you be, you are still my children, and I will come to your rescue.' My dear friends, as I always say, remember that you have a dual duty in this world. You have a dual duty in this land of Africa.

You represent to my people, to the coloured people and to the black people the traditions of British liberty, of British justice which have made the glory of Britain, but you represent even more another also—the Christian tradition. Someone some years ago, I think it was Stead wrote a book entitled *If Christ Came to Chicago*, but what would He say if he came to Natal and to Durban, to the country which the Portuguese sailors discovered on His Natal day, Christmas day? Would He say you were carrying out His will by crucifying Him, not once but cross after cross, a million times? This is your responsibility and I appeal to you not as one who has come with a message of conflict, but with an appeal for peace, the gospel of peace from my country, whose message is peace to the world. Christ's message was peace and goodwill to the world and I appeal to you not to let the law of expediency—the law of self-preservation—blind you to your duty as disinterested exponents of the law of Christ who died on the Cross to save your sins. If those thieves who were with him could enter into his paradise, men who stole and murdered—are not my people, who are neither thieves nor murderers, but meek and loyal and lowly men of a country that gave civilisation to the world—are not they good enough to enter into the paradise of South Africa with the whiter races of South Africa whom they have served for so many years in the past, building up a great heritage from which the forsaken children of Europe will seek a sign, and which will transmute a world of despair into a world of hope and brotherhood.

PRESIDENTIAL ADDRESS

40th Indian National Congress

Friends, were I to ransack all the treasuries of human language I fear I should fail to discover words of adequate power or beauty to translate my deep and complex emotion in acknowledging the signal honour you have done me, by entrusting to my unskilled hands the high burden and responsibility of so exalted an office, which for two score years has been ennobled by the brilliant and memorable achievement of my distinguished predecessors, both of our own and of alien race. I am fully aware that you have bestowed upon me the richest gift in your possession, not merely as gracious recompense for such trivial service as I may have been privileged to render at home or abroad; but rather in generous tribute to Indian womanhood and as token of your loyal recognition of its legitimate place in the secular and spiritual counsels of the nation. In electing me to be the chief among your chosen servants, through a period so fraught with grave issues and fateful decisions, you have not created a novel precedent. You have only reverted to an old tradition and restored to Indian woman the classic position she once held in a happier epoch of our country's story: symbol and guardian alike of the hearth-fires, the altar-fires and the beacon-fires of her land. Poignantly conscious as I am of my own utter unworthiness to interpret so exquisite, so austere an ideal of wisdom, devotion, and sacrifice, as embodied through the ages in the radiant heroines of our history and legend, I trust, that to the fulfilment of the lofty task you have allotted me, even I might bring some glowing ember of the immortal faith that illumined the vigil of Sita in her forest exile, and bore the feet of Savitri undaunted to the very citadels of Death.

The accepted convention of this august assembly imposes upon me, alas, the duty of placing before you a formal document of plans and policies of work for the coming year. I, therefore, contrary to the impulse and custom of a lifetime, am vainly groping for appropriate phrases that might serve dimly to foreshadow some of the thoughts that can only find spontaneous expression when I stand in your midst and the inspiration of your living presence shall give to my heart its voice of hope, and to my words their wings of fire.

Before we reach the central purpose of our labours in this northern city, to which we have journeyed from the farthest ends of India, let us offer our mournful homage to the memory of our illustrious dead—to that great patriarch of our national renaissance, Surendranath Bannerjea, who for well-nigh half a century assailed the heavens with the thunders of his splendid oratory in indignation at the burning wrongs of his people; to Ramakrishana Bhandarkar, the famous scholar of the Deccan, who with patient and dedicated hands rekindled the lamp of our ancient Sanskrit culture, and lifted it high above the clamour and conflict of political throngs, to Deshbandhu Chitta Ranjan Das, kingliest of dreamers, whose whole being was a Vaishnavite rhapsody of incomparable passion for the liberty of his Motherland, who died with his hand outstretched in a royal gesture of reconciliation towards a powerful antagonist against whom he had fought so often with such reckless and victorious chivalry.

Would that he were with us today to guide us aright in our anxious deliberations and help us to apprehend the true and tragic significance of the stupendous problems that call for immediate settlement and cannot with impunity be deferred to a more convenient season. A singular combination of domestic and international circumstances has conspired to implicate us against our will and almost without our knowledge in a labyrinth of intricate and unparalleled difficulties that threaten the stability and integrity of our national existence. Our imperative duty, therefore, is to survey with eyes unhooded of their habitual illusion, the sinister and melancholy spectacle of our abject helplessness born of our foolish disunion and nourished by our long dependence upon the caprice or the compassion of imperial policies. What means shall we devise, what schemes shall we evolve to deliver ourselves from the manifold dangers that encompass us? How shall we combat the deadly forces of repression that challenge our human rights of liberty, how defeat the further encroachment of ruthless and rapacious imperialist exploitation that despoils the remnants of our moral and material heritage? How circumvent the insidious and ingenious aggression of other foreign races eager to profit by the conditions of our economic and intellectual servitude? How shall we avert the implacable doom that menaces our unfortunate kindred in the colonies, how quell the rampant forces of reaction or divert the disaster of our internecine feuds?

The answers that we need are fully enshrined in the magnificent gospel of sacrifice enunciated by Mahatma Gandhi, in which he vainly strove to teach us the heroic secret of national self-redemption. But we, so long disinherited from the epic faith that sustained our brave forefathers, were too weak and unworthy to respond for more than a brief period to the demands of that noble and exacting creed. Whatever may be the verdict of history, it cannot be gainsaid that the movement of non-violent non-cooperation that swept like a tempest over the country shook the very foundations of our national life, and though today it is quiescent and its echoes are almost still, it has irrevocably changed the aspect of our spiritual landscape.

However remote may be all our programmes for the future from the principles and ideals of Mahatma Gandhi, they must inevitably be permeated by the influence of these recent years which have permanently shifted the currents of our political thought and altered the direction of our political destiny.

We need today some transcendent miracle of intrepid and enduring statesmanship to enable us to remobilise, reconcile and discipline our scattered and demoralised energies to a supreme unanimous effort for the final deliverance of India from the last shackles of her political subjection; and to devise a comprehensive scheme that shall act as a natural and indispensable auxiliary of political emancipation, and include within the scope of its interest or benediction all the enterprises and endeavours that substantially contribute to the social, economic, industrial and intellectual advancement of India, consistently with the requirements of her own peculiar conditions and in accordance with the finest ideals of modern progress.

To give concrete expression to our decisions in regard to these ancillary activities, the Indian National Congress should create definite departments to be governed by groups of men and women specially qualified by their capacity or enthusiasm to administer to the vital and divergent wants of the people. The main divisions might be few but should include within their sphere of responsibility all cognate matters. To my mind it is of paramount importance to formulate a practical scheme of village reconstruction on the lines of Deshbandhu Das's dream. For this purpose we must try to enlist a large band of missionary patriots of burning zeal who set free from material wants by the pious charity of the householders of the country as in ancient times, should carry through the length and breadth of the land the beneficent evangel of self-reliance and self-respect, taking the immemorial twin symbols of the plough and the spinning-wheel as the central text of the teaching that shall liberate our unhappy peasantry from the crushing misery and terror of hunger, ignorance and disease. Closely allied to the task of village reorganisation is the task of organising the industrial workers in the crowded cities, who are so often compelled to live under conditions that degrade and brutalise them; and who, dislocated from the steadying influences of the familiar traditions and associations of the rural homes they leave in search for bread, are so hopelessly exposed to the temptations of immorality and vice. It should be our endeavour to assist in securing for them improved housing conditions, better wages and a cleaner atmosphere, and to establish an equitable and harmonious cooperation between capital and labour as a valuable joint asset of national progress.

I am appalled at the criminal apathy of our general attitude towards the urgent problem of Indian education. The surpassing evil of foreign domination has been to enslave our imagination and intellect and alienate us from the glorious tradition of our national learning. We are today no more than the futile puppets of an artificial and imitative system of education which, entirely unsuited to the special trend of our racial genius, has robbed us of our proper mental values and perspectives, and deprived us of all true initiative and originality in seeking authentic modes of self-expression. It is pre-eminently our duty towards the young generation to so recreate our educational ideals as to combine in felicitous, and fruitful alliance, all the lovely regenerating wisdom of our Eastern culture with all the highest knowledge of art and science, philosophy and civic organisation evolved by the younger peoples of the West.

In addition, I would insist with all the force at my command on including a complete course of military training as an integral part of national education. Is it not the saddest of all shameful ironies that our children whose favourite lullabies are the battle songs of Kurukshetra and whose little feet march gaily to the stirring music of Rajput ballads, should be condemned to depend for the safety of their homes, the protection of their sanctuaries, the security of their mountain and ocean frontiers, on the fidelity and strength of foreign arms? The savage Massai, the primitive Zulu, the Arab and the Afridi, the Greek and the Bulgar may all carry their tribal weapons and claim their inalienable right to defend the honour of their race, but we whose boast it is that we kindled the flame of the world's civilisation are alone defrauded of our privilege and have become cowards by compulsion, unfit to answer the world's challenge to our manhood, unable to maintain the sanctity of our homes and shrines.

Whatever the experiments recommended by the Commission now sitting to explore the avenues of military advancement for our people, it is incumbent upon the Congress to form forthwith a national militia by voluntary conscription, of which the nucleus might well be the existing volunteer organisations. Further we should also carefully consider the question of nautical as well as naval and aerial training to equip the nation for all purposes of defence against invasion or attack.

Let it not be said of us, however, that our selfish absorption in our own domestic affairs has made us oblivious to the distress and difficulty of our kinsmen in foreign lands. Our adventurous compatriots, who have crossed the seas to seek their livelihood in the dominions and colonies, have from time to time been subjected to restrictive and repressive legislation. The White Paper still stands as a reproach against our failure to redress the wrongs of the Indian community in Kenya. But in the whole chronicle of civilised legislation there has never been so cruel and relentless an outrage against humanity as is deliberately embodied in the anti-Asiatic Bill, which is calculated to exterminate the Indian community from South Africa.

Shall we not send across the seas a loving and ready response to their heart-rending cry for succour, and, through their ambassadors whom we welcome today, offer to our harassed and afflicted brothers in South Africa the assurance that India stands behind their courageous struggle to vindicate their inherent civic and human rights against the onslaught of such terrific injustice and oppression?

Never before has our duty to our kindred in foreign countries been so vividly brought home to our minds; nor the necessity of establishing a close and living contact with all their changing fortunes. We should not lose a single moment in forming an Overseas Department in the Congress manned by those who can keep themselves vigilantly aware of all the legislations and enactments that adversely or otherwise affect Indian settlers abroad.

Here my heart pleads with me to remember those sorrowful and lonely exiles, pining in strange and far off corners of the earth, consumed with a desperate hunger and nostalgia for a glimpse of their motherland, to which they cannot return because, once they sought to serve her and win her freedom in ways unrecognised by the common law. But many amongst them surely have made fullest atonement for all the fervent folly of their too impatient youth. Surely they, who have been chastened in the searching crucibles of dreadful suffering and privation, have been refashioned to become consecrated vessels of selfless service for the amelioration of the poor, the fallen, and the depressed.

I cannot conceive how we have allowed ourselves to be so heavily handicapped by the lack of an efficient publicity which is the first essential of any campaign. We should therefore take immediate steps to form a department for widespread political propaganda and for the education of the masses in all matters pertaining to their civic and social interests, to the wrongs under which they labour, the struggles in which the nation is engaged, the iniquitous and unstable fiscal and financial policies so ruinous to the prosperity of the country. I am confident that we could secure the willing cooperation of those who, otherwise prevented from active participation in public affairs, would gladly place their expert knowledge at our disposal, to advise us on questions connected with the revival of cottage industries, on commerce, railway, shipping, cooperative banking, and all other branches of development necessary for our material welfare.

The nationalist press, both vernacular and English, should be amongst the accredited channels of our propaganda; above all a reliable foreign news service should be established to transmit to all the chief centres of the world the correct version of Indian affairs, and friendly embassies appointed to foster feelings of goodwill and understanding between India and the people of other lands.

And now I approach with the utmost hesitation and regret the most baffling and most tragic of all the problems before us. I, who have dedicated my life to the dream of Hindu-Muslim unity, cannot contemplate without tears of blood the dissensions and divisions between us that rend the very fabric of my hope. I have tried to arrive at a just appreciation of the many unfortunate causes that have brought about so deep a gulf between the two communities, and tended to quicken such a sharp and importunate sense of aloofness on the part of my Muslim brothers, which, to the profound alarm and resentment of the Hindu community, manifests itself in a growing and insistent demand for separate and preferential rights and privileges in academic, official, civic and political circles of life. Though I am convinced that the principle of communal representation, whether through a joint or a separate electorate, frustrates the conception of national solidarity, I am compelled to recognise that situated as we are today, in an atmosphere so tense and dark and bitter with unreasoning communal jealousy, suspicion, fear, distrust and hatred, it is not possible to reach any satisfactory or abiding readjustment without the most earnest and patient collaboration between Hindu and Muslim statesmen of undeniable patriotism to whom we should entrust the delicate and difficult task of seeking some sovereign remedy for so devastating a disease.

I beseech my Hindu brothers to rise to the height of their traditional tolerance which is the basic glory of our Vedic faith and try to comprehend how intense and far-reaching a reality is the brotherhood of Islam, which constrains seventy million of Indian Mussalmans to share with breathless misery the misfortunes that are so swiftly overtaking the Islamic countries and crushing them under the heel of the military despotism of foreign power.

In their turn I would implore my Muslim comrades not to permit their preoccupation with the sorrows of Syria, Egypt, Iraq and Arabia; to obliterate the consciousness of their supreme duty to India their motherland, who must always have the first claim upon their devotion and allegiance.

If Hindus and Mussalmans would both learn to practise the divine qualities of mutual forbearance and accord to one another perfect liberty of worship and modes of living, without the tyranny of fanatical interruptions of one another's appointed rituals and sacrifices, if they would but learn to revere the beauty of each other's creeds and the splendour of each other's civilisations, if the women of the two communities would but join together in the intimate friendship of their common sisterhood, and nurture their children in an atmosphere of mutual sweetness and harmony, how near we should come to the fulfilment of our hearts' desire!

We should grossly fail in our duty to our neighbours were we to omit to try and foster cordial ties of sympathy and trust between ourselves and the princes and the people of the great Indian states, scrupulously refraining from all interference in their internal concerns but always ready to serve in their wider interests.

Nor can we afford to ignore the claims of the Frontier Provinces, which, owing to their peculiar geographical and strategic position on the map, are governed by a form of perpetual martial law. We should render them all the assistance in our power, in their efforts to obtain the normal civic and social amenities which are so abundantly enjoyed by their sister provinces.

These are some of the accessory features of our work. The real function however of the Indian National Congress is the speedy attainment of Swaraj.

There is a large and influential section of Congressmen who still cling with touching and jealous loyalty to the orthodox creed of non-cooperation. Sternly refusing to take cognisance of legislative bodies they devote themselves to the pursuit of

Mahatma Gandhi's benevolent mission, propagating the cult of the spinning-wheel and ministering to the lowly and pitiful outcastes of our society whom, in our arrogance, we have so long deprived of their elementary human rights.

Today, therefore, the Swaraj Party with its highly disciplined organisation and its striking record of success is the only political body within the Congress engaged in actual combat with bureaucratic authority. Is it not in this crucial hour the unmistakable duty of all the other political parties in the country, irrespective of their particular labels and particular beliefs, to return to the Congress, which invites them with open doors, and coalesce all their divided energies and talents in devising a common programme of action in pursuance of a common goal?

All of them have openly acknowledged that the Reforms of 1919 which were to have created a new era of progress have proved nothing but a mirage and the powers they professed to transfer to the people nothing but a deceptive myth. All of them, surely, are tacitly agreed upon some common maximum of the wrongs they are still prepared to endure, some common minimum of the rights they are now determined to enforce. And whatever be my own personal conviction, they, at all events, are all in favour at least as an initial form of self-government, of the ideal of Dominion Status, so elaborately ex-pounded in the Commonwealth of India Bill, and more succinctly and emphatically embodied in the national demand which has been endorsed by the representatives of all political schools in the Legislative Assembly. Below the limits of that demand the Indian nation cannot descend without irretrievable damage to its dignity and self-respect. It is now for the Government to make the responsive gesture that shall decide our future attitude. If the response be sincere and magnanimous, with ample guarantees of goodwill and good faith on its part, it will necessitate an immediate revision of our present policy. But if by the end of the Spring Sessions we receive no answer or an answer that evades the real issues, or proves unworthy of our acceptance, the National Congress must clearly issue a mandate to all those who come within its sphere to vacate their seats in the Central and Provincial Legislatures and inaugurate from Kailash to Kanyakumari, from the Indus to the Brahmaputra an untiring and dynamic campaign to arouse, consolidate, educate and prepare the Indian people for all the progressive and ultimate stages of our united struggle and teach them that no sacrifice is too heavy, no suffering too great, no martyrdom too terrible, that enables us to redeem our Mother from the unspeakable dishonour of her bondage, and bequeath to our children an imperishable legacy of Peace.

In the battle for liberty, fear is the one unforgivable treachery and despair, the one unforgivable sin.

With palms uplifted in ardent supplication, I pray that, to us, in our coming hour of travail, may be granted in sufficient measure an invincible faith and an inflexible courage, and that He in whose name we begin our labours today will in the hour of our triumph keep us humble and in the beautiful words of our ancient invocation.

> Lead us out of the Unreal into the Real,
> Out of the Darkness into the Light,
> Out of Death into Immortality.

PRESIDENTIAL ADDRESS

Asian Relations Conference

Pandit Nehru's speech was followed by Sarojini Naidu's presidential address. Rising amidst continued cheering and hailing the audience as 'Comrades and Kindred of Asia' she said:

You will wonder why a mere woman has been chosen to occupy the great place of honour today. The answer is simple. India has always honoured her women. I am so deeply moved when I behold this marvellous gathering of the nations of Asia, that almost, but only almost, I am stricken dumb. It takes so much to strike a woman dumb. My brother and leader and the hero of India, Pandit Jawaharlal Nehru, has said all that could be said, and said it beautifully. I can only paraphrase and re-echo in my own poor manner the great thoughts that he has put into words in welcoming you today.

I wonder how many of you who have come journeying across steep mountain passes, floating on the vast bosom of many-coloured seas, riding amid the clouds of dawn and darkness realise that we stand today, here and now, not only in the heart of Asia, but the very core and centre of India's heart. This *Purana Qila*, this historic ruin, the broken arches—what do they signify? They signify the dawn of history, the history of many forgotten ages. And they also symbolise the dawn of a new era beckoning today. Here was the capital of Hindu supremacy many centuries ago, that now lives only in song and legend. Here are monuments raised by those who came to conquer, but stayed to become children of the soil. The mosque of Sher Shah is here. Other monuments are here. The dreamer, the great dreamer, Humayun, gazing at the stars used to sit up at his watch tower and dream of the destiny of unborn ages. History is in every stone, history sleeps hidden but living in every acre, in every patch of the soil of Hindustan. Kings have walked here, warriors have walked there, where little children are playing today. But today, because it is not the time for children's play, we have summoned you to a great gathering of the nations of Asia to make a great declaration for the future of Asia. We may have our own movements of freedom, but we have come here to take an indestructible pledge of the unity of Asia so that the world in ruin could be redeemed from sorrow, unhappiness, exploitation, misery, poverty, ignorance, disaster and death.

What has Asia always stood for? We have read so many things about the deeds of Asia, cruel, barbarous—it all depends upon who writes our history. But there is one thing—it is the most authentic feature of this great continent—that beckons every nation of Asia to come and partake of the common ideal of peace—not the peace of negation, not the peace of surrender, not the peace of coward, not the peace of the dying, not the peace of the dead, but the peace, militant, dynamic, creative, of the human spirit which exalts. Pandit Jawaharlal Nehru has told us of the human spirit being but a demonstration of the renaissance of the spirit of Asia. Has human spirit ever died? Human spirit may sometimes be defeated, but it can never die. But today, across the length and breadth of our great continent, in the small, far off, inaccessible places and mountains, the little known hamlets in the far off clime of Asia, these little mountain heights of Tibet, in the great, mysterious country known as China, in that exquisitely poetic country known as Iran, that great country known as Afghanistan, in that country of splendid tradition known as

Egypt—in all those and other countries, great and small, there is today a spirit that says "we are alive." We had been buried for centuries, we had forgotten the splendours of our past, the teachings of our ancestors, the writings of our poets, the banners of our heroes. We had forgotten them for a little while and we believed that we were dead. But when the spring time calls to us, the heart throbs.

Is there any man so dead, so deeply buried in the tomb that his heart does not beat to the calls of the birds of spring time? Is there anyone so dead, whose spirit is not enchanted—whether living or dying—by the first fragrance and first blossoms of the spring? It stirs such people as are divided from one another, as the Kashmiri and the Telugu—the Kashmiri Pandit Jawaharlal Nehru, and the gentleman of Andhra *desa* whom I have married. Spring time has no date. It does not confine itself to the flowering of trees and singing of birds; it depends upon the attitude to life and the approach to life.

And what will Asia do with her renaissance? Will she arm herself for battles to conquer, to annex and exploit, or rather, will she forge new weapons and refashion her armoury in accordance with ancient ideals, as soldiers of peace and missionaries of love? My great and beloved leader, Mahatma Gandhi, has taught us that not through bitterness and hate, not through anger and strife, but through compassion, love and forgiveness shall the world be redeemed. And this is not a new message. It is an old message of Asia reinforced by the experience, adventure, suffering and hope of the Indian people. By love and not by hate shall the world be redeemed.

Therefore, India has beckoned to her kindred of Asia to come and understand the new message and hope of the whole world. When we started the idea of this Conference, I remember with amusement and pain a variety of emotions that emerged from the unexpressed questions that were looked at, because they were not spoken. 'What is this? An Asian bloc against Europe? A conspiracy of Asian people against Western civilisation?' I said how great a compliment it is to one poor woman who signs a humble invitation—that she should symbolise red to centuries of Western civilisation! I thought of all the countries whose names thrilled me when I was small. What was the picture that came before my eyes when I thought of those names? China, Egypt, Mongolia, Afghanistan, Persia and all those other countries—Bali with its great sculpture and painting, the Japanese dancers with their fingers, Egypt mysterious with the pyramids of the Pharaohs, and now a modern nation. I still do not know the physical position of many countries, whether they are contiguous or whether they are divided. But one thing I know—that mountain passes and riverways of the world cannot divide the heart of Asia. The differences of tongue, of costumes, customs, food, ways of enjoyment—all those things that make for the social life of people—and it seems so curious in many ways—cannot divide the heart of Asia. Rather, the great diversity of Asian culture has cemented the unity of the Asian people. Who wants a monotonous culture? Who wants a uniform culture? Who wants a colourless culture? Who wants one country to imitate another? It is rather the richness and variety, the diversity and sometimes the conflict of one culture with another that is the guarantee and prophecy of a real, abiding and dynamic unity. And that is what we want, what he wants—Pandit Jawaharlal Nehru—and what Mahatma Gandhi wants, what my people who speak for the Indian nation want. Diversity of culture, unity of heart and pursuit; because Asia must bring to the pool its own contribution, its own particular mode of life, its own particular vision of life, its own approach to life. And it is all these varieties of human experience that make for a great civilisation.

India is not a civilisation of one unit. India today is not a Hindu India of the Vedic ages. My ancestors, the ancestors of Pandit Nehru, were influenced by the streams that came from western Asia, the streams that came with all their depths from the Arab world, the great democratic ideals that came through the Arab traders of India—all those influenced our introspective philosophy, taught us the great ideal of brotherhood and enriched the dreams of our own philosophers. And you have a great philosopher sitting there, Sir S. Radhakrishnan, and I hope he is nodding his head at what I am saying. The Western stream of culture that came with the message of the Prophet, the great democratic ideal became in time an inalienable part of our national culture. Those streams of culture came and fed as tributaries the vast ocean of India. The great band that fled from Persia, the Chinese travellers that came painfully and piously across the mountain groups, the great scholars that came from all over, from across the seas and the wastes, to learn at various schools in India—all these came as seekers of truth. Even those who came to spoil, plunder and loot brought with them—in spite of themselves, unawares—the gifts of civilisation and became part of Indian life and culture. So, today if India, my India, has issued an invitation and summoned the people of the east and west of Asia to come to this great gathering, has she—who has been the custodian of our own cultures as of yours, one of the great achievements of Asia—not the right to do so? Did we not in our own turn send to southeast Asia the great treasure of ours in India, Gautama Buddha—the teaching of peace? Did we not send to China, to Japan, to Ceylon, to Burma, the influence, philosophy and wisdom of India and the teachings of Gautama Buddha? Did we not send to Babylon, to Egypt, to the furthermost corners of Asia with our merchandise, the treasure of our arts, the teachings of our literature, the wisdom of our sages and the splendour of our ideals? Then did we not take willingly and gladly, whether from friend or foe, from any part of the world—from friend or foe I repeat—all that knowledge would give, for we have never been a people so limited in our vision that we said, 'this knowledge belongs to us; that knowledge does not belong to us.' We have always said that knowledge is universal and therefore we shall disseminate our knowledge and render it back to the world, because India has been the universal custodian of many influences which other nations had created but had forgotten.

I bid you welcome to my Mother's Home. I bid you welcome so that once more you may re-remember your ancient greatness and so that you and we together may dream a common dream of our Asia and how our Asia can redeem the world. Asia shall not be a country of enemies. Asia should be a country of fellowship of the world. How should you and I, speaking different tongues and bringing interpreters, sufficiently understand one another, may I ask, to make a common charter for the Asian people for their freedom and the freedom of the world? I have never found that a lack of vocabulary, a lack of dictionary knowledge of words, ever prevented true understanding between hearts that were agreed and were ready to understand and cooperate.

Therefore, we are at the first spring time of the world; when the birds sing; when waters smile at the sight of the sun; when flowers blossom and young brides put flowers on their hair and children make garlands of them; and when you remember all those who have gone before. I bid you, arise from your grave; I bid you, become the bard of the eternal spring time; I bid you, arise and say, 'There is no death, there shall be no death for those who move onward, united in a spirit of undefeatable hope and courage.' We shall move together, the people of Asia, undefeated by disaster and not discouraged by anything that may befall other people. It is part of my creed and tradition, part of my heritage to believe that nothing can die that is good. When my father who was one of the great men of the world was about to die, his last words to young friends were, 'There is no birth, there is no death, there is only the spirit seeking evolution in higher and higher stages of life.' That is the history of India, that is the history of Asia. And I bid you, whatever your creed, whatever your faith, whatever your tongue, remember there is no birth, there is no death; we move onward and onward, higher and higher till we attain the stars. Let us move on to the stars. Who can hamper our ascent? Who will bid us and say, 'halt, thus far and no further?' No. The birds have said, 'Why do you cry for the moon?' We do not cry for the moon. We pluck it from the skies and wear it upon the diadem of Asia's freedom.

MY FATHER, DO NOT REST!

Homage to Mahatma Gandhi on His Death

Like Christ of old on the third day he has risen again in answer to the cry of his people and the call of the world for the continuance of his guidance, his love, his service and inspiration. And while we all mourn, those who loved him, knew him personally, and those to whom his name was but a miracle and a legend, though we are all full of tears and though we are full of sorrow on this third day when he has risen from his own ashes, I feel that sorrow is out of place and tears become a blasphemy. How can he die, who through his life and conduct and sacrifice, who through his love and courage and faith has taught the world that the spirit matters, not the flesh, that the spirit has the power greater than the powers of the combined armies of the earth, combined armies of the ages? He was small, frail, without money, without even the full complement of garment to cover his body, not owning even as much earth as might be held on the point of a needle, how was he so much stronger than the forces of violence, the might of empires and the grandeur of embattled forces in the world? Why was it that this little man, this tiny man, this man with a child's body, this man so ascetic, living on the verge of starvation by choice so as to be more in harmony with the life of the poor, how was it that he exercised over the entire world, of those who revered him and those who hated him, such power as emperors could never wield?

It was because he did not care for applause; he did not care for censure. He only cared for the path of righteousness. He cared only for the ideals that he preached and practised. And in the midst of the most terrible disasters caused by violence and greed of men, when the abuse of the world was heaped up like dead leaves, dead flowers on battlefields, his faith never swerved in his ideal of non-violence. He believed that though the whole world slaughter itself and the whole world's blood be shed, still his non-violence would be the authentic foundation of the new civilisation of the world and he believed that he who seeks his life shall lose it and he who loses his life shall find it.

His first fast in 1924 with which I associated was for the cause of Hindu-Muslim unity. It had the sympathy of the entire nation. His last fast was also for the cause of Hindu-Muslim unity, but the whole nation was not with him in that fast. It had grown so divided, it had grown so bitter, it had grown so full of hate and suspicion, it had grown so untrue towards the tenets of the various creeds in this country that it was only a section of those who understood the Mahatma, who realised the meaning of that fast. It was very evident that the nation was divided in its loyalty to him in the fast. It was very evident that it was not any community but his that disapproved so violently and showed its anger and resentment in such a dastardly fashion. Alas for the Hindu community, that the greatest Hindu of them all, the only Hindu of our age who was so absolutely and unswervingly true to the doctrine, to the ideals, the philosophy of Hinduism should have been slain by the hand of a Hindu! That indeed, that indeed is almost the epitaph of the Hindu faith that the hand of a Hindu in the name of Hindu rights and a Hindu world should sacrifice the noblest of them all. But it does not matter. It is a personal grief, that is, loss, day in and day out, year in and year out, for many of us who cannot forget, because for more than 30 years some of us have been so closely associated with him that our lives and his life were an integral part of one another. Some of us are indeed dead to the faith; some of us indeed have had vivisection performed on us by his death, because fibres of our being, because our muscles, veins and heart and blood were all intertwined with his life.

But, as I say, it would be the act of faithless deserters if we were to yield to despair. If we were indeed to believe that he is dead, if we were to believe that all is lost, because he has gone, of what avail would be our love and our faith? Of what avail would be our loyalty to him if we dare to believe that all is lost because his body is gone from our midst? Are we not there, his heirs, his spiritual descendants, the legatees of his great ideals, successors of his great work? Are we not there to implement that work and enhance it and enrich and make greater achievements by joint efforts than he could have made singly? Therefore, I say the time is over for private sorrow.

The time is over for beating of breasts and tearing of hair. The time is here and now when we stand up and say, 'We take up the challenge!' to those who defied Mahatma Gandhi. We are his living symbols. We are his soldiers. We are the carriers of his banner before an embattled world. Our banner is truth. Our shield is non-violence. Our sword is a sword of the spirit that conquers without blood. Let the people of India rise up and wipe their tears, rise up and still their sobs, rise up and be full of hope and full of cheer. Let us borrow from him, why borrow, he has handed it to us, the radiance of his own personality, the glory of his own courage, the magnificent epic of his character.

Shall we not follow in the footsteps of our master? Shall we not obey the mandates of our father? Shall not we, his soldiers, carry his battle to triumph? Shall we not give to the world the completed message of Mahatma Gandhi? Though his voice will not speak again, have we not a million, million voices to bear his message to the world, not only to this world, to our contemporaries, but to the world generation after generation? Shall sacrifice be in vain? Shall his blood be shed for futile purposes of mourning? Or, shall we not use that blood as a *tilak* on our foreheads, the emblem of his legion of peace-loving soldiers to save the world? Here and now, here and now, I for one before the world that listens to my quivering voice pledge myself and you, as I pledged myself more than 30 years ago, to the service of the undying Mahatma.

What is death? My own father, dying, just before his death with the premonition of death on him, said: 'There is no birth. There is no death. There is only the soul seeking higher and higher stages of truth.' Mahatma Gandhi who lived for truth in this world has been translated, though by the hand of an assassin, to a higher stage of the truth which he sought. Shall we not take up his place? Shall not our united strength be strong enough to preach and practise his great message for the world? I am here one of the lowliest of his soldiers, but along with me I know that there are his beloved disciples like Jawaharlal Nehru, and his trusted followers and friends like Vallabhbhai Patel, and Rajendra Babu, who was like St. John in the bosom of Christ, and those others of his associates who at a moment's notice flew from all ends of India to make their last homage at his feet. Shall we not all take up his message and fulfil it? I used to wonder very often during his many fasts in which I was privileged to serve him, to solace him, to make him laugh, because he wanted the tonic laughter of his friends—I used to wonder, supposing he died in Sevagram, supposing he died in Noakhali, supposing he died in some far off place, how should we reach him?

It is therefore right and appropriate that he died in the city of kings, in the ancient site of the old Hindu empires, in the site on which was built the glory of the Moghuls, in this place that he made India's capital wresting it from foreign hands, it is right that he died in Delhi; it is right that his cremation took place in the midst of the dead kings who are buried in Delhi, for he was the kingliest of all kings. And it is right also that he who was the apostle of peace should have been taken to the cremation ground with all the honours of a great warrior; far greater than all warriors, who led armies to battle was this little man, the bravest, the most triumphant of all. Delhi is not only today historically the Delhi of seven kingdoms; it has become the centre and the sanctuary of the greatest revolutionary who emancipated his enslaved country from foreign bondage and gave to it its freedom and its flag.

May the soul of my master, my leader, my father rest not in peace, not in peace, but let his ashes be so dynamically alive that the charred ashes of the sandalwood, let the powder of his bones be so charged with life and inspiration that the whole of India will after his death be revitalised into the reality of freedom.

My father, do not rest. Do not allow us to rest. Keep us to our pledge. Give us strength to fulfil our promise, your heirs, your descendants, your stewards, the guardians of your dreams, the fulfillers of India's destiny. You, whose life was so powerful, make it so powerful—in your death. Far from mortality you have passed mortality by a supreme martyrdom in the cause most dear to you.

CONVOCATION REMARKS

PANDIT JAWAHARLAL NEHRU

Now how shall I describe you? Crusader, poet, statesman, dreamer, political and spiritual heir to our beloved Mahatma Gandhi, you who have raised the stature of India to the very stars, you who are not only our undoubted leader, but also our playmate and our friend, and my brother and my son. I hope that you will some day find leisure and pleasure to write another book, like your *Autobiography* and your *Discovery of India*, in which you will yearn no longer, but say, 'I have fulfilled my destiny; India has fulfilled her destiny.'

MAULANA ABUL KALAM AZAD

I am sorry that my old friend and colleague and leader, Abul Kalam Azad, is not here to take this diploma. You, sir, (addressing the Dean of the Faculty of Arts) have enumerated a long list of virtues and gifts of this scholar. But I think it is enough to say that in the whole length and breadth of India, it would be difficult to find a patriot so staunch, a believer in his idealism so unyielding, a man so steeped in learning, a man so burning with the desire for freedom, a man so free from the virus of that awful, that terrible, communalism that has almost destroyed our country, one of the greatest scholars in Asia, one of the greatest thinkers in India, one of the greatest writers in any continent. In absentia, I am proud to confer this degree on Maulana Abul Kalam Azad.

PROFESSOR S. RADHAKRISHNAN

Do philosophers need praise? No. Then I accord you that praise. I was travelling in Africa and later in America. One of the first questions I was asked was, 'Do you know Radhakrishnan?' These were the students that had been to Oxford and heard your speeches, and also American scholars at whose universities you had interpreted the golden wisdom of ancient India. Only yesterday we were thrilled by your words of magic, so gracious that not a single heart was left untouched. You have earned much praise and much distinction. You have been a great ambassador of Indian genius abroad. But I may mention the most golden of your gifts, which lightens your work and enchants your activities, and that is, your gift of humour. I know many people talk of Mahatmaji's many gifts. But to me the climax of all his greatness was his sense of humour, which meant understanding, compassion, kindliness and friendliness towards humanity. I am very proud that in addition to all your great gifts of intellect, you have the delightful, endearing quality of humour, which makes you not only a philosopher, but also a companion, a comrade and a friend. May I give you this scrap of paper as a token of our admiration for your gifts?

DR SAMPURNANAND

I am sorry that my Education Minister has not come here today. I do not think that in any province of free India there is a Minister who has a greater sense of responsibility or fulfils his duty within the limitations of possibilities. I wish very much that the students, who are exhibiting a very misplaced sense of humour at this moment, would realise the difficulties of administering so great a province as the United Provinces and would realise that, night and day, Sampurnanandji works for the welfare of the students of this province. No students, nor those who incite them, have a right not to believe that their Ministers are doing their utmost, and that he, Sampurnanandji, who is an intellectual of the intellectuals, a man of letters (at this stage a section of the students started shouting and addressing them Her Excellency said: 'You will keep quiet while I am speaking.' Then followed complete silence), a man honoured for his intellectual integrity, would not do his best for the young students of the country on whom lies the future destiny of India. Therefore I ask you to accord with me a tribute of praise to Sampurnanandji, our Education Minister.

DR RADHA KUMUD MOOKERJI

Dr Mookerji, you are a fortunate person. I have brothers also, but nobody has called me 'my learned sister'. I have not been praised by any member of my family, but you are a very lucky man. You know for how many years you and I have been friends and how you have been very kind and presented me with your writings and also how much I have appreciated them. I am not going to enter into any learned discourse on your writings, for they are almost too learned for me to understand sometimes. But I have realised what scholarship can mean—what patient, devoted scholarship can mean—year in and year out working amidst tremendous difficulties and often without proper appreciation. But the knowledge you have imparted to your own countrymen and to the people abroad is, I think, for you a sufficient reward, even if that was the only reward. But you have a place among the scholars of the world where Indian history is concerned. I have very great pleasure in giving you this Diploma and in endorsing all that your learned brother said about, his learned brother.

PANDIT HAZARI PRASAD DWIVEDI

Panditji, you have enriched Hindi literature in the days when Hindi was not so fashionable as it is going to be now. So you have earned double praise because you are one of the pioneers of Hindi literature. You are one of those who caused the renaissance of Hindi, and now, today, you are in the proud position of realising that you have helped to make Hindi the national language. I am praising you for your work in Hindi, and if you become a teacher in Hindi, I like a teacher like you. Please do not accept any other job, but teach me how to read and how to write the beautiful language that law, custom, sentiment and tradition have made the national language of India.

PROFESSOR W. SIERPINSKI

Sir, you may or may not understand the gist of what I am going to say to you, but we honour you for being a great mathematician. I understand that you lectured here in Polish the other day and it was translated into English for this illiterate audience. But in the years to come we shall learn Polish as well as other languages to cement our international fellowship. But apart from your own knowledge and talent and fame, I think I may be bold enough to say that the whole audience here honours in you and through you the great genius of Poland. I hope whatever vicissitudes may befall her, brave Poland will for ever continue to contribute to the culture and knowledge of the world.

PROFESSOR MEGHNAD SAHA

Dr Saha, you know that you are young enough for me to have followed your career. I and scientists who are of my age watched you with great pride from the early days when you began your work in India. You are among those who have brought honour to India. Services are of so many kinds; political service, social service, all kinds of services; but knowledge is the greatest of all services, in accordance with Indian genius. He who brings knowledge brings life. He who uses knowledge for the enrichment of the nation brings dignity to the nation. I am proud that it is my privilege to confer this one superfluous Degree on you who have already won so many honorary degrees like other leaders. I hope that I shall live to see the day when you acquire greater and greater honours for greater and greater work.

PROFESSOR K.S. KRISHNAN

It is less than a month ago, Dr Krishnan, that I gave you a very valuable piece of advice, which I hope you have taken to heart. You have had so much praise in your life that I think my piece of advice was very timely and very practical. Shall I tell them (the audience) what it was? You have done wonderful work for many years. You have laboured for science with a disinterested love, and with great ability, and your work has brought you great fame. I am too stupid to understand all the learned implications of your work. But I have seen with dismay as well as pride your one great fault, and that is, you are too modest and too unassuming; and in the cause of science you must be arrogant! Do not believe that being assertive in science is being conceited yourself. You have a gift to the world; give it with pride and give it with certainty. Your work will live I know. I am not so stupid as not to know that. And I wish you great success in the new work which you have undertaken and which I believe will bring great glory to India. But do not let me have to remind you a second time to hold up your chin and face the world, because you have brought a message for the world.

SIR SHANTI SWARUP BHATNAGAR

I have a grouse against you. How dare you become a rival to me by writing poetry? As if it is not enough that you have conquered a large part of the scientific world, must you also invade my territory? Anyhow, I should not grudge you your success in poetry, although you have not read to me a single poem of yours. But we have all known your work. I have known it since your student days and I have literally seen you grow from strength to strength and achieve distinction after distinction. I owe you personally a great debt, which I would like to pay you in words in public. That is the great help you gave to me and the organisers of the first Asian Cultural Conference, leaving aside your most important scientific work. Because of your help, the conference was supremely successful. Men who have so much work to do in their own field are not always so generous in giving their personal help. But your knowledge, your learning and your interests are so wide that you could afford the leisure to help. I know this new department of scientific research, of which the Prime Minister is the head, is going to mean a great deal to India. I know that every item of work that you undertake will meet with inspired success. It will not be your success, but it will be an asset to the country. May I present to you this Diploma.

PROFESSOR H. J. BHABHA

Now what am I to say about you, Homi Bhabha? For three generations I have known your family, your grandfather and your grandmother, then your mother and father, and now you, and I do not know, if I live long, how many generations of Bhabhas I will see. When you were a school boy, your father, who was really a very great friend of mine, used to tell me all about you. When you went to Cambridge and became so illustrious, I was amazed and asked your father, 'Well, Jehanghir, how did you manage to produce such a brilliant son?' It is very refreshing and very inspiring to the people of my generation, the grandmother generation, to see how India has progressed. She is free today, but you are one of those whose knowledge and skill in science has brought glory to her. You are today in a position when you can fulfil your own genius. The other day someone said that scientists are so narrow and so self-centred that they work in water-tight compartments. But Sir Shanti Swarup Bhatnagar is a poet and you are an artist. And you are a true artist. Less than a month ago (addressing the audience) he produced a picture of me. Though I do not praise myself, I do praise his talent. He made me look as ugly as I am. You are young and youth is the greatest of all gifts. I look upon you as one of those who have far to go and to raise the country and to let the country realise that knowledge is power and to use knowledge in the service of humanity is the beginning of wisdom. May this carry the grandmother's blessings to you.

PROFESSOR LAKSHMANASWAMI MUDALIAR

I am struck dumb now. What more have I to say about you? You are too great a senior to me to be in a position to give me good advice. You have blessed so many thousands of people in distress. There is hardly a home in southern India that has not in one way or another to bless you. You have used your knowledge for the service of humanity and you have rendered this service gladly, proudly and affectionately, especially to women and children and thus have helped in preserving many a happy home. Now you have undertaken the great responsibility of guiding the affairs of your University. It is seldom that a man of one profession has gifts equal to another vocation in life; but the students of the Madras Presidency have realised your great gifts and your worth. You have so raised the status of Vice-Chancellors by your occupation of that position that you have become, if I may say so without disrespect to anybody, almost an exemplar for other Vice-Chancellors to emulate. I am not an academician. I have no degrees. I have very little education. But when I utter words, Dr Mudaliar, they are words of sincerity, and with utmost sincerity I pay you a tribute of praise for the great things you have done during the past so many years in the service of your country. The whole country will need your services, more and more young people, more and more women and children. I know you can impart a new kind of knowledge to your pupils that will enable them to guide the health of the country not only physically, but also mentally and morally. May I offer you this Diploma?

DR KAILAS NATH KATJU

My fellow-Governor, when you arrived this morning, you said to me, 'I hear that some of the most learned men in India are staying with you. I do not know why I have been asked. They are getting honorary degrees for good reasons, but I am only a joker.' Well, if you are a joker, I am a joker too. The Governors at present are only jokers.

You have always been praised as a lawyer, as a man of great intellectual gifts. But lately I am hearing so much about you from men and women who have visited Calcutta for one reason or another and for whom you have offered hospitality. They are also attracted by your other gifts, by just those qualities that have just been enumerated—by your kindliness, your humility and unassuming charm and by the background of your knowledge which is not always known. You are known as a lawyer; you are known as an administrator, but are you known for some of those things which are so deep in you? For your mystic qualities, for your inner spiritual convictions, for your ideals? During the few days that I spent with you in your terrible palace in Calcutta, in your enormous palace, not fit for simple people like me, in the few moments you could spare to have conversation with us,

I discovered just those qualities in you which are not always known in your own native province, for you are too good a lawyer to mystify your other qualities. But in that land of mysticism, my original homeland, your mysticism has come to the fore. I do not know what special value this diploma will have for you, excepting as a symbol of our affection, respect and honour. But take it from us who belong to your province—not your province, but now my province. And believe it or not, all of us are very proud of you for your more explicit as well as your implicit qualities. And may you live long and keep peace and harmony in your province of Bengal and let your province be as nice as my province, the United Provinces.

PANDIT GOVIND BALLABH PANT

Now if I begin praising my Premier, it will be like offering bribery and corruption. But I am not afraid, because he has given me all that he could and I know he would be only too glad if he could do more. There is nothing more that I demand of him, excepting that he continue to be the Premier of the United Provinces for many, many years to come. All of you know, or should know, that had it not been for his great mental as well as physical stature, your province—my province—would not have slept in peace, as it does today. At a most critical time when the passions of men and women had been roused and when in some parts of the country they were suffering mutual recriminations, reprisals, death and destruction, this man stood like a light-house, like a wise man not yielding to the demon, and the province was safe. I watched him. I watch him still. As a matter of fact, I am my own spy. I watch his work in this province from day to day and I do not know when he sleeps. I only know he has a bath, but I do not know who allows him to sleep. I know that this man is a living symbol of vigilance for this province. As an administrator I see his worth. As a counsellor, I saw his worth for many years in the Congress Working Committee. He is one of those men who has transcended all personal, sectarian feeling, even when personal, sectarian feeling might have some vestige of excuse. It is because of his impartial courage, because he is free from personal ambition in all that matters, that he became the hero of the United Provinces. He has much vision; he has large schemes. I do not believe, and will never believe, that he discriminates between one community and another. I believe that he has an impartial outlook, and as far as events and circumstances today will permit of any administrator redeeming his pledges to the people, he has tried to do so, and I hope that the people of the United Provinces will realise what a jewel of a Premier we have.

He is a lawyer of course. Many people are lawyers, and there are many Prime Ministers, but he is Govind Ballabh Pant and that is the highest tribute that he could have.

SHAIKH MOHAMMAD ABDULLAH

I am glad that you are the last person on whom I am conferring the Degree. My throat is bad; my limbs are unsteady. But, Sher-e-Kashmir, how am I going to greet you? Your deeds have brought you world fame. Your courage has been like a beacon fire. Your faith has been a banner. I am glad that we, who have so far been distributing diplomas on administrators, scientists, lawyers and poets, are also giving a diploma to one whose science and art is concentrated patriotism, exemplified and expressed in freedom form. Life is not only academic knowledge; life is the art of knowing how to live, how to die and how not to die. During the many years I have known you, I have seen you in various aspects. But now, when you are still a young man, you have brought your country to the forefront in the estimation of the world and you have drawn the sympathy of all free nations towards you. May you in the near future be rewarded for all the suffering and pain through which you and your people have passed, and the next time you are honoured at a convocation in any one of our universities in the United Provinces, may I hope that I shall say, 'Sher-e-Kashmir Zindabad; Kashmir Zindabad.' May I now give you this Diploma not only as a token of recognition of your merits by the University of Lucknow, but also as a token of appreciation and homage of the entire country for you, Sher-e-Kashmir.

SELECT BIBLIOGRAPHY AND WORKS CITED

BIBLIOGRAPHICAL GUIDES

A bibliography on Sarojini Naidu compiled by Sarala Magal and Fatima Sarvar. Unpublished, but available in xerox at the Sarojini Naidu Memorial Museum and Trust, Hyderabad.

Singh, Amritjit, Rajiva Verma, and Irene Joshi, eds. *Indian Literature in English, 1827-1979: A Guide to Information Sources*. Detroit: Gale Research Company, 1981.

Also see the annual listings on Indian English literature in *Journal of Commonwealth Literature* and *Indian Literature*.

PRIMARY WORKS (in chronological order)

Poetry

Mehir Muneer: A Poem in Three Cantos by a Brahmin Girl. Madras: Srinivasa, Varadachari and Co, 1893.

Songs by Miss S. Chattopadhyaya. Hyderabad: for private circulation, 1896.

The Golden Threshold. Introd. Arthur Symons. London: Heinemann, 1905.

The Bird of Time: Songs of Life, Death and the Spring. Introd. Edmund Gosse. London: Heinemann, 1912.

The Broken Wing: Songs of Love, Death and the Spring, 1915-1916. London: Heinemann, 1917.

The Sceptred Flute: Songs of India. New York: Dodd, Mead and Co., 1928; Indian ed., Allahabad: Kitabistan, 1943, 1946, 1958, 1979.

Select Poems. Ed. H.G. Dalway Turnbull. Calcutta: Oxford University Press, 1930.

The Feather of the Dawn. Ed. Padmaja Naidu. Bombay: Asia Publishing House, 1961.

Prose
Gokhale the Man. (Booklet). Hyderabad: A.V. Pillai and Sons, 1915.
The Soul of India. (Booklet). Madras: Ganesh and Co, 1917; 2nd. ed., Madras: The Cambridge Press, 1919.
Speeches and Writings of Sarojini Naidu. Ed. G. A. Natesan. Madras: Natesan, 1918; 2nd. ed., 1921; 3rd ed., 1925.
Ideals of Islam. (Booklet). Dacca: Matri Bhandar, 1921.
Presidential Address Delivered at the 40th National Congress. (Pamphlet). Kanpur: Reception Committee of the Indian National Congress, 1925.

Letters
Paranjape, Makarand, ed. *Sarojini Naidu: Selected Letters, 1890s-1940s.* New Delhi: Kali for Women, 1996.

SECONDARY WORKS
Biographical
Abbas, K.A. *Sarojini Naidu.* Bombay: Bharatiya Vidya Bhavan, 1980.
Ayyar, Subramanya P.A. *Sarojini Devi.* Madras: Cultural Books, 1957.
Baig, Tara Ali. *Sarojini Naidu.* New Delhi: Publications Division, 1974.
—— *Portraits of an Era.* New Delhi: Roll Books, 1986.
Chattopadhyaya, Harindranath. *Life and Myself.* Bombay: Nalanda, 1948.
Home, Amal. *Sarojini Naidu: The Poet, the Patriot, the Orator, the Woman; Reminiscences.* Calcutta: Privately published by the author, 1949.
Jha, Amarnath. *Sarojini Naidu: A Personal Homage.* Allahabad: n.p., n.d.
Natesan, G.A. and Co. *Mrs Sarojini Naidu: A Sketch of Her Life and an Appreciation of Her Books.* Madras: Natesan and Co, 1914.
National Archives. *Sarojini Naidu: Some Facets of her Personality.* Booklet New Delhi: National Archives, n.d.
Sengupta, Padmini. *Sarojini Naidu.* Bombay: Asia Publishing House, 1966.

Critical

Alexander, Meena. *The Shock of Arrival: Reflections on Postcolonial Experience*. New York: South End Books, 1996.

Anand, Mulk Raj. *The Golden Breath: Studies in Five Poets of the New India*. London: John Murray, 1933.

Basu, Lotika. *Indian Writers of English Verse*. Calcutta: University of Calcutta, 1933.

Basu, Aparna and Bharati Ray. *Women's Struggle: A History of the All India Women's Conference 1927-2002*. New Delhi: Manohar, 2003.

Bhatnagar, Ram Ratan. *Sarojini Naidu: The Poet of a Nation*. Allahabad: Kitabistan, 1954.

Bhushan, V.N. *The Peacock Lute*. Bombay: Padma Publication, 1945.

Boehmer, Elleke. "East Is East and South Is South: The Cases of Sarojini Naidu and Arundhati Roy." *Women: a Cultural Review*. 11: 1-2, 1 (April 2000): 61-70; also in *Stories of Women: Gender and Narrative in the Postcolonial Nation*. Manchester UP, 2005: 158-171.

Chatterjee, Partha. *The Nation and Its Fragments: Colonial and Postcolonial Histories*. Princeton: UP, 1993.

Chavan, Sunanda. *The Fair Voice: A Study of Indian Women Poets in English*. New Delhi: Sterling, 1984.

Cousins, James H. *The Renaissance of India*. Madras: Ganesh and Co, 1918.

Dustoor, P. E. *Sarojini Naidu and Her Poetry*. Mysore: Rao and Raghavan, 1961.

Edmonds, Paul N. *Guerdon: Song from the Album 'The Bird of Time' (Four Indian songs)/the Poem by Sarojini Naidu; the music by Paul Edmonds*. London: Enoch & Sons, c1924.

Fakhr-Rohani, M. R, ed. *Ashura Poems in English, Explained and Annotated*. Vol. 1. Karbala, Iraq: Imam Al Husain Sacred Sancturary, 1976.

Gupta, A. N. and Satish Gupta, eds. *Sarojini Naidu: Select Poems*. Bareilly: Prakash Book Depot, 1982.

Gupta, Rameshwar. *Sarojini: The Poetess*. Delhi: Doaba House, 1975.

Huggan, Graham. *The Postcolonial Exotic: Marketing the Margins*. London: Routledge, 2001.

Iyengar, K. R. Srinivasa. *Indian Writing in English*. 3rd ed. New Delhi: Sterling, 1983.

Khan, Izzat Yar. *Sarojini Naidu: The Poet*. New Delhi: S. Chand and Co, 1983.

Kotoky, P. C. *Indo-English Poetry: A Study of Sri Aurobindo and Four Others*. Gauhati: Gauhati University, 1969.

Lehmann, Lehman and Sarojini Naidu. The Golden Threshold: An Indian Song-Garland, for Four Solo Voices: (Soprano, Contalto, Tenor and Baritone), Chorus And Orchestra. London: Boosey, 1907.

Murthy, K. V. Suryanarayana. *Kohinoor in the Crown: Critical Studies in Indian English Literature*. New Delhi: Sterling, 1987.

Nagarajan, S. 'Sarojini Naidu and the Dilemma of English in India.' *Kavya Bharati*. 1 (1989): 23-43.

Nageswara Rao, G. *Hidden Eternity: A Study of the Poetry of Sarojini Naidu*. Tirupati: S.V. University, 1986.

Naik, M. K. et al. eds., *Critical Essays on Indian Writing in English*. Madras: Macmillan, 1977.

——, ed. *Perspectives on Indian Poetry in English*. New Delhi: Abhinav Publishers, 1984.

Nair, K. R. Ramachandran. *Three Indo-Anglian Poets: Henry Derozio, Toru Dutt, and Sarojini Naidu*. New Delhi: Sterling, 1987.

Narasimhaiah, C. D. *The Swan and the Eagle*. Simla: Indian Institute of Advanced Studies, 1969.

Naravane, V. S. *Sarojini Naidu: An Introduction to Her Life, Work, and Poetry*. New Delhi: Vikas, 1980.

Nicholson, D. H. S. and A. H. E. Lee. *The Oxford Book of Mystic* Verse. Oxford: The Clarendon Press, 1917.

Raghavacharyulu, D. V. K., ed. *The Two-Fold Voice: Essays on Indian Writing in English*. Guntur: Navodaya, 1971.

Rahman, Anisur. "Counterposing Exotica and Stereotype: Finding a New Context for Sarojini Naidu,' *New Bearings in English Studies*. Eds. R. Azhagarasan, Bruce Bennett et. al., New Delhi: Orient Longman, 2008.

Rajyalakshmi, P. V. *The Lyric Spring: A Study of the Poetry of Sarojini Naidu*. New Delhi: Abhinav Publishers, 1977.

Ramanujan, A. K. The Interior Landscape. Bloomington: Indiana University Press, 1967.

Sengupta, Padmini. *Sarojini Naidu*. New Delhi: Sahitya Akademi, 1981.

Shahane, V. S. and M. N. Sharma, eds. *The Flute and the Drum*. Hyderabad: Osmania University, 1980.

Shaw, Martin. *Song of the Palanquin Bearers* / [words by] Sarojini Naidu; [music by] Martin Shaw. Publisher: London : Curwen, 1917.
Tilak, Raghukul. *Sarojini Naidu: Select Poems*. New Delhi: Rama Brothers, 1981.
Verghese, C. Paul. *Problems of the Indian Creative Writer in English*. Bombay: Somaiya, 1971.
Viswanatham, K. 'The Nightingale and the 'Naughty Gal.' *Banasthali Patrika*. 12 (1969): 127-40.
Walker, Benjamin. *The Hindu World*. Vol 2. London: George Allen and Unwin, 1968.
Wilhelm, J. J. *Ezra Pound in London and Paris:* 1908-192. University Park: The Pennsylvania State University Press, 1990.

ABBREVIATIONS USED IN THE COMMENTARY

BT	*The Bird of Time*
BW	*The Broken Wing*
dt	dated
GT	*The Golden Threshold*
FD	*The Feather of the Dawn*
MGN	M. Govindarajulu Naidu
MS	Manuscript
NA	National Archives, New Delhi
NML	Nehru Memorial Library, New Delhi
PN	Padmaja Naidu
PS	*Sarojini Naidu* by Padmini Sengupta. Bombay: Asia, 1966
SF	*The Sceptred Flute*
SN	Sarojini Naidu
SWSN	*Speeches and Writings of Sarojini Naidu*, 3rd ed. Madras: Ganesh and Co, 1925

COMMENTARY

POETRY*

The selections have been made from the various books of SN's poetry arranged in chronological order. However, for selections within each collection, I have followed SN's own sub-headings and order. All footnotes are SN's and have been printed without alteration even if some of them seem quaint today.

Mehir Muneer
A printed copy of this poem is in the PN papers, NML.

The Golden Threshold
SN's first collection, published at Arthur Symons' behest, by Heinemann in London in 1905. Izaat Yar Khan could not find the MS of GT at the National Library, Calcutta; he concludes that it is lost. But several MSS are at the NA, New Delhi. Some of the poems were also set to music by Liza Lehmann and published as *The Golden Threshold: An Indian Song-Garland, for Four Solo Voices: (Soprano, Contalto, Tenor And Baritone), Chorus And Orchestra* (London: Boosey, 1907).

---

*Also see Izzat Yar Khan for commentary on several individual poems

Palanquin Bearers
MS dated 1899 in NA.
 See Anand's discussion of the poem in *The Golden Breath* 106-109.

Wandering Singers
The nostalgic longing of the singers for the chivalry of times past is typical of SN's poetry. This is an expression of the deeper conflict within the poet between the modern India of the future that she was fighting to bring into being as a national leader and the decadent Hyderabad of her childhood which appealed to her aesthetically.

Indian Weavers
Garments aren't woven at the fall of night or at midnight. SN's poetic licence makes the weavers more symbolic than realistic. The three times of day correspond not only to the three ages of childhood, youth, and old age, but also to three aspects of the biological cycle, birth, procreation and death. SN sees the human condition as a part of the larger process of nature. Again, we see how a static poetic structure, without internal debate or tension, still manages to provide a sense of balance and multifacetedness.

Corn-Grinders
The poem emphasises the continuity between nature and culture. Human sorrow is seen as continuous with and similar to sorrow in nature: the mouse, the deer, and the woman mourn the loss of their loved ones similarly. The mourning, however, is ritualistic and conventionalised; the mourner is always a female, lamenting over the death of her 'lord.' In this sense, the poem is a part of the sati cycle.

Village-Song
MS dated 1896 in NA, entitled, 'A Folk Song of the Deccan.'

Last two stanzas added on 14 December 1903. Another copy entitled 'Song,' in NA.

The choice before the adolescent girl is between two versions of romanticism. One is the more domestic and less exotic choice of a sequestered and luxurious married life; the other is the more exotic and romantic escape to the 'wild forest' where the 'fairy-folk' are calling her. Predictably, the girl chooses the latter. The poem, thus, becomes an example of SN's aesthetics of excess.

Indian Love Song
MS dated Sept 1902 in NA; original title: 'Indian Nocturne.'

Suttee
MS in NA.
See note to 'Corn-Grinders'. One of her several poems on the same topic.

Autumn Song
MS in NA. According to PS, the poem was written 'in the woodlands of Girton in Nov. 1896,' (30).

This poem, like 'Alabaster,' and 'To My Fairy Fancies' (SF: 26), and 'In the Forest,' is pensive and elegiac, lamenting the passing of youth and the loss of dreams. In that sense, it' indicates a rite of passage over the 'Golden Threshold' to the hard realities of life afterwards.

Alabaster
MS dated 30 October (1896?) in NA.

Ecstasy
MS in NA; original title: 'Song.'

The first of SN's three 'Ecstasy' poems; the other two are found in BT and 'Temple' in BW respectively.

The poem, paradoxically, can be read as expressing a death wish or desire for the cessation of experience. A one-word summary of it would be, 'Enough!'

Ode to H. H. The Nizam of Hyderabad
Two copies of MS in NA, one entitled, 'Asafia,' and the other with the present title.

Leili
MS in SN's letter to MGN, 16 May 1896, NML; also in NA.
   'Leili' means 'dark,' in Persian; the title refers to the night. The first two lines of the second stanza contains one of the most celebrated images in SN's poetry wherein she compares the moon to 'a caste-mark in the azure brown of Heaven.'

In the Forest
MS in NA.
   See commentary on 'Autumn Song'. However, the poem goes further to suggest a recovery and renewal of the struggle with sorrow.

Past and Future
MS in letter to MGN of 16 October 1896, NML.
   Each stanza contains an extended simile. The solitary and retiring hermit (stanza one), who stands for the past, contrasts with the new and unknown bride (stanza two), who is the future. The latter image is far more striking, capturing the shrinking timidity of a traditional Indian bride and the expectancy and suspense of the bridegroom, both of whom may never have seen each other before. SN plays on the idea of the *ashramas* in Hindu life; the past, it would seem, corresponds to the retreat from life, while the future is like the crossing over to the estate of being a householder.

To the God of Pain
MS in correspondence file with MGN in NML.

SN's health was delicate throughout her life. Her letters to MGN written when she was in England often complain of exhaustion and illness.

Indian Dancers
Two copies of MS in NA, one with a title, 'Eastern Dancers.'

Perhaps, the best example of SN's aesthetic of excess. Every sense is pushed to a point beyond satiety in this poem through an overabundance of lush and overripe imagery.

My Dead Dream
MS dated 13 December 1903, at NA, with the same title.

The poem is in anapestic pentameter and lends itself to a Freudean interpretation as a description of the return of the repressed.

Damayanti to Nala in the Hour of Exile
MS in NA as 'Damayanti to Nala.'

The Queen's Rival
MS dated 1905 in NA.

The story of Gulnaar (literally, 'pomegranate flower') and Feroz is Persian in origin, but is well-known and popular in India.

The Poet to Death
Two MS copies in NA, one with the title, 'The Sick Poet to Death,' dated 16 December 1903.

A poem which is best read with the Spring poems of SN. It shows the poet's zest for life as we know it, with all its transience and pain. She prefers this to any denial of the world as illusion or attempt to transcend it. Here SN contrasts with several male poet-mystics like Swami Vivekananda, Sri Ananda Acharya, or even Nissim Ezekiel who, at some point or the other, express their complete disgust with the world.

The Indian Gipsy
MS in NA.
  The subject of this poem seems to belong more to 'Folk Songs,' except that the speaker is not the gipsy, but the poet. Again, we see an attempt not to portray the gipsy realistically, but to idealise her into a symbol of raw courage and untamable primitivism. SN makes no attempt to see the gipsy as dispossessed or marginalised member of her society.

Nightfall in the City of Hyderabad
MS in NA.
  Another of the Hyderabad poems, celebrating the city's grandeur and romance. The construction of Hyderabad as an enchanted, medieval fortress-city is shaped by the rich imagery in rhyming couplets. The images emphasise the pristineness, seclusion, security, leisure, oriental sensuality and opulence of the city.

Street Cries
MS in NA.
  Another poem which has a cyclical structure. The morning, which corresponds to 'bread,' is a time of work and activity; the afternoon ('fruit'), of leisure and relaxation, and night (flowers), of love and sex. Each facet has its place and together constitute the totality of life.

To India
MS in NA.

The Royal Tombs of Golconda
MS in NA as 'The Tombs of Golconda.'

To a Buddha Seated on a Lotus
MS in NA.

The Bird of Time
PS indicates that the MS of this collection is at the National Library, Calcutta (see the facsimile of the title poem in the illustrations after page 160). Also see Khan: 'Manuscripts of all the poems in this volume, with the exception of the last poem, "Guerdon," are available at the National Library, Calcutta,' (137). Actually, two other poems, 'The Dance of Love,' and 'In the Night' are also missing from this MS. The MS has been copy edited; there are occasional minor changes, and several untitled poems have titles inserted in pencil.

Dirge
Another sati poem which apparently eroticizes the ritual stripping of the widow of all signs of matrimony, effectively desexualizing and dehumanizing her. The last stanza, however, relents from this debasement of the widow, arguing that it is better not to inflict more suffering on one who is already so distraut.

An Indian Love Song
See commentary on 'Indian Love Song' under **The Golden Threshold**. The poem depicts an inter-caste, inter-religious romance. The man is a Muslim or, at any rate someone who professes one of the Abrahamic faiths which disallow idol worship, while the woman is Hindu. SN sidesteps the communal implications of such a romance simply by asserting the supremacy of love.

At Twilight
Another poem which starts with a death wish and ends with the reaffirmation of life. See commentary on 'The Poet to Death.'

A Song in Spring
Spring is the most appropriate of seasons for love according to classical Indian aesthetics. The poems on Spring appear to draw heavily on Kalidasa and on the Indian tradition of love poetry. An appropriate landscape for love is offered in these Spring poems, reminding us of specifications of place, time, objects, seasons, and themes laid down in texts like the Tolkappiyam. See A. K. Ramanujan's *The Interior Landscape* (Bloomington: Indiana University Press, 1967).

Ecstasy
A poem of the same title appears in both GT and BW.
   The poem is a celebration of transience and temporariness. Behind it is a profound philosophical conviction in their liberating power: if everything is fleeting, why worry about sorrow and death? They too, like all natural phenomena, must be temporary. SN believes in revelling in the present because the present joy of Spring is the overwhelming reality which shuts out all remembrance of sorrow.

Songs of My City
MS in NA as 'Two Folk Songs.'
   The second part is more interesting because we see an attempt to, once again, exoticise Hyderabad as a place of oriental mystery and magic.

Spinning Song
There is a common pattern in the utterances of the three fictional speakers, Padmini, Mayura, and Saraswati. Each shifts the focus from the public celebration of the festival to a private revelling in the joy of an intimate relationship. The personal domain of love is, thus, paramount to SN; this shows her emphasis on individual rather than on the communal.

COMMENTARY   315

Hussain Sagar
MS in NA, dated May 1905, entitled, 'The Hussain Sagar Lake.'
   An artificial lake in the heart of Hyderabad.

The Faery Isle of Janjira
This is just the sort of place which held fascination for SN. Janjira, like Hyderabad, is a romantic island where, much as she is attracted by it, SN cannot stay because the larger cause of the freedom struggle ('the drum beat of destiny') calls her.

The Soul's Prayer
MS in NA entitled, 'The Soul's Progress.'

Guerdon
MS in NA. This poem was set to song by Paul N. Edmonds in a volume called Four Indian Songs (1924). Love, Truth, and Song are the slogans of the poem which, in a sense, constitute a credo of what SN wanted from life.

The Broken Wing
MS in NML.

The Temple
MS in NML.
   SN also has a long sequence of poems with the same title. The poem is devotional in a self-effacing Tagorean way, with the pilgrim stressing how he has no material possessions but only his sincerity to offer.

The Imam Bara and A Song from Shiraz
MS of 'The Imam Bara' in NML.

Memorial Verses

MS of 'II. Gokhale,' in NML dated 9 September 1915, with SN's note, 'Composed on the Tank Bund for D. G. Wacha's book.'

'I. Ya Mahbub!' mourns the death of Mir Mahboob Ali Khan. (See commentary on 'Ode to H.H. the Nizam of Hyderabad.')

'II. Gokhale.' Gopal Krishna Gokhale was SN's political guru before Gandhi. See 'Gokhale the Man.'

The Lotus

S. Nagarajan criticises this poem for not fully exploiting the deeper mythological and spiritual connotations of the lotus as a symbol (see Bibliography for reference). But he neglects to see that the poem is addressed to Mahatma Gandhi who, like the mystical lotus, is inviolable and immaculate, though assailed by worldly events.

The poem is a sonnet in which the turn comes somewhat late, in the third line of the sestet.

Bells

MS in NML.

The different bells represent various aspects of life—love, work, and worship—which together make for completeness and fulfilment.

The Pearl

The poem possibly refers to Jawaharlal Nehru (Jawahar means pearl) before he was married to Kamala.

June Sunset

Possibly one of the two or three poems that SN wrote in the realistic mode. Stanzas two and three, especially, offer a fairly unexaggerated 'slice of life.'

The Time of Roses
MS in correspondence with MGN, dated 1896, NML.

Destiny
MS in NML.
    Like in 'Caprice,' the speaker of this poem expresses with bitter irony her sense of being used in an intimate relationship with a man. As in 'The Temple,' the gender of the speaker is hard to identify, but in this poem, Love is specifically referred to as 'he.'

The Temple
    A sequence of twenty-four poems with eight in each of the three parts, 'The Gate of Delight,' 'The Path of Tears,' and 'The Sanctuary.'

The Gate of Delight

'2. The Feast'
    MS in NML.

'3. Ecstasy'
    MS in NML, entitled, 'Spring.'

'4. Lute-Song'
    MS in NML, entitled, 'Song.'

'6. The Sins of Love.'
    MS in NML.

The Path of Tears
'3. The Menace of Love'
    MS in NML, entitled, 'Retribution.'

'4. Love's Guerdon'
   MS in NML.

'5. If You Were Dead'
   MS in NML.

'7. The Slayer.'
   MS in NML.

'8. The Secret.'
   MS in NML, entitled, 'The Welcome.'

The Sanctuary
'4. Love Triumphant'
   MS in NML.

'8. Devotion'
   MS in NML

The Feather of the Dawn
The MS is at the National Library except for five poems, 'Gujarat,' 'The Glorissa Lily,' 'Mimiary,' 'Blind,' and 'Unity.' Some poems have been copied on the Taj Mahal Hotel letter paper and dated July 1927.
PN's note says that the poems were composed during July-August, 1927.

The Amulet
MS in PN papers along with other MSs of PN's poems in NML. This and the other love poems in FD, to me, indicate a thematic advance over the earlier love poems.

Songs of Radha
These poems attempt to bring into English verse the rich tradition of Bhakti or devotional poetry dedicated to Krishna.

Prose

Mah Rukh Begum: A Romance of Fate
MS dated 6 May, 1897, in NA.
   This unpublished narrative is the earliest available example of SN's prose.

Nilambuja: The Fantasy of a Poet's Mood
First Published in *The Indian Ladies' Magazine,* December 1902, and reprinted in SWSN.
   Nilambuja (literally, 'blue lotus') is a version of SN herself (Sarojini means 'lotus born'). PN says as much: 'Nilambuja could well be Sarojini herself just stepping out of her world,' (38).
   The piece is fascinating for its dense texture of dreamlike imagery, which can well be interpreted in psychoanalytic terms as a young woman's discovery of her sexuality. There is a touch of the occult in it too, which adds to its tantalising appeal.
   This piece, again, shows the protagonist at a threshold, unable to decide which way to go. There is a movement from the freedom of vast spaces outside to the enclosed and secure world of the woman's quarters. Nilambuja chafes at the closing of her world, but is unable to decide to abandon it. The piece ends on an uncertain note of indecision.
   SN faced a similar choice after she was married. She could have sunk into an obscure and comfortable wifehood and motherhood, but chose, instead, to enter public life. As in 'Mah Rukh Begum,' the choices in real life were more radical than in her writing.

Women's Education and the Unity of India
My title; untitled MS. in NML. This is a speech SN gave at a function to celebrate the fiftieth anniversary of a Gujarati reformist journal, *Stree Bodh,* in March 1908, Bombay (see PS 69).

Gokhale the Man
First published as a tribute to Gokhale in *The Bombay Chronicle* on 5 March 1915.

The tribute is not without a definite note of hero-worship. Gokhale was one of the foremost leaders of India, known internationally, while SN's public career was just fledging. Gokhale guided and encouraged her, extracting a promise from her to dedicate her life to the nation. SN sees Gokhale as a combination of worldly wisdom and practicality and Brahminical integrity and detachment. The tribute is personal because she owes her rise partly to Gokhale. All her life, SN was close to people who were important; Gokhale was the first of them and was followed by Gandhi and Nehru.

The Soul of India
This essay traces the evolution of the Indian people from the accounts in the Hindu myths, through the period of Muslim rule, to British colonialism, and projects from thence a future of freedom and resurgence. SN was not a major author in the theoretical construction of the new India as were Gandhi or Nehru, but she reflected, in her poetic manner, ideas which were current at her time. Like the other nationalistic leaders, SN resorts to a certain fabrication of the past to justify the project of independent India.

Ideals of Islam
Speech delivered at the Young Men's Muslim Association, Madras, 19 December 1917. Published as a booklet by Matri Bhandar, Dacca, 1921. Reprinted in SWSN.

Considers brotherhood to be the chief ideal of Islam upon which all its other strengths—respect for women, sense of justice, equality, pan-Islamic identity, and so on—are predicated. The main thrust of the speech, however, is how these inherent strengths of Islam can contribute to the making of the Indian nation. Here, SN follows a line first propounded by Swami Vivekananda, who argued that the new India would be born with Hindu brains and Muslim sinews. SN would like the activism of Islam to be used to bring about a brotherhood of all Indians, not just Muslims. The speech is an apt illustration of a cause SN worked for all her life: Hindu-Muslim unity. The problem is that SN's case is based not on questions of power but on emotional appeal.

Indian Women and the Franchise
From SWSN; Natesan's title. This section contains two resolutions which SN moved within forums inside the Congress and one before the Joint Committee of the Lords and Commons, England. SN played a leading role for ensuring equal voting rights for women. The ground was laid as early as 1889 when Pandita Ramabai led a delegation of women to the Indian National Congress to press for various rights for women. So, when independent India granted equal rights to women from its inception, it was no surprise because the Congress party was always favourable to the idea. But this achievement was the result of a long struggle by women both against the colonial administration which opposed equal rights and within the Congress itself, which needed considerable persuasion to endorse the idea wholeheartedly. (See PS 152-157.)

I: SN moved the following resolution on 'Woman's Franchise' at the eighteenth session of the Bombay Provincial Conference held at Bijapur: 'This conference welcomes the requisition of the ladies of Bombay inviting the support of this conference for women's franchise should be given to women, but under suitable conditions, and recommends that this Resolution be forwarded to the Congress through the Provincial Congress Committee.' The speech in the text was given in moving the resolution.

II: This speech was given in support of the following resolution which SN moved at the Bombay Special Congress on 1 September 1918: 'Woman possessing the same qualifications as are laid down for man in any part of the scheme shall not be disqualified on account of sex.'

Ill: When SN was in England, she submitted a Memorandum before the Joint Committee of the Lords and Commons of the British Parliament, which was considering the Government of India Bill on reforms. The Committee heard SN's evidence on Thursday, 7 August 1919. Referring to her speech, the Chairman thanked her and remarked: 'If I may be allowed to say so, it illuminates our prosaic literature with a poetic touch.'

Speech at Trichur
From SWSN, delivered at Trichur on 11 May 1923.

The speech shows SN in a role she played for the greater part of her public life. Here she is an apostle of Gandhi, whose task is to spread his message to the public. The speech also shows her sense of humour and zest for public life.

Speech at Durban Town Hall
From SWSN, delivered on 10 March 1924.

The main thrust is against apartheid. This eloquent, charged emotional appeal, is nevertheless based on the underlying belief in the equality of all races and communities of human beings. SN doesn't dilute her criticism of the white South Africans. This speech, like some of the others she delivered in South Africa, provoked a lively controversy as evidenced by the press reports of her visit.

Presidential Address, Indian National Congress
Delivered at the 40th annual session of the Indian National Congress on 26 December 1925, at Kanpur.

Presidential Address, Asian Relations Conference
Delivered at the Asian Relations Conference, 23 March 1947, at New Delhi. The conference, organised by Nehru, was an assembly

of the prominent leaders of Asia, and meant to soon-to-be-independent India's leadership role in the continent. Though SN was made the President, she was more or less just a figurehead. Yet she, in her own poetic way, reiterates the sense of India's special destiny in her speech.

My Father, Do Not Rest
This tribute was broadcasted from the Delhi station of All India Radio on 1 February 1948.

Convocation Remarks
These remarks were made while conferring honorary degrees at the Silver Jubilee Special Convocation of the Lucknow University on Friday, 28 January 1949; typed copy of MS in NML.

As the Governor of United Provinces (now Uttar Pradesh), SN was required to preside over the Convocations of all its universities. This is one of the last public functions she attended because she died a month later, on 2 March 1949.

SN's remarks show not only her sense of humour, originality, wit, frankness, and irreverence, but also her zest for life, energy, *joie de vivre*.

www.ingramcontent.com/pod-product-compliance
Lightning Source LLC
Chambersburg PA
CBHW021801220426
43662CB00006B/143